THE COMIC BOOK STORY
OF VIDEO GAMES

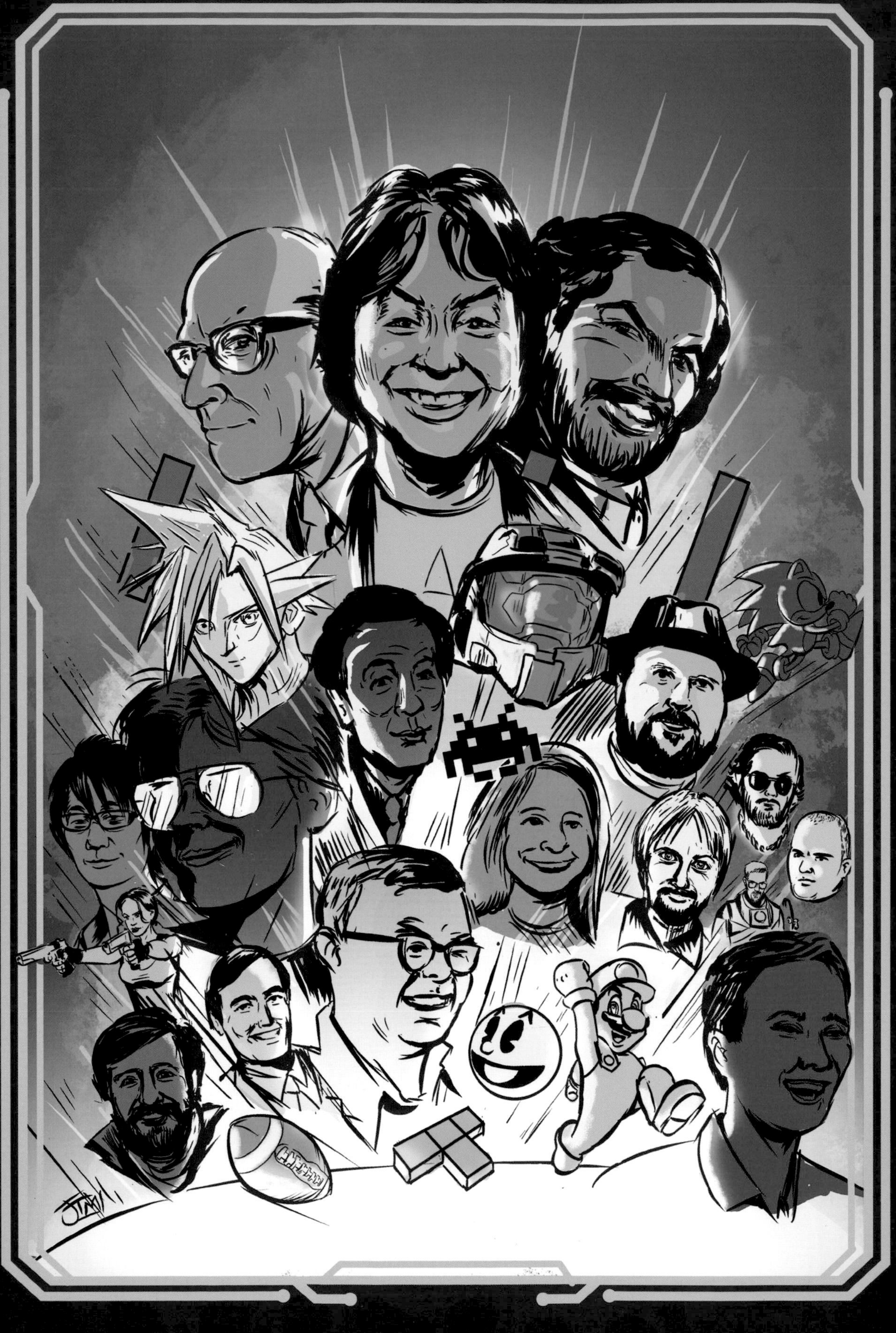

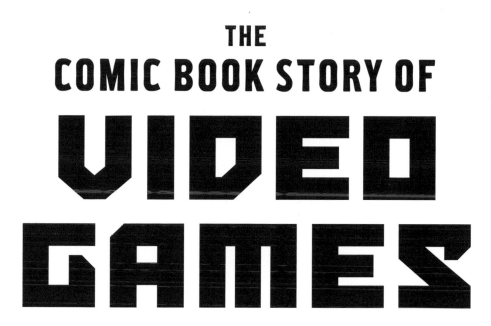

THE
COMIC BOOK STORY OF
VIDEO GAMES

The Incredible History of the
Electronic Gaming Revolution

Jonathan Hennessey
Art by **Jack McGowan**

**Coloring by William Smith IV and Jason Wordie,
with additional colors by Dan Blaushild**

Lettering by Tom Orzechowski

TEN SPEED PRESS
California | New York

CHAPTER ONE

TOTALLY TUBULAR

The Tech Evolution That Made Gaming Possible

It is pitch black. You are likely to be eaten by a Grue.

IN THE BIBLICAL TELLING, *"LET THERE BE LIGHT"* IS THE PHRASE THAT CORONATES CREATION ITSELF.

THOSE *SAME FOUR WORDS* CAN ALSO BE SAID TO HERALD THE GENESIS OF...

VIDEO GAMES

WHY IS "LIGHT" SO *INDISPENSABLE* TO THE HISTORY OF VIDEO GAMES?

LET'S FIRST DEFINE OUR TERMS.

THE QUESTION OF *WHAT MAKES A VIDEO GAME A VIDEO GAME* IS SENSITIVE ENOUGH TO BAIT PURISTS INTO VICIOUS *FLAME WARS*.

YOUR PEDANTIC ARGUMENT ON *"CREATOR INTENT"* IS MOST UNDERWHELMING, GOOMBA_PIMP666!!

tap t-tap
tap t-tap

SOME MIGHT GET HUNG UP ON THE MATTER OF A GAME OR GAME SYSTEM'S "GUTS"--THAT IS, WHETHER THE GAME IS GENERATED BY...

MICROPROCESSING CHIPS,

A TRACK-SKIPPING LASER DISC PLAYER, OR

A SOLDERED-TOGETHER, FRANKENSTEIN ASSEMBLAGE OF PARTS AND CIRCUITRY.

BUT SUCH ISSUES ARE BESIDE THE POINT. WHAT *QUALIFIES SOMETHING AS A VIDEO GAME* IS FIRST AND FOREMOST THAT IT DELIVERS A *HUMAN EXPERIENCE* THROUGH THE PHENOMENON OF *PLAY*.

FOR TRUTH! FOR BEAUTY! FOR ART!

CHAARGE!

GAME DESIGNER *CHRIS CRAWFORD'S* "DRAGON" SPEECH, 1992 COMPUTER GAME DEVELOPER'S CONFERENCE.

STILL, ONE *TECHNICAL POINT* IS UNAVOIDABLE.

"VIDEO." (Ahem.) "THAT WHICH IS DISPLAYED OR TO BE DISPLAYED ON A TELEVISION SCREEN OR OTHER CATHODE-RAY TUBE."

--OXFORD ENGLISH DICTIONARY

CAPTAIN VIDEO

BEFORE VIDEO GAMES CAN BE POSSIBLE, THERE MUST BE A METHOD TO BRING *LIGHT* TO A *SCREEN INTERFACE*--AND MAKE THAT LIGHT *RESPONSIVE* TO HUMAN CONTROL.

COMPUTERS ARE GREAT. BUT THIS POINT BEARS REPEATING: THEY ARE NOT A "MUST HAVE" TO MAKE OR PLAY VIDEO GAMES. THE PLAY EXPERIENCE OF THE BELLWETHER TITLE *PONG*, AS WE SHALL SEE, WAS 100% COMPUTER-FREE.

LIKEWISE, NOT ALL *ELECTRONIC GAMES* ARE *VIDEO GAMES*. WERE THAT THE CASE, THEN WE WOULD HAVE TO EQUATE ARCADE FAVORITE *TECMO SUPER BOWL*...

WHAT KIND OF ALCOHOL DO YOU PREFER? WHISKEY, WINE, OR BEER?

ALCOHOL IS VERY IMPORTANT TO GAME DEVELOPMENT--I LIKE THEM ALL!

GAME DEVELOPER *TOMONOBU ITAGAKI*

...WITH A SCREENLESS DOOZY THAT SWAPS OUT LIGHTBULBS AND AN *X-Y TABLE OF PLOTTED FUNCTIONS* FOR THE VISCERAL EXCITEMENT OF THE GRIDIRON ON GAME DAY.

IN THESE HEADY DAYS, WHEN YOU'RE PLAYING *EDGE OF NOWHERE* ON A *VR HEADSET* BOASTING A RESOLUTION OF 2160x1200 PIXELS, A FULL 110° FIELD OF *3-D VISION*, AND UPWARD OF *16.7 MILLION COLORS*...

...IT'S EASY TO LOSE SIGHT OF THE *HYPNOTIC ALLURE* MERE *LIGHTED BLIPS ON BLACK FIELDS* ONCE HAD.

SO TO UNDERSTAND HOW AND WHY VIDEO GAMES EMERGED IN THE FIRST PLACE, LET'S *TIMEWARP OUR BRAINS* TO A AN *EXOTIC* AND *RETROGRADE* FRAME OF MIND.

...WHERE EVEN *PREPOSTEROUSLY CRUDE* "GRAPHICS" AND "GAME-PLAY" WOULD HAVE BEEN *FASCINATING* AND *HABIT FORMING*.

FOR THAT MATTER, WHY STOP THERE?

TO GET AT THE *DEEP TECHNOLOGICAL ROOTS* FROM WHICH VIDEO GAMES SPROUT, LET'S RETURN TO AN ERA WHEN *ARTIFICIAL LIGHT* OF ALMOST *ANY KIND* WAS DEEMED *MIRACULOUS*.

RRRRRRRR!!!

???

?

THE MIDDLE OF THE 19TH CENTURY SHOULD DO.

CLICK

FOR MUCH OF THE 1800s, *STEAM POWER* RULED THE DAY. AND, JUST LIKE IN OUR OWN TIMES, IT WAS COMMON FOR CONTEMPORARIES TO "GEEK OUT ON" TECHNOLOGY--AND *WAX POETIC* ABOUT THE FUTURE OF HUMANKIND.

THE CORLISS ENGINE DOES NOT LEND ITSELF TO DESCRIPTION; ITS PERSONAL ACQUAINTANCE MUST BE SOUGHT BY THOSE WHO WOULD UNDERSTAND ITS VAST AND ALMOST SILENT GRANDEUR.

WILLIAM DEAN HOWELLS, 1876.

THE "CENTENNIAL ENGINE," BUILT TO POWER ALL THE EXHIBITS AT THE 1876 CENTENNIAL EXHIBITION IN PHILADELPHIA. THE FESTIVAL MARKED THE ONE HUNDREDTH 4th OF JULY AND CELEBRATED THE ACHIEVEMENTS OF THE UNITED STATES SINCE INDEPENDENCE.

BUT SOME IN THE STEAM AGE SAW *CHANGE* COMING. THE HARNESSING OF ANOTHER FORM OF ENERGY WOULD *TRANSFORM THE WORLD.*

FOR THE WONDERFUL FORCE OF *ELECTRICITY* EXCELS IN READINESS OF APPLICATION AND UTILITY ALL OTHER FORCES OF NATURE.

GERMAN PHILOSOPHER *LUDWIG BÜCHNER,* 1898.

ELECTRICITY WON'T READILY FLOW THROUGH AIR.

NOT UNLESS WE'RE TALKING *EXTREMELY HIGH VOLTAGES* LIKE IN THE CONDITIONS AROUND A *LIGHTNING STRIKE.*

BUT IN 1857, A GERMAN WITH WHAT WE MIGHT THINK OF AS AN ODDBALL DUO OF SKILL SETS, *GLASSBLOWING* AND *PHYSICS...*

...RAN *ELECTRIC VOLTAGE* THROUGH GLASS TUBES FILLED NOT WITH AIR, BUT WITH GASES LIKE *HYDROGEN* OR *SODIUM VAPOR.*

TO PUMP?

Na

or

H

?

CATHODE

VALVE

GLASS

− HV +

ANODE

THE RESULTS *HEINRICH GEISSLER* ACHIEVED WERE A DOWNRIGHT WONDER.

THE TUBES GLOWED WITH COLORED LIGHT.

SCIENCE AND MYSTICISM, NOW POLAR OPPOSITES, HAD ONCE OVERLAPPED. THE AURA OF THIS NEARLY VANISHED AGE STILL CLUNG TO...

...FLAMBOYANT ENGLISHMAN, *SIR WILLIAM CROOKES. HE* BELIEVED IN *MAGNETISM, SPIRIT CONJURING,* AND *TELEPATHY.*

ETHER VIBRATIONS HAVE POWERS AND ATTRIBUTES ABUNDANTLY EQUAL TO ANY DEMAND-- EVEN TO THE TRANSMISSION OF THOUGHT.

IN 1878, CROOKES RAN ELECTRIC VOLTAGE THROUGH AN "EVACUATED" GLASS TUBE-- AS NEAR TO A *VACUUM* AS RESEARCHERS COULD ACHIEVE AT THE TIME.

PHOSPHORESCENT MATERIAL COATING THE FAR END OF THE TUBE GLOWED.

A GLOWING SPOT OF LIGHT CAUSED BY A RAY OF *ELECTRONS* SHOOTS FROM A POSITIVELY CHARGED FILAMENT PAST A NEGATIVELY-CHARGED METAL PLATE...

...AND EXCITES WHAT IT STRIKES THERE.

REALLY?

THIS IS THE MUSE THAT INSPIRED A $64 BILLION GLOBAL INDUSTRY?!

CALL IT A TESTAMENT TO THE *DEPTH OF HUMAN IMAGINATION.* MOST CAN EASILY BE SEDUCED INTO ADOPTING THIS GLOWING SPOT AS A *SYMBOL* OR *SURROGATE* FOR... *SOMETHING ELSE.*

AND IT'S FAR EASIER TO LET THAT SPOT BECOME OUR PROXY--OUR *PROTO-AVATAR,* EVEN--WHEN WE ARE ABLE TO *MOVE IT AROUND THE SCREEN AT OUR WILL.*

THAT'S EXACTLY WHAT *KARL FERDINAND BRAUN* MADE IT DO...

CHOOSE YOUR INVENTOR

K. FERDINAND BRAUN NAME

M. DIECKMANN

J.A. FLEMING

J.W. HITTORF

A.A. CAMP -SWINTON

...AND IN DOING SO, BROUGHT US A *QUANTUM LEAP* CLOSER TO VIDEO GAMES.

THE *CATHODE RAY TUBE,* OR *CRT*--BRAUN'S 1897 IMPROVEMENT ON THE INVENTIONS OF GEISSLER AND CROOKES--USED *MAGNETIC FIELDS* TO *DEFLECT* THE ELECTRON RAY AND *FOCUS* THE LIGHT.

BRAUN SHUTTLED THE LIGHT UP, DOWN, LEFT, AND RIGHT-- TRACING PATTERNS, SUGGESTING SHAPES, AS IT WENT.

INCREMENTAL UPGRADES TO BRAUN'S EXPERIMENTS CONTINUED.

7

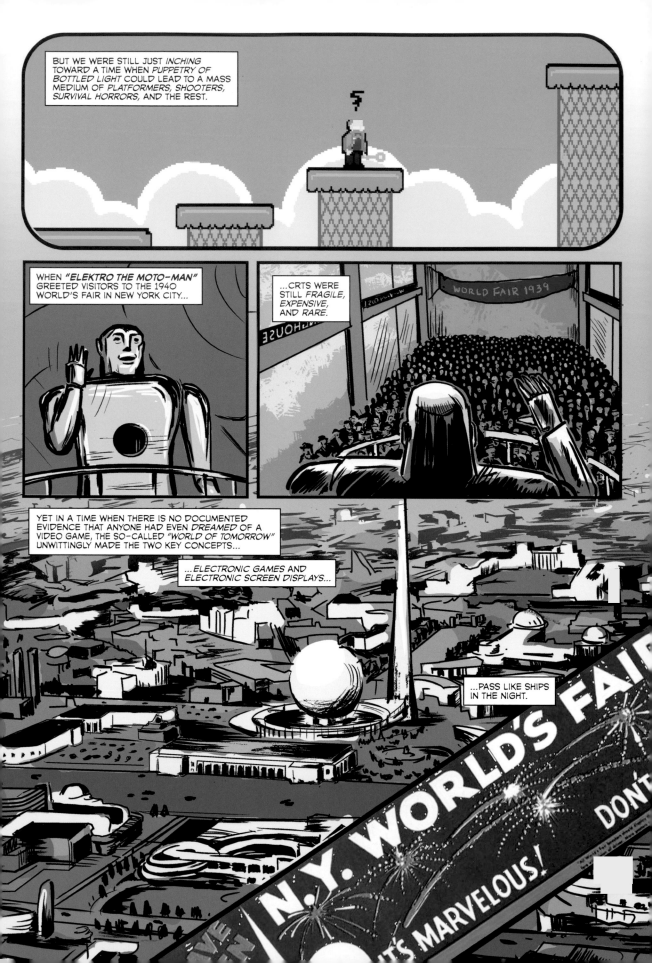

BUT WE WERE STILL JUST *INCHING* TOWARD A TIME WHEN *PUPPETRY OF BOTTLED LIGHT* COULD LEAD TO A MASS MEDIUM OF *PLATFORMERS, SHOOTERS, SURVIVAL HORRORS,* AND THE REST.

WHEN *"ELEKTRO THE MOTO-MAN"* GREETED VISITORS TO THE 1940 WORLD'S FAIR IN NEW YORK CITY...

...CRTS WERE STILL *FRAGILE, EXPENSIVE,* AND *RARE.*

WORLD FAIR 1939

YET IN A TIME WHEN THERE IS NO DOCUMENTED EVIDENCE THAT ANYONE HAD EVEN *DREAMED* OF A VIDEO GAME, THE SO-CALLED *"WORLD OF TOMORROW"* UNWITTINGLY MADE THE TWO KEY CONCEPTS...

...ELECTRONIC GAMES AND ELECTRONIC SCREEN DISPLAYS...

...PASS LIKE SHIPS IN THE NIGHT.

N.Y. WORLD'S FAIR

IT'S MARVELOUS!

DON'T

IN THE *RADIO CORPORATION OF AMERICA*, OR *RCA*, BUILDING, CROWDS SWARMED TO THE LATEST HOT TECH DEMO.

THESE NEW "MIRACLES OF ENGINEERING SKILL" WERE 8x9-INCH BLACK-AND-WHITE MONITORS CALLED *TELEVISIONS*.

THEY USED CATHODE RAY TUBES NOT TO PRODUCE DOTS, BUT *ENTIRE MOVING IMAGES*.

WHICH IS WHY INDULGING IN TV IS STILL SOMETIMES CALLED "WATCHING THE TUBE."

MEANWHILE, JUST DOWN GRAND CENTRAL PARKWAY IN THE WESTINGHOUSE PAVILION...

WESTINGHOUSE

...FOLKS EAGERLY WAITED IN LINE FOR THEIR TURN AT A BOXY APPARATUS OF RELAYS AND LAMPS.

THIS WAS THE *"NIMATRON"*--AN "ELECTRICAL BRAIN" PLAYERS COULD TRY TO BEAT AT AN ANCIENT MATH GAME KNOWN IN ENGLISH AS *NIM*.

THE NIMATRON USUALLY WON. BUT IF AN OPPONENT *PWNED* ITS ARCHAIC "AI," SHE WOULD BE GIFTED WITH A SOUVENIR TOKEN ACCLAIMING HER A "NIM CHAMP."

WORLD'S FAIR 1940
NIM CHAMP
NEW YORK

THE TWO HALVES OF THE *LAUNCH CODE* FOR THE *ENTIRE VIDEO GAMES MEDIUM* WERE JUST WAITING FOR THE RIGHT *GENIUS* TO COME ALONG AND ADD THEM TOGETHER.

ALBERT EINSTEIN WAS AT THE FAIR. NOT EVEN *HE* CONNECTED THE DOTS.

NEVERTHELESS, ACROSS THE ATLANTIC AT THAT VERY MOMENT, TREMORS OF *WORLD-HISTORICAL UPHEAVAL* WERE SURGING. THE LIVES OF TENS OF MILLIONS, THE DESTINIES OF NATIONS, WERE AT STAKE.

NOUS NOUS BATTRONS JUSQU'À LA DERNIERE CARTRIDGE!

ACK-A-ACK-A!

BLAM!

BLAM!

ACK-ACK-ACK!

K-BOOM!

THIS CLASH OF CIVILIZATIONS WAS

WORLD WAR II.

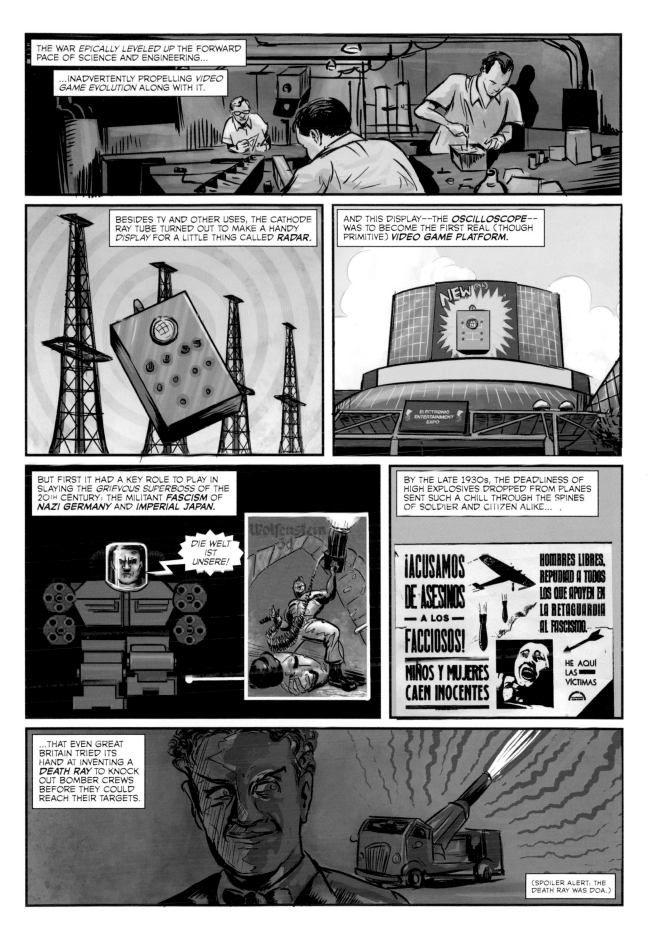

THE WAR *EPICALLY LEVELED UP* THE FORWARD PACE OF SCIENCE AND ENGINEERING...

...INADVERTENTLY PROPELLING *VIDEO GAME EVOLUTION* ALONG WITH IT.

BESIDES TV AND OTHER USES, THE CATHODE RAY TUBE TURNED OUT TO MAKE A HANDY *DISPLAY* FOR A LITTLE THING CALLED *RADAR*.

AND THIS DISPLAY--THE *OSCILLOSCOPE*-- WAS TO BECOME THE FIRST REAL (THOUGH PRIMITIVE) *VIDEO GAME PLATFORM*.

NEW (ISA)

ELECTRONIC ENTERTAINMENT EXPO

BUT FIRST IT HAD A KEY ROLE TO PLAY IN SLAYING THE *GRIEVOUS SUPERBOSS* OF THE 20TH CENTURY: THE MILITANT *FASCISM* OF *NAZI GERMANY* AND *IMPERIAL JAPAN*.

DIE WELT IST UNSERE!

Wolfenstein 3D

BY THE LATE 1930s, THE DEADLINESS OF HIGH EXPLOSIVES DROPPED FROM PLANES SENT SUCH A CHILL THROUGH THE SPINES OF SOLDIER AND CITIZEN ALIKE... .

¡ACUSAMOS DE ASESINOS A LOS FACCIOSOS! NIÑOS Y MUJERES CAEN INOCENTES

HOMBRES LIBRES, REPUDIAD A TODOS LOS QUE APOYEN EN LA RETAGUARDIA AL FASCISMO.

HE AQUÍ LAS ▓▓ VICTIMAS

...THAT EVEN GREAT BRITAIN TRIED ITS HAND AT INVENTING A *DEATH RAY* TO KNOCK OUT BOMBER CREWS BEFORE THEY COULD REACH THEIR TARGETS.

(SPOILER ALERT: THE DEATH RAY WAS DOA.)

11

WHEN THE NAZI REGIME'S AIR FORCE, OR *LUFTWAFFE*, BEGAN ATTACKING GREAT BRITAIN IN 1940, RADAR WAS STILL A *GLITCHY, TECHNOLOGICAL NOOB.*

R-R-RUMBLE...

BUT BRITAIN'S HIGH COMMAND HAD A *REVOLUTIONARY, ULTRASECRET RADAR INVENTION* UP ITS SLEEVE.

...THE MICROWAVE-PRODUCING *CAVITY MAGNETRON.*

Obtained Cavity Magnetron!

YET UNDER THE STRESS OF DEFENDING ITSELF FROM A PLANNED GERMAN INVASION, GREAT BRITAIN LACKED THE REQUIRED *MANPOWER* AND *MANUFACTURING MUSCLE...*

...TO TURN THE CAVITY MAGNETRON'S PROTOTYPES INTO A NEXT-GENERATION SYSTEM FOR SPOTTING WARPLANES, WARSHIPS, AND SUBMARINES BEFORE THEY COULD *WREAK HAVOC.*

PRIME MINISTER *WINSTON CHURCHILL* SENT AGENTS ON A HIGHLY SENSITIVE ASSIGNMENT TO THE UNITED STATES.

THIS *TIZARD MISSION* OFFERED THE AMERICANS A TREASURE CHEST FULL OF BRITAIN'S ULTRACLASSIFIED HIGH TECH IN EXCHANGE FOR RADAR AID.

THE YANKS ACCEPTED...

(IN 1940, AMERICA WAS NOT YET EMBROILED IN THE WAR.)

12

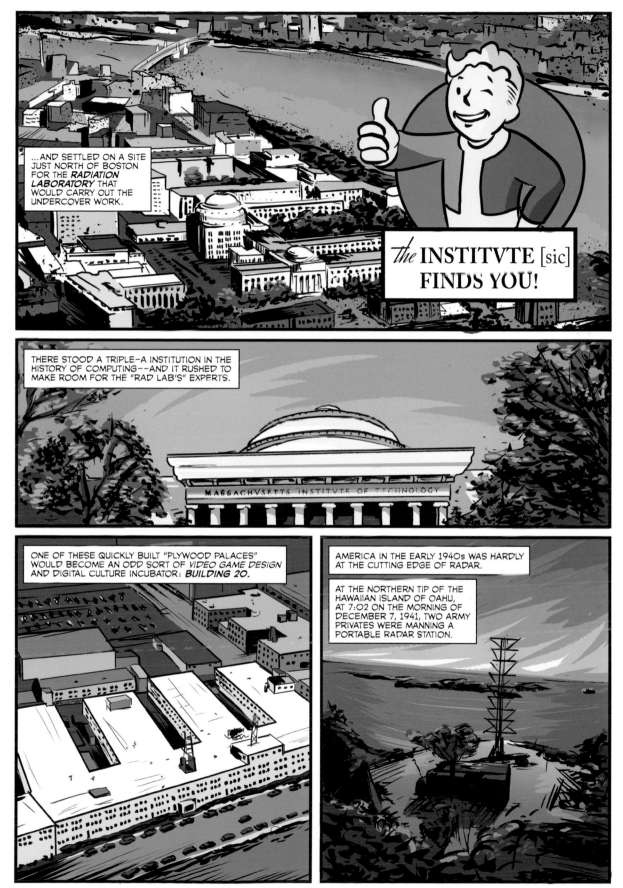

...AND SETTLED ON A SITE JUST NORTH OF BOSTON FOR THE *RADIATION LABORATORY* THAT WOULD CARRY OUT THE UNDERCOVER WORK.

the INSTITVTE [sic] FINDS YOU!

THERE STOOD A TRIPLE-A INSTITUTION IN THE HISTORY OF COMPUTING--AND IT RUSHED TO MAKE ROOM FOR THE "RAD LAB'S" EXPERTS.

MASSACHVSETTS INSTITUTE OF TECHNOLOGY

ONE OF THESE QUICKLY BUILT "PLYWOOD PALACES" WOULD BECOME AN ODD SORT OF *VIDEO GAME DESIGN* AND DIGITAL CULTURE INCUBATOR: *BUILDING 20.*

AMERICA IN THE EARLY 1940s WAS HARDLY AT THE CUTTING EDGE OF RADAR.

AT THE NORTHERN TIP OF THE HAWAIIAN ISLAND OF OAHU, AT 7:02 ON THE MORNING OF DECEMBER 7, 1941, TWO ARMY PRIVATES WERE MANNING A PORTABLE RADAR STATION.

FOR THE STORY OF THE "TMRC" AND *SPACEWAR!*--THE GAME THAT LAUNCHED A THOUSAND GAMES--*READ ON.*

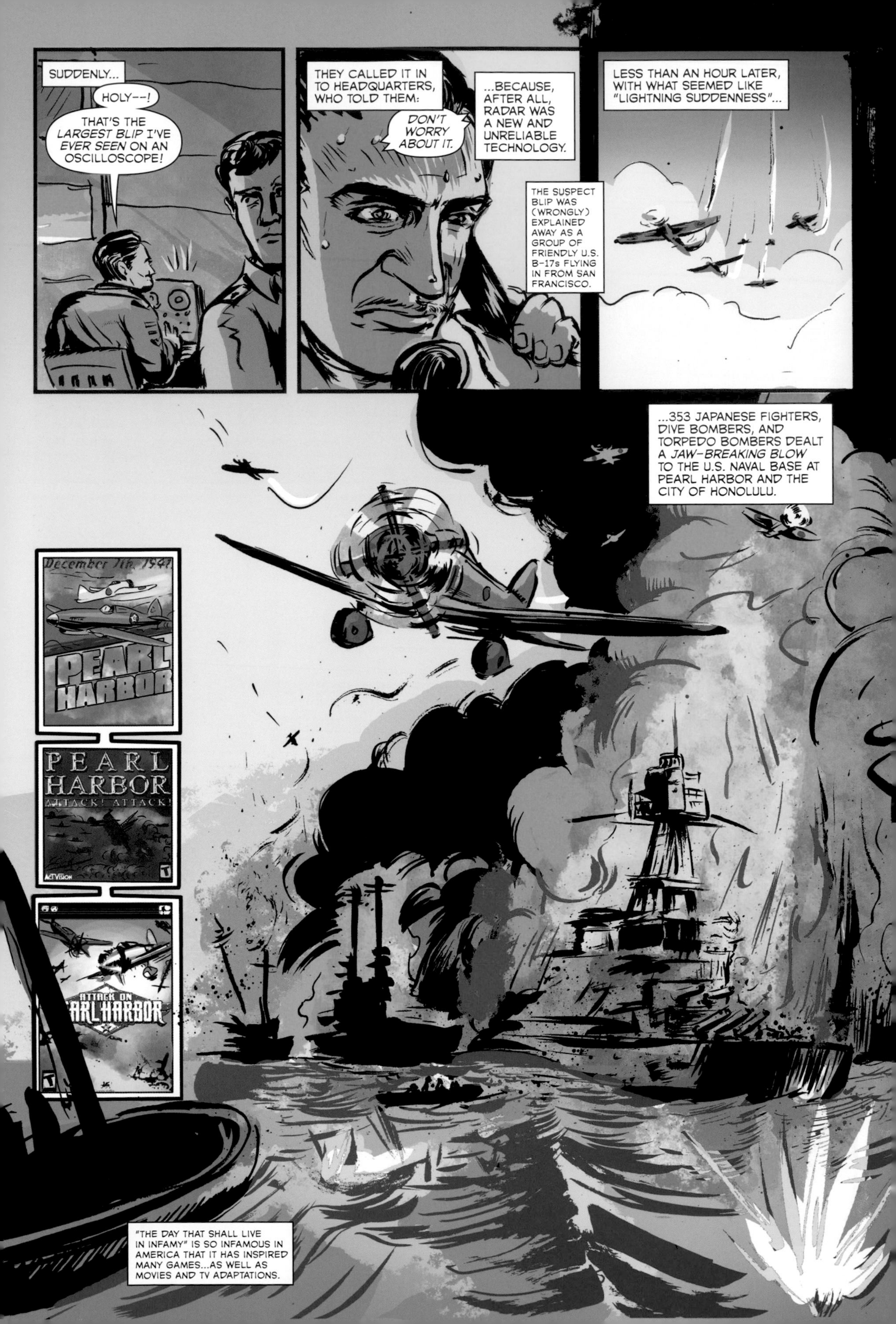
SUDDENLY...
HOLY--!
THAT'S THE LARGEST BLIP I'VE EVER SEEN ON AN OSCILLOSCOPE!
THEY CALLED IT IN TO HEADQUARTERS, WHO TOLD THEM:
DON'T WORRY ABOUT IT.
...BECAUSE, AFTER ALL, RADAR WAS A NEW AND UNRELIABLE TECHNOLOGY.
THE SUSPECT BLIP WAS (WRONGLY) EXPLAINED AWAY AS A GROUP OF FRIENDLY U.S. B-17s FLYING IN FROM SAN FRANCISCO.
LESS THAN AN HOUR LATER, WITH WHAT SEEMED LIKE "LIGHTNING SUDDENNESS"...
...353 JAPANESE FIGHTERS, DIVE BOMBERS, AND TORPEDO BOMBERS DEALT A JAW-BREAKING BLOW TO THE U.S. NAVAL BASE AT PEARL HARBOR AND THE CITY OF HONOLULU.
PEARL HARBOR
PEARL HARBOR
ATTACK! ATTACK!
ACTIVISION
ATTACK ON PEARL HARBOR
"THE DAY THAT SHALL LIVE IN INFAMY" IS SO INFAMOUS IN AMERICA THAT IT HAS INSPIRED MANY GAMES...AS WELL AS MOVIES AND TV ADAPTATIONS.

THE U.S. CONGRESS DECLARED WAR ON JAPAN THE NEXT DAY--AND GERMANY FOUR DAYS LATER. PRESIDENT FRANKLIN ROOSEVELT WARNED:

THERE IS NO BLINKING AT THE FACT THAT OUR PEOPLE, OUR TERRITORY, AND OUR INTERESTS ARE IN GRAVE DANGER.

THE COUNTRY'S TOP SCIENTISTS AND INDUSTRIAL BUSINESS GIANTS DROPPED EVERYTHING TO GIVE THE UNITED STATES A SORELY NEEDED TECHNOLOGICAL EDGE.

ALL OUR FACILITIES AND PERSONNEL ARE READY AND AT YOUR INSTANT SERVICE.

PRESIDENT FRANKLIN D. ROOSEVELT.

WAR (EVEN THE "COLD" VARIETY, AS WE WILL SEE) HAS TYPICALLY DRIVEN TECHNOLOGY FORWARD.

BRONZE DAGGERS AND SWORDS-- CIRCA 5,000 BCE

SPEAR--CIRCA 40,000 BCE

FLINTLOCK MUSKET--CIRCA 1612

DARKBURST--(INVENTION DATE REDACTED BY THE LUMINOTH)

HAMMER OF DAWN--1 BE

BOW AND ARROW-- CIRCA 20,000 BCE

EARLY GUNPOWDER WEAPONS-- CIRCA 904 CE

THIS WOULD BE ESPECIALLY TRUE IN THE 1940s.

DURING WORLD WAR II, THE SIZE OF THE SCIENTIFIC COMMUNITY INCREASED BY A FACTOR OF 10.

THE AMOUNT OF MONEY THAT THE FEDERAL GOVERNMENT WAS INVESTING IN SCIENCE INCREASED BY A FACTOR OF 10.

PROFESSOR ROBERT CREASE, 2013

THE ADVANCED WEAPONS OF THE 20TH CENTURY AND BEYOND REQUIRE ADVANCED KNOWLEDGE AND TECHNIQUES. FOR EXAMPLE, TO MOST EFFECTIVELY USE A HEAVY GUN LIKE A *HOWITZER,* THE OPERATOR MUST CONSIDER A STAGGERING NUMBER OF VARIABLES: THE HEIGHT AND DISTANCE OF THE TARGET, AIR TEMPERATURE, WIND, DRAG COEFFICIENT OF THE PROJECTILE USED, EVEN THE ROTATION OF THE EARTH!

SPOTLIGHT: ALAN TURING

BESIDES IMPROVED RADAR, THE *ALLIES* OF WWII HAD *ANOTHER* SECRET WEAPON OF SORTS...

...IN THE PERSON OF COMPUTER LEGEND *ALAN TURING*.

UNITED
THE UNITED NATIONS FIGHT FOR FREEDOM

TURING--AN ENGLISHMAN--GETS CREDIT FOR *WRITING THE FIRST COMPUTER GAME PROGRAM.*

THE BRILLIANT, SOLITARY TURING HELPED DESIGN METHODS TO DECODE SENSITIVE NAZI RADIO TRANSMISSIONS SCRAMBLED BY THEIR *ENIGMA* CIPHER MACHINES.

LATER, IN SEARCH OF EVIDENCE THAT A POWERFUL COMPUTER MIGHT DEVELOP *ARTIFICIAL INTELLIGENCE*, TURING BEGAN WORK ON "TUROCHAMP."

DEVISED TO BEAT A HUMAN BEING AT CHESS, THE PROGRAM WAS WRITTEN WITH PEN AND PAPER.

TURING WAS TOO FAR AHEAD OF HIS TIME.

HE NEVER LIVED TO SEE A COMPUTER POWERFUL ENOUGH TO ACTUALLY RUN TUROCHAMP.

TURING DIED OF CYANIDE POISONING IN 1954. MAINSTEAM SPECULATION HAS IT THAT HE COMMITTED SUICIDE AFTER PLEADING GUILTY TO "GROSS INDECENCY" CHARGES DUE TO HIS HOMOSEXUALITY.

SOME HOLD THAT THE POISONING WAS *AN ACCIDENT*-- THE RESULT OF TURING WORKING WITH TOXIC CHEMICALS IN ORDER TO GOLD-PLATE A SPOON.

BUT WORKING OUT THIS COMPLICATED MATH ON THE FLY--*UNDER FIRE*--WAS, LET'S SAY, LESS THAN IDEAL.

SSSSSSSSSIPP

KLOOOM!!

ARTILLERY CREWS WERE BETTER OFF CONSULTING *FIRING TABLES** IN WHICH THIS DIZZYING NUMBER OF NUMBERS HAD BEEN CALCULATED AND RECORDED.

* OFTEN ON WOODEN *SLIDE RULES* OR BOOKS OF CARDS.

BEFORE THE DIGITAL REVOLUTION, LEGIONS OF *LIVING NUMBER-CRUNCHERS*--MEN AND (MOSTLY) WOMEN LITERALLY REFERRED TO AS *"COMPUTERS"*--PRODUCED FIRING TABLES.

BUT THIS SYSTEM'S *HUMAN ELEMENT* MADE IT PRONE TO ERROR AND GRINDINGLY SLOW.

IT WAS TO *PERFECT* AND *SPEED UP* THE CREATION OF FIRING TABLES THAT THE FIRST COMPUTERS--*THE TOOLS THAT WOULD EVOLVE TO MAKE MOST VIDEO GAMES POSSIBLE*--WERE CREATED.

ONE EARLY COMPUTER--THAT OF M.I.T. ALUMNUS *VANNEVAR BUSH*--THE ANALOG, ELECTROMECHANICAL *DIFFERENTIAL ANALYZER*, WAS BUILT IN 1931.

17

ANOTHER EARLY COMPUTER, THIS ONE FROM 1945, IS THE GAMESTOP-SIZED *ENIAC*. IT WAS POWERED BY 17,468 *VACUUM TUBES*--THE *LINEAL DESCENDANTS* OF THE GEISSLER, CROOKE, AND BRAUN TUBES.

THE ENIAC AND DIFFERENTIAL ANALYZER WERE *STATE OF THE ART* IN THEIR TIMES.

AGAIN, AT WAR'S START, VACUUM TUBES WERE *FRAGILE, EXPENSIVE,* AND *RARE*.

THE ENEMY CAN'T HIDE FROM **RADAR**

PHILCO CORPORATION

BUT WITH SUCH INVENTIONS IN THE HANDS OF U.S. ELECTRONICS FIRMS, *BOOMING* WITH *LUCRATIVE DEFENSE CONTRACTS* AND *FIRING ON ALL CYLINDERS* WITH *PATRIOTIC FERVOR,* THINGS CHANGED.

AND CHANGED *FAST*.

MASS PRODUCTION OF NEW WAVE RADAR SYSTEMS LIKE BELL LABS' *SCR-717*-- WHICH MENACED NAZI U-BOATS IN THE ATLANTIC--MADE COMPONENTS LIKE CRTS *EASIER* AND *CHEAPER* TO MANUFACTURE.

BY 1944, *H2X "MICKEY"* RADAR UNITS, HAND-BUILT AT M.I.T., WERE INSTALLED IN SOME OF THE FIRST U.S. BOMBERS TO CONDUCT DAYLIGHT RAIDS ON THE NAZI CAPITAL OF BERLIN.

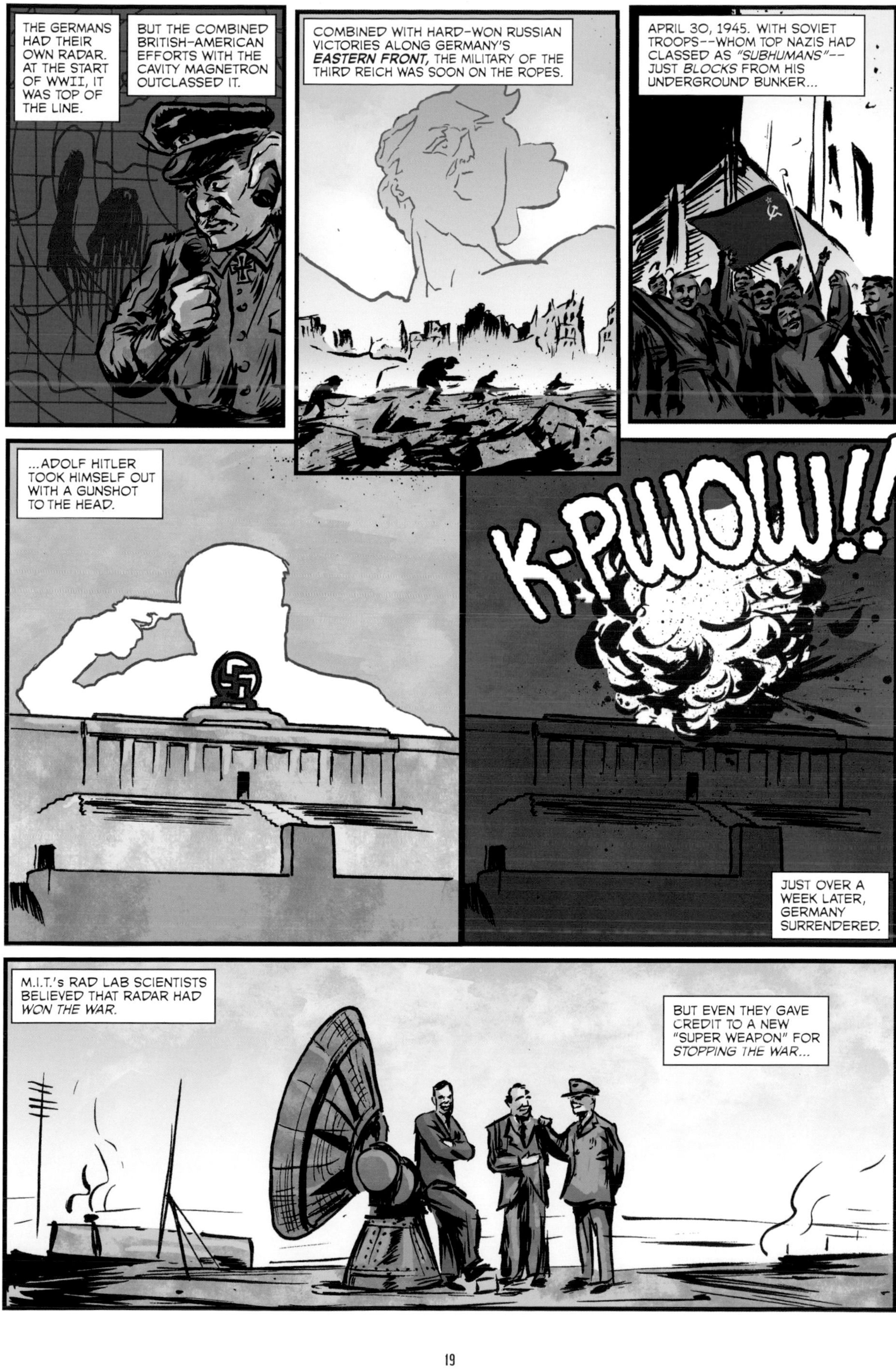
THE GERMANS HAD THEIR OWN RADAR. AT THE START OF WWII, IT WAS TOP OF THE LINE.
BUT THE COMBINED BRITISH-AMERICAN EFFORTS WITH THE CAVITY MAGNETRON OUTCLASSED IT.
COMBINED WITH HARD-WON RUSSIAN VICTORIES ALONG GERMANY'S *EASTERN FRONT,* THE MILITARY OF THE THIRD REICH WAS SOON ON THE ROPES.
APRIL 30, 1945. WITH SOVIET TROOPS--WHOM TOP NAZIS HAD CLASSED AS *"SUBHUMANS"*--JUST *BLOCKS* FROM HIS UNDERGROUND BUNKER...
...ADOLF HITLER TOOK HIMSELF OUT WITH A GUNSHOT TO THE HEAD.
K-PWOW!!
JUST OVER A WEEK LATER, GERMANY SURRENDERED.
M.I.T.'s RAD LAB SCIENTISTS BELIEVED THAT RADAR HAD *WON THE WAR.*
BUT EVEN THEY GAVE CREDIT TO A NEW "SUPER WEAPON" FOR *STOPPING THE WAR...*

...THE *ATOMIC BOMB.*

THE DEADLIEST WEAPON IN HUMAN HISTORY, DEVELOPED BY THE PERSONNEL OF THE TOP-SECRET *MANHATTAN PROJECT,* AND FIRST TESTED IN THE NEW MEXICO DESERT ON JULY 16, 1945.

THE BOMB RELEASED BETWEEN TWO AND FOUR TIMES AS MUCH ENERGY AS MOST MANHATTAN PROJECT SCIENTISTS PREDICTED.

ENRICO FERMI   VANNEVAR BUSH   JOHN VON NEUMANNN   J. ROBERT OPPENHEIMER   ERNEST LAWRENCE   WILLIAM HIGINBOTHAM

1943
THE BATTLE OF MIDWAY

EVEN WITH GERMANY DEFEATED, JAPAN CONTINUED TO WAGE WAR WITH NO END IN SIGHT.

ITS MILITARY CULTURE HARBORED A SENSE OF *HONOR* AND *COLLECTIVISM* ALMOST *BAFFLING* TO THE WESTERN MIND.

WE HAVE NO CHOICE BUT TO SEEK LIFE IN DEATH...

THE *ENTIRE JAPANESE PEOPLE* [SHOULD] *PERISH WITH THE HOMELAND...* BY CONTINUING TO FIGHT, THEREBY KEEPING THE PRIDE OF THE YAMATO RACE FOREVER.

GENERAL *TORASHIRŌ KAWABE.*

TO COMPEL "THE EMPIRE OF THE SUN" TO LAY DOWN ITS ARMS, U.S. BOMBERS WERE DIRECTED TO DROP ATOMIC BOMBS ON THE CITIES OF HIROSHIMA AND NAGASAKI.

THE FORCE FROM WHICH THE SUN DRAWS ITS POWER HAS BEEN LOOSED AGAINST THOSE WHO BROUGHT WAR TO THE FAR EAST.

THE SHOCKING DEVASTATION OF THE RADIOACTIVE WARHEADS* COMBINED FATALLY WITH THE U.S.S.R.'S DECLARATION OF WAR AGAINST JAPAN.

THE JAPANESE SURRENDERED.

*ON TOP OF THE EARLIER, DESTRUCTIVE FIREBOMBING OF TOKYO, OSAKA, AND OTHER CITIES.

THE USE OF NUCLEAR WEAPONS ON ITS PEOPLE LEFT AN INDELIBLE MARK ON JAPAN.

I SAW IT
A SURVIVOR'S TRUE STORY

KONAMI

METAL GEAR SOLID 3

FOR GENERATIONS, JAPANESE POP CULTURE-- AND MOST DEFINITELY ITS VIDEO GAMES-- WOULD BEAR THE IMPRINT OF BECOMING WHAT ARTIST TAKASHI MURAKAMI DESCRIBED AS...

..."THE WORLD'S FIRST POST-APOCALYPTIC SOCIETY."

GAME DESIGNER HIDEO KOJIMA.

BRITISH AND AMERICAN RESEARCH--AND INVESTMENT IN THEIR *GOVERNMENT, MILITARY, ACADEMIC,* AND *INDUSTRIAL SECTORS*--PRODUCED A *JACKPOT PAYOFF.*

whir whir whir

THUNK! THUNK! THUNK!

RADAR | NUCLEAR ENERGY | JET PROPULSION | DIGITAL COMPUTING

BY WAR'S END IN 1945, CRTs (AND MANY OTHER ELECTRONICS) WERE CHEAPER THAN EVER BEFORE. THEIR MASS PRODUCTION WAS READY TO GO "PRIME TIME."

NEW ERA of PEACE WORK

WAR OVER

TELEVISION--SO RECENTLY IN THE HANDS OF NONE BUT A SMATTERING OF HOBBYISTS-- WAS POISED TO GO *VIRAL.*

...AND THE *VERY FIRST VIDEO GAME* WOULD RIDE IN ON TELEVISION'S COATTAILS.

Patented Dec. 14, 1948

2,455,99

UNITED STATES PATENT OFFICE

2,455,992

CATHODE-RAY-TUBE AMUSEMENT DEVICE

Thomas T. Goldsmith, Jr., Cedar Grove, and Estle Ray Mann, Upper Montclair, N. J., assignors to Allen B. Du Mont Laboratories, Inc., Passaic, N. J., a corporation of Delaware

Application January 25, 1947, Serial No. 724,444

8 Claims. (Cl. 315—26)

CHAPTER TWO — THEY'RE HERE...!
The Earliest Early Video Games

DUMONT TELEVISION

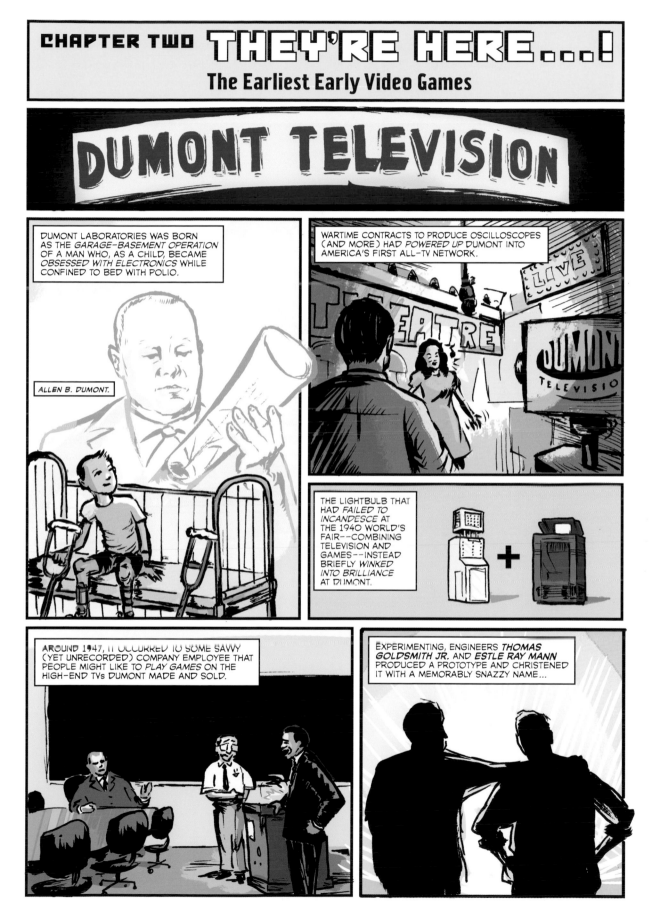

DUMONT LABORATORIES WAS BORN AS THE *GARAGE-BASEMENT OPERATION* OF A MAN WHO, AS A CHILD, BECAME *OBSESSED WITH ELECTRONICS* WHILE CONFINED TO BED WITH POLIO.

ALLEN B. DUMONT.

WARTIME CONTRACTS TO PRODUCE OSCILLOSCOPES (AND MORE) HAD *POWERED UP* DUMONT INTO AMERICA'S FIRST ALL-TV NETWORK.

THE LIGHTBULB THAT HAD *FAILED TO INCANDESCE* AT THE 1940 WORLD'S FAIR--COMBINING TELEVISION AND GAMES--INSTEAD BRIEFLY *WINKED INTO BRILLIANCE* AT DUMONT.

AROUND 1947, IT OCCURRED TO SOME SAVVY (YET UNRECORDED) COMPANY EMPLOYEE THAT PEOPLE MIGHT LIKE TO *PLAY GAMES* ON THE HIGH-END TVS DUMONT MADE AND SOLD.

EXPERIMENTING, ENGINEERS *THOMAS GOLDSMITH JR.* AND *ESTLE RAY MANN* PRODUCED A PROTOTYPE AND CHRISTENED IT WITH A MEMORABLY SNAZZY NAME...

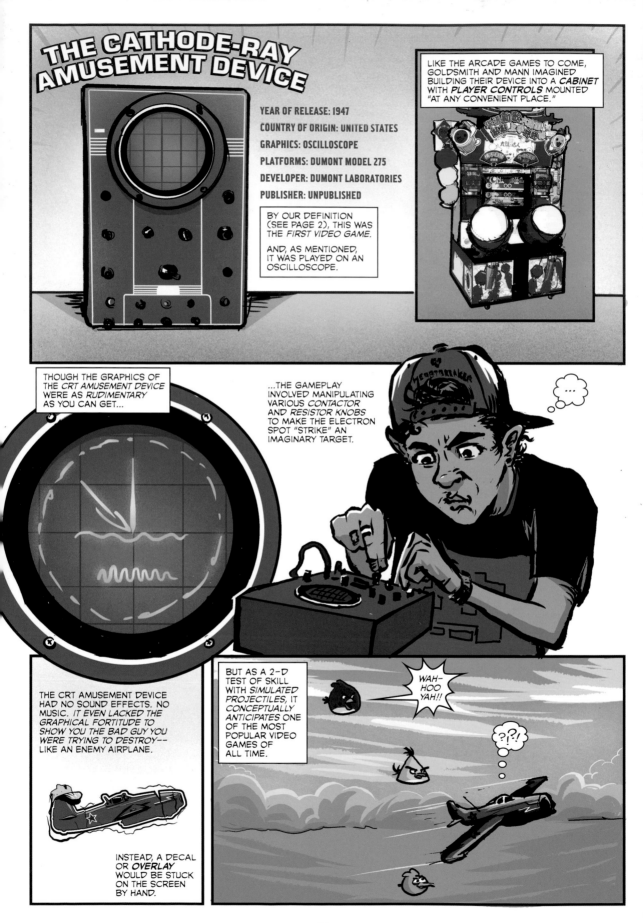

THE CATHODE-RAY AMUSEMENT DEVICE

YEAR OF RELEASE: 1947

COUNTRY OF ORIGIN: UNITED STATES

GRAPHICS: OSCILLOSCOPE

PLATFORMS: DUMONT MODEL 275

DEVELOPER: DUMONT LABORATORIES

PUBLISHER: UNPUBLISHED

BY OUR DEFINITION (SEE PAGE 2), THIS WAS THE *FIRST VIDEO GAME.*

AND, AS MENTIONED, IT WAS PLAYED ON AN OSCILLOSCOPE.

LIKE THE ARCADE GAMES TO COME, GOLDSMITH AND MANN IMAGINED BUILDING THEIR DEVICE INTO A *CABINET* WITH *PLAYER CONTROLS* MOUNTED "AT ANY CONVENIENT PLACE."

THOUGH THE GRAPHICS OF THE *CRT AMUSEMENT DEVICE* WERE AS *RUDIMENTARY* AS YOU CAN GET...

...THE GAMEPLAY INVOLVED MANIPULATING VARIOUS *CONTACTOR* AND *RESISTOR KNOBS* TO MAKE THE ELECTRON SPOT "STRIKE" AN IMAGINARY TARGET.

....

THE CRT AMUSEMENT DEVICE HAD NO SOUND EFFECTS. NO MUSIC. *IT EVEN LACKED THE GRAPHICAL FORTITUDE TO SHOW YOU THE BAD GUY YOU WERE TRYING TO DESTROY--* LIKE AN ENEMY AIRPLANE.

INSTEAD, A DECAL OR *OVERLAY* WOULD BE STUCK ON THE SCREEN BY HAND.

BUT AS A 2-D TEST OF SKILL WITH *SIMULATED PROJECTILES,* IT *CONCEPTUALLY ANTICIPATES* ONE OF THE MOST POPULAR VIDEO GAMES OF ALL TIME.

WAH-HOO YAH!!

?!?!

THIS CRUDE PROGENITOR (WHICH NEVER LAUNCHED AS A CONSUMER ITEM) FORETOLD *EVEN MORE* ABOUT HOW GAMING WOULD DEVELOP.

SSSHHHHFFFFFF

PARAMOUNT PICTURES BEGAN BUYING INTO DUMONT AS EARLY AS 1939. WHEN THE CRT AMUSEMENT DEVICE WAS PATENTED, THE MOVIE STUDIO OWNED A CONTROLLING STAKE IN THE BUSINESS.

HOLLYWOOD

SO EVEN IN ITS CRADLE, GAMING-- LIKE MOVIES--WAS LARGELY DEVELOPED AS A *FOR-PROFIT VENTURE* DESTINED TO COMMINGLE WITH HOLLYWOOD.

Stanford

NOW PLAYING
1. MORTAL KOMBAT
2. SILENT HILL

AND ALSO *COMPETE WITH* HOLLYWOOD. IN THE UNITED STATES, VIDEO GAME REVENUE EXCEEDED MOTION PICTURE BOX OFFICE REVENUE IN 1981. IT WAS 2009 IN THE U.K.

I THINK THE REAL INDICATOR WILL BE WHEN SOMEBODY CONFESSES THAT THEY CRIED AT LEVEL 17.

STEVEN SPIELBERG, COMMENTING IN 2004.

SOON AFTER THE CRT AMUSEMENT DEVICE WAS SHELVED, A GAMING PIONEER THEN ALSO AT WORK AS A TV ENGINEER *INDEPENDENTLY* HIT ON THE NOTION...

...OF USING *ELECTRONIC SCREEN GRAPHICS* TO PLAY GAMES.

RALPH BAER, 1951.

THE "SUITS" IN CHARGE WERE, HOWEVER, TYPICALLY SLOW ON THE UPTAKE.

FORGET IT. JUST BUILD THE DAMN TV SET. YOU'RE BEHIND SCHEDULE AS IT IS.

NOTHING AT ALL WAS SLOW, ON THE OTHER HAND...

...ABOUT BUDAPEST-BORN MATH WIZARD AND ALL-AROUND BRAINIAC *JOHN VON NEUMANN.*

VON NEUMANN WAS THE PRODUCT OF AN ALL-TOO-BRIEF *SUPERNOVA* OF *CULTURAL AND INTELLECTUAL ADVANCEMENT* IN THE LATE AUSTRO-HUNGARIAN EMPIRE.

IN THE 1930s, HE WAS KNOWN AROUND PRINCETON, NEW JERSEY,* FOR *UPROARIOUS, DRUNKEN COCKTAIL PARTIES* AND *BAT-OUT-OF-HELL RECKLESSNESS* BEHIND THE WHEEL.

WHIRRRR!!!

*HOME OF *THE INSTITUTE FOR ADVANCED STUDY,* RESERVED FOR "FUNDAMENTAL INQUIRY INTO THE UNKNOWN."

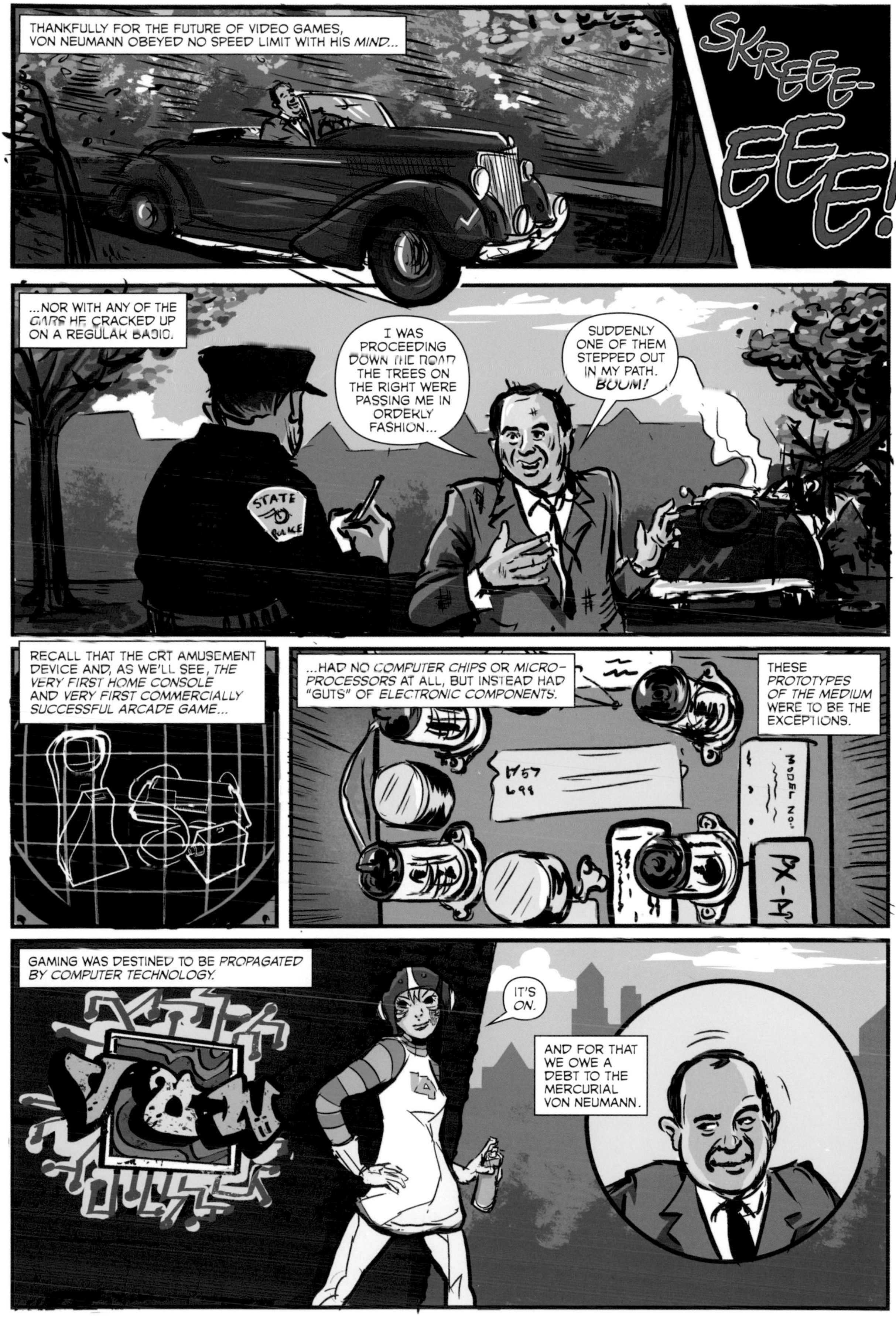
THANKFULLY FOR THE FUTURE OF VIDEO GAMES, VON NEUMANN OBEYED NO SPEED LIMIT WITH HIS *MIND*...
SKREEE-EEEE!
...NOR WITH ANY OF THE CARS HE CRACKED UP ON A REGULAR BASIS.
I WAS PROCEEDING DOWN THE ROAD THE TREES ON THE RIGHT WERE PASSING ME IN ORDERLY FASHION...
SUDDENLY ONE OF THEM STEPPED OUT IN MY PATH. *BOOM!*
STATE
RECALL THAT THE CRT AMUSEMENT DEVICE AND, AS WE'LL SEE, *THE VERY FIRST HOME CONSOLE* AND *VERY FIRST COMMERCIALLY SUCCESSFUL ARCADE GAME*...
...HAD NO *COMPUTER CHIPS* OR *MICRO-PROCESSORS* AT ALL, BUT INSTEAD HAD "GUTS" OF *ELECTRONIC COMPONENTS.*
THESE *PROTOTYPES OF THE MEDIUM* WERE TO BE THE EXCEPTIONS.
GAMING WAS DESTINED TO BE *PROPAGATED BY COMPUTER TECHNOLOGY.*
IT'S *ON.*
AND FOR THAT WE OWE A DEBT TO THE MERCURIAL VON NEUMANN.

MOTIVATED IN PART BY HIS HATRED OF THE NAZI REGIME, THE JEWISH VON NEUMANN BECAME A KEY SCIENTIST FOR THE U.S. MILITARY DURING WWII. THIS INCLUDED CRITICAL PARTICIPATION IN THE MANHATTAN PROJECT. SUCCESS THERE HINGED ON SUCH COMPLICATED MATH THAT IT MADE PRODUCING ARTILLERY FIRING TABLES...

LOS ALAMOS PROJECT MAIN GATE PASSES MUST BE PRESENTED TO GUARDS

POST No. 1

MANHATTAN PROJECT A BOMB

...LOOK LIKE CHECKING YOUR STEAM WALLET BALANCE AFTER PUNCHING IN THE CODE OF A PAYPAL GIFT CARD.

MATH WOES IMPOSED *DELAYS* TO THE A-BOMB THAT SOMETIMES SEEMED *INSURMOUNTABLE*.

OUR PREVIOUS HOPES THAT AN IMPLOSION TYPE OF BOMB MIGHT BE DEVELOPED IN THE LATE SPRING OF 1945 HAVE NOW BEEN DISSIPATED BY SCIENTIFIC DIFFICULTIES...

clak
k-clak
clak

THEN IN 1944 VON NEUMANN, IN A CHANCE TRAIN STATION ENCOUNTER, LEARNED OF THE ENIAC COMPUTER...

ABERDEEN

...WHICH COULD PERFORM 333 MULTIPLICATIONS PER SECOND.

TICKETS

HE MANEUVERED HIS WAY ONTO THE TEAM DESIGNING ENIAC'S SUCCESSOR AND SOON AUTHORED *THE* SEMINAL COMPUTER SCIENCE PAPER...

First Draft
of a Report
on the EDVAC

by
John von Neumann

...WHICH MINTED THE "ARCHITECTURE" BEHIND EVEN CURRENT PCs, GAME CONSOLES, MOBILE DEVICES, AND *NEARLY EVERY COMPUTER IN EXISTENCE.*

AS THE 1950s APPROACHED, IN A FEW ENVIABLE PLACES WHERE GREAT MINDS (AND GREAT MONEY) CONGREGATED, A *NEW WAVE OF COMPUTERS* WAS BEING ENGINEERED.

THE IDEAS ATTRIBUTED TO VON NEUMANN RIPPLED BACK TO GREAT BRITAIN--THE SEEDBED OF *COMPUTER VISIONARIES* LIKE *CHARLES BABBAGE* AND *ADA LOVELACE.*

MACHINES SUITED FOR A VAST EXPANSE OF PURPOSES-- NOT JUST *FAST, ACCURATE, BRUTE-FORCE ARITHMETIC*-- EXQUISITELY REALIZED THE DREAMS OF LOVELACE.

...WHO DIED IN 1852.

THE FIRST SLATE OF VIDEO GAMES ALL CAME ABOUT AS *EXPLORATIONS INTO* THE CAPABILITIES OF THIS UNPROBED FRONTIER...

...(WHICH IS TO SAY--UNLIKE THE CRT AMUSEMENT DEVICE--THEY WERE NOT CONCEIVED FOR COMMERCIAL RELEASE OR FOR PROFIT.)

Manchester, Cathedral & Cromwell Monument.

ONE SUCH GAME WAS *DRAUGHTS* ("CHECKERS" IN NORTH AMERICA), REALIZED IN 1951 IN MANCHESTER, ENGLAND.

THE DEPICTION OF MANCHESTER CATH IN VIOLENT *RESISTANCE: FALL OF MAN* (INSOMNIAC GAMES, 2006) SPARKED A MAJOR GAMING CONTROVERSY, PROMPTING SONY TO ISSUE AN APOLOGY TO THE CHURCH OF ENGLAND.

THE COMPUTER THAT RAN *DRAUGHTS*-- THE VON NEUMANN ARCHITECTURE-BASED FERRANTI MARK I...

...HAD ITS PROGRAMS *CODED* ON AND *LOADED* IN VIA HOLE-PUNCHED PAPER TAPE.

CHRISTOPHER STRACHEY, THE AUTHOR OF *DRAUGHTS,* WAS A WELL-BORN ENGLISHMAN WHO...

...LIKE HIS ACQUAINTANCE ALAN TURING, STRUGGLED AS A GAY MAN IN A TIME AND PLACE WHEN HOMOSEXUALITY WAS *LITERALLY* ILLEGAL.

DRAUGHTS IS IMPORTANT FOR THREE REASONS. IT IS THE FIRST PROGRAM TO USE ANY KIND OF GRAPHICAL DISPLAY. IT ALSO CONTAINS THE EARLIEST FUNCTIONAL AI.*

*IN DRAUGHTS, YOU PLAYED AGAINST THE COMPUTER, NOT ANOTHER HUMAN OPPONENT.

GOD SAVE THE KING

LASTLY, IT WAS THE FIRST VIDEO GAME TO INCORPORATE MUSIC. UPON TERMINATION, DRAUGHTS WOULD UTTER A LEADEN RENDERING OF "GOD SAVE THE KING."

1952 SAW *OXO*,* A TIC-TAC-TOE PROGRAM WRITTEN BY ENGLISHMAN ALEXANDER (SANDY) SHAFTO DOUGLAS, WHO STUDIED HUMAN-COMPUTER INTERACTION.

*AKA *NOUGHTS AND CROSSES*.

THE VERY EXISTENCE OF THESE GAMES SORT OF GOES *AGAINST THE GRAIN* OF WHAT COMPUTING WAS FIRST *SUPPOSED* TO BE *ABOUT*.

AND FIRST GENERATION PROGRAMMERS PROBABLY WROTE *MORE GAMES* THAT NO ONE TOOK *SERIOUSLY ENOUGH* TO PRESERVE.

UNIVERSITIES, RESEARCH INSTITUTES, *CORPORATIONS*, AND *GOVERNMENTS* WERE ALL STRIVING TO ADVANCE THE PACE AND POWER OF DIGITAL COMPUTATION.

BECAUSE OF ITS EXCLUSIVE SELF-CHECKING FEATURES, *UNIVAC* CANNOT MAKE A MISTAKE!

AND NEVER AMONG THE STATED PURPOSES OF THEIR WORK DID THEY *MENTION* "ENTERTAINMENT."

THEN WHY CAN'T I GET MY BLUETOOTH TO CONNECT?!

THEY WANTED TO TAKE THE SAME *SWEEPING* ENHANCEMENT TO *HUMAN BRAINPOWER* THAT HAD PERFECTED FIRING TABLES...

U.S. ARMY BALLISTICS LAB, 1962.

...AND APPLY IT TO *ECONOMICS, METEOROLOGY, BUSINESS, PUBLIC POLICY,* AND THE MANAGEMENT OF *INFORMATION*.

Bendix

G-15

ALL

PURPOSE

COMPUTER

YET MANY PROGRAMMERS KEPT RETURNING TO MAKING--AND PLAYING--*GAMES*.

ARTHUR SAMUEL PROGRAMMING A CHECKERS GAME FOR THE IBM 701, "AFFECTIONATELY" CALLED "THE HULKING GIANT" BY PROGRAMMERS.

OFTEN ANYONE DARING THIS FELT THEMSELVES PLACED ON THE *WRONG SIDE* OF A "CULTURAL DIVIDE" IN COMPUTING.

[YOU] MIGHT WELL ASK WHY WE BOTHER TO USE THESE EXPENSIVE AND COMPLICATED MACHINES IN SO TRIVIAL A PURSUIT...

BUT GAMES PROVED TO BE *ELEGANT* AND *USEFUL* METAPHORS FOR THE VERY ASPECTS OF LIFE THAT COMPUTING ADVOCATES WANTED TO INFLUENCE.

THE MACHINE CANNOT LOOK AT THE WHOLE OF THE CHESS BOARD AT ONCE.

IT HAS TO PEER SHORT-SIGHTEDLY AT EVERY SQUARE IN TURN.

RESEARCH INTO THE TECHNIQUES OF PROGRAMMING A MACHINE TO TACKLE COMPLICATED PROBLEMS OF THIS TYPE MAY IN FACT LEAD TO QUITE IMPORTANT ADVANCES.

YOU CAN SAY THAT AGAIN.

ACM Chess Challenge
Garry Kasparov vs

IBM'S DEEP BLUE, WHICH IN 1997 DEFEATED...

...CHESS WORLD CHAMPION *GARRY KASPAROV* IN TOURNAMENT PLAY.

GAMES, TOO, PROVED TO BE *SENSATIONAL DIGITAL DIPLOMATS*...

...TOOLS FOR DEMONSTRATING TO OUTSIDERS WHAT COMPUTERS COULD DO.

PR WAS NEEDED BECAUSE NO SMALL NUMBER OF THOSE OUTSIDERS WERE *SUSPICIOUS* AND *MYSTIFIED* ABOUT WHERE THIS SO-CALLED *NEW INDUSTRIAL REVOLUTION* WAS TAKING THEM.

Lewis Yablonsky
ROBOPATHS
PEOPLE AS MACHINES

WHO EXACTLY WERE THE *SUITED, JARGON-SPOUTING EGGHEADS* DOING *UNEXPLAINABLE* THINGS WITH *INEXPLICABLE* TECHNOLOGY?...

...OFTEN BEHIND CLOSED DOORS?

Fweet!!

IT WAS ENOUGH TO MAKE CERTAIN PEOPLE *PARANOID.*

MP

AND IN THE POST WWII ATOMIC AGE...

...THERE WAS PLENTY OF PARANOIA TO GO AROUND.

MILITARY AREA
WEAPONS · AMMUNITION · EXPLOSIVES
CAMERAS · FIELDGLASSES · LIQUORS
TELESCOPES · RADIO TRANSMITTERS
PROHIBITED
ALL VEHICLES & PASSENGERS
SUBJECT TO SEARCH

The ATOM BOMB!

IS THIS TOMORROW

AMERICA UNDER COMMUNISM!

THEY PUSH A BUTTON AND VAST CITIES VANISH BEFORE YOUR VERY EYES!

INVASION U.S.A.

IT WASN'T JUST *MOORE'S LAW*--THE FORECASTED *RAPID EXPANSION OF COMPUTER PERFORMANCE*--SPURRING INNOVATION.

CHEMIST *GORDON MOORE.*

The Beginning of the Cold War

BLAM!
POW!

GUNSHOTS? CHEERING? *HUH?!*

IT WAS ALSO BECAUSE THE UNITED STATES, BRITISH COMMONWEALTH, AND WESTERN EUROPE WERE RACING TO KEEP A TECHNOLOGICAL EDGE...

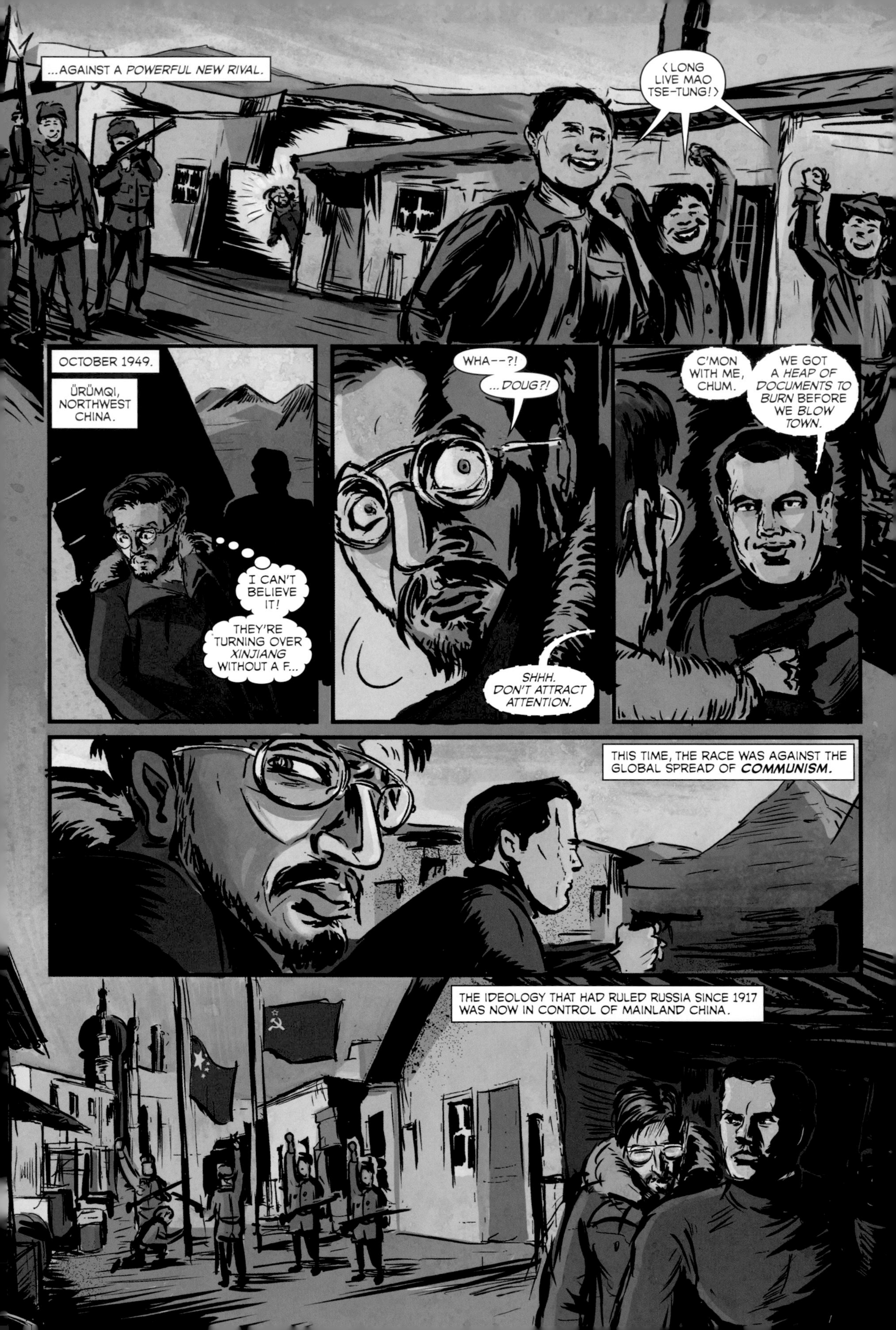

...AGAINST A POWERFUL NEW RIVAL.
‹LONG LIVE MAO TSE-TUNG!›
OCTOBER 1949.
ÜRÜMQI, NORTHWEST CHINA.
I CAN'T BELIEVE IT!
THEY'RE TURNING OVER XINJIANG WITHOUT A F...
WHA--?!
...DOUG?!
SHHH. DON'T ATTRACT ATTENTION.
C'MON WITH ME, CHUM.
WE GOT A HEAP OF DOCUMENTS TO BURN BEFORE WE BLOW TOWN.
THIS TIME, THE RACE WAS AGAINST THE GLOBAL SPREAD OF COMMUNISM.
THE IDEOLOGY THAT HAD RULED RUSSIA SINCE 1917 WAS NOW IN CONTROL OF MAINLAND CHINA.

HAVING LOST 20 MILLION PEOPLE IN ITS OWN FIGHT AGAINST THE NAZIS, THE SOVIET UNION WAS DETERMINED TO ENSURE THAT GERMANY WOULD NEVER AGAIN INVADE THE RUSSIAN HOMELAND.

TO CREATE A PROTECTIVE "BUFFER ZONE," THE U.S.S.R. TOOK CONTROL OF POLAND, BULGARIA, CZECHOSLOVAKIA-- NEARLY THE WHOLE OF *EASTERN EUROPE*-- AND A LARGE CHUNK OF GERMANY, TOO.

POWERFUL FIGURES IN AMERICA SAW THIS NOT ONLY AS THE UGLY ASCENT OF *TOTALITARIANISM* BUT ALSO AS DEPRIVING THE *CAPITALIST* UNITED STATES OF KEY TRADING PARTNERS.

BALANCE of POWER

Geopolitics in the nuclear age
by Chris Crawford

MINDSCAPE

oftware that challenges the mind.

BALANCE of POWER
Geopolitics in the nuclear age
by Chris Crawford

1985'S *BALANCE OF POWER* WAS A PC STRATEGY GAME FOR THE APPLE MACINTOSH. IT ALLOWED PLAYERS TO ASSUME THE ROLE OF U.S. PRESIDENT OR SOVIET PREMIER AND TRY THEIR HAND AT WORLD DOMINATION. BRASH ACTIONS COULD END IN *NUCLEAR NIGHTMARE.*

COMPUTER GAMING WORLD CALLED IT "ONE OF THE MOST INNOVATIVE COMPUTER GAMES OF ALL TIME."

MEANWHILE, THE *COMMUNIST DREAM* OF ENDING THE ENDLESS DOMINATION OF THE *POOR* BY THE *RICH* WAS ALLURING TO MANY...

...OFTEN IN COUNTRIES LIKE CHINA, WHICH HAD ENDURED YEARS OF EXPLOITATION BY POWERFUL COUNTRIES LIKE GREAT BRITAIN, JAPAN, AND GERMANY.

EVEN THE MANHATTAN PROJECT WAS TINGED WITH COMMUNIST SYMPATHY IN THE PERSONS OF PHYSICIST *EMIL JULIUS "KLAUS" FUCHS*, CHEMIST *HARRY GOLD*, AND MACHINIST *DAVID GREENGLASS*...

...WHO WERE AMONG THOSE WHO LEAKED *ATOMIC SECRETS* TO RUSSIA IN HOPES THEY WOULD HELP THAT COUNTRY DEFEAT THE NAZIS.

"I COME FROM JULIUS."

THE PRECISE VALUE OF SUCH LEAKS IS UNCLEAR. BUT THE U.S.S.R. DETONATED ITS FIRST NUCLEAR WEAPON AT A TEST SITE IN MODERN KAZAKHSTAN IN AUGUST 1949.

FROM THAT POINT ON THROUGH TO THE PRESENT, AMERICANS AND RUSSIANS HAVE *SHUFFLED BACK AND FORTH* BETWEEN *HOT-TEMPERED ARMS RACE* AND SOBER *DIPLOMACY*.

THE *COLD WAR* LEFT THE WORLD FACING THE LOOMING POSSIBILITY OF *APOCALYPTIC DESTRUCTION* THAT HAS SERVED AS A *TROPE* IN SO MANY GAMES, BOTH VINTAGE AND CONTEMPORARY.

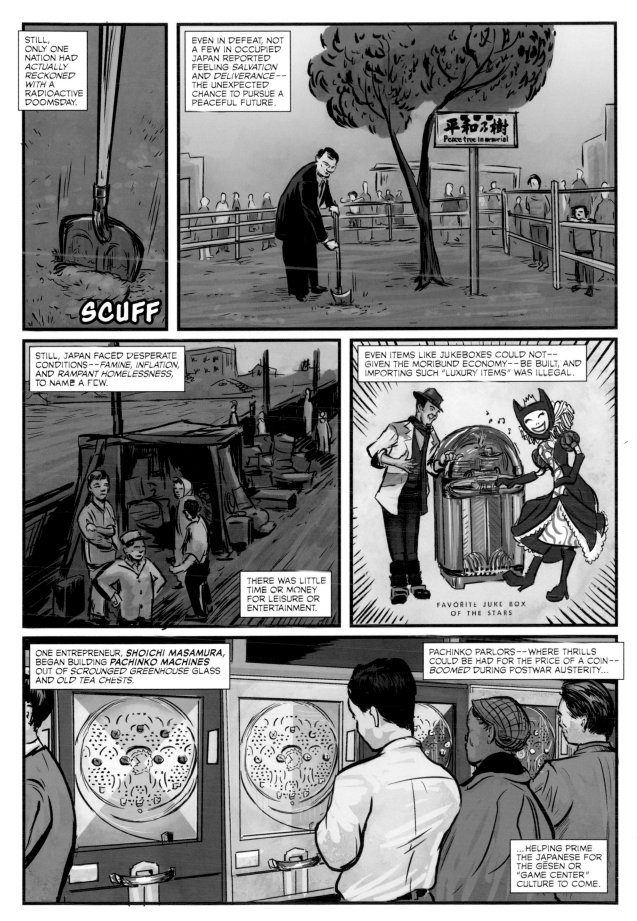

STILL, ONLY ONE NATION HAD *ACTUALLY RECKONED WITH* A RADIOACTIVE DOOMSDAY.

SCUFF

EVEN IN DEFEAT, NOT A FEW IN OCCUPIED JAPAN REPORTED FEELING *SALVATION* AND *DELIVERANCE*-- THE UNEXPECTED CHANCE TO PURSUE A PEACEFUL FUTURE.

平和乃樹
Peace tree in memorial

STILL, JAPAN FACED DESPERATE CONDITIONS--*FAMINE, INFLATION,* AND *RAMPANT HOMELESSNESS,* TO NAME A FEW.

THERE WAS LITTLE TIME OR MONEY FOR LEISURE OR ENTERTAINMENT.

EVEN ITEMS LIKE JUKEBOXES COULD NOT-- GIVEN THE MORIBUND ECONOMY--BE BUILT, AND IMPORTING SUCH "LUXURY ITEMS" WAS ILLEGAL.

FAVORITE JUKE BOX OF THE STARS

ONE ENTREPRENEUR, *SHOICHI MASAMURA,* BEGAN BUILDING *PACHINKO MACHINES* OUT OF *SCROUNGED GREENHOUSE* GLASS AND *OLD TEA CHESTS.*

PACHINKO PARLORS--WHERE THRILLS COULD BE HAD FOR THE PRICE OF A COIN-- *BOOMED* DURING POSTWAR AUSTERITY...

...HELPING PRIME THE JAPANESE FOR THE GĒSEN OR "GAME CENTER" CULTURE TO COME.

JAPAN HAD COMMUNISTS, TOO. THE FASCISTS HAD JAILED THEM. BUT POSTWAR, THEY STROVE FOR CLOUT IN SOCIETY.

YET NATIVE CAPITALISTS AND WESTERN POWERS WOULD NOT STAND FOR THE *NIPPONESE* FOLLOWING THE LEAD OF CHINA AND NORTH KOREA.

THE UNITED STATES DECIDED TO POSITION JAPAN AS A *REGIONAL ALLY* TO *HALT COMMUNISM IN ITS TRACKS.*

IN JAPAN, WE HAVE AN ILLUSTRATION THAT WE CAN COOPERATE ON A BASIS OF EQUALITY EVEN WITH FORMER ENEMIES OF ANOTHER RACE.

WE SHALL SHOW THAT...THE FREE WEST CAN JOIN HANDS WITH THE FREE EAST...TO PRESERVE OUR COMMON FREEDOM.

JOHN FOSTER DULLES, U.S. SECRETARY OF STATE, 1951.

THE UNITED STATES USED JAPAN AS A LOGISTICS BASE TO FIGHT THE *KOREAN CONFLICT*...

...AGAINST OPPOSING FORCES COMBINING NORTH KOREANS, CHINESE, AND (SECRETLY) *ELITE RUSSIAN JET-FIGHTER PILOTS.*

OWING IN PART TO THE COLD WAR, JAPAN BEGAN TO *RESURGE.*

MONEY *FLOODED IN,* FOR EXAMPLE, WHEN THE U.S. MILITARY ORDERED THOUSANDS OF TRUCKS AND JEEPS FROM TOYOTA...

...WHICH HAD ALSO SUPPLIED THE IMPERIAL FORCES THEY FOUGHT IN WORLD WAR II.

WAR'S MANY SIDE EFFECTS INCLUDE A YEARNING FOR THE FAMILIAR AND VEXING WAITS FOR ORDERS OR ACTION.

A TRUE VIDEO GAME INDUSTRY POWER PLAYER AROSE DURING THE KOREAN CONFLICT TO CAPITALIZE ON THIS.

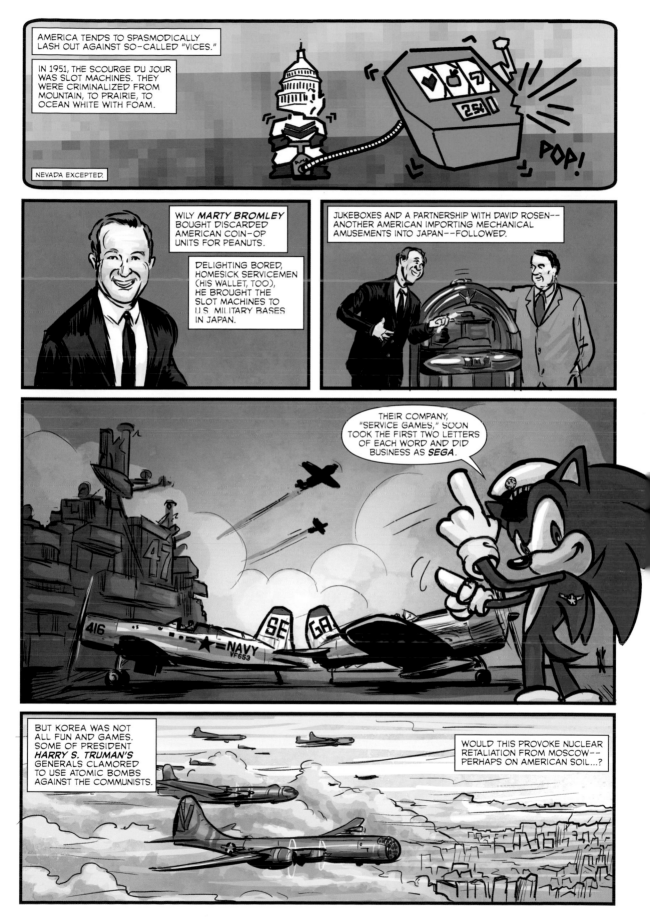

AMERICA TENDS TO SPASMODICALLY LASH OUT AGAINST SO-CALLED "VICES."

IN 1951, THE SCOURGE DU JOUR WAS SLOT MACHINES. THEY WERE CRIMINALIZED FROM MOUNTAIN, TO PRAIRIE, TO OCEAN WHITE WITH FOAM.

NEVADA EXCEPTED.

POP!

WILY *MARTY BROMLEY* BOUGHT DISCARDED AMERICAN COIN-OP UNITS FOR PEANUTS.

DELIGHTING BORED, HOMESICK SERVICEMEN (HIS WALLET, TOO), HE BROUGHT THE SLOT MACHINES TO U.S. MILITARY BASES IN JAPAN.

JUKEBOXES AND A PARTNERSHIP WITH DAVID ROSEN-- ANOTHER AMERICAN IMPORTING MECHANICAL AMUSEMENTS INTO JAPAN--FOLLOWED.

THEIR COMPANY, "SERVICE GAMES," SOON TOOK THE FIRST TWO LETTERS OF EACH WORD AND DID BUSINESS AS *SEGA*.

BUT KOREA WAS NOT ALL FUN AND GAMES. SOME OF PRESIDENT *HARRY S. TRUMAN'S* GENERALS CLAMORED TO USE ATOMIC BOMBS AGAINST THE COMMUNISTS.

WOULD THIS PROVOKE NUCLEAR RETALIATION FROM MOSCOW-- PERHAPS ON AMERICAN SOIL...?

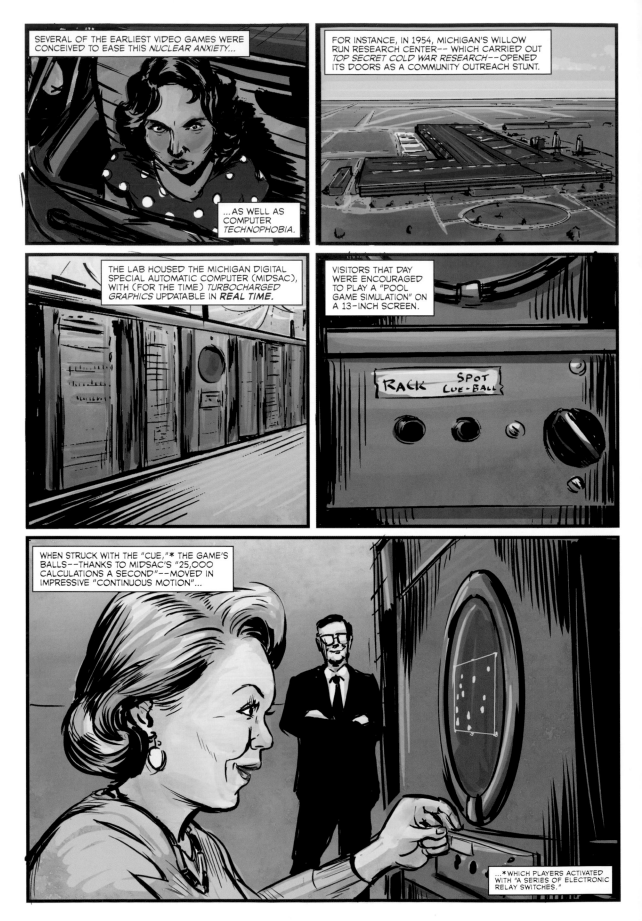

SEVERAL OF THE EARLIEST VIDEO GAMES WERE CONCEIVED TO EASE THIS *NUCLEAR ANXIETY*...

...AS WELL AS COMPUTER *TECHNOPHOBIA.*

FOR INSTANCE, IN 1954, MICHIGAN'S WILLOW RUN RESEARCH CENTER-- WHICH CARRIED OUT *TOP SECRET COLD WAR RESEARCH*--OPENED ITS DOORS AS A COMMUNITY OUTREACH STUNT.

THE LAB HOUSED THE MICHIGAN DIGITAL SPECIAL AUTOMATIC COMPUTER (MIDSAC), WITH (FOR THE TIME) *TURBOCHARGED GRAPHICS* UPDATABLE IN **REAL TIME.**

VISITORS THAT DAY WERE ENCOURAGED TO PLAY A "POOL GAME SIMULATION" ON A 13-INCH SCREEN.

RACK   SPOT
         CUE-BALL

WHEN STRUCK WITH THE "CUE,"* THE GAME'S BALLS--THANKS TO MIDSAC'S "25,000 CALCULATIONS A SECOND"--MOVED IN IMPRESSIVE "CONTINUOUS MOTION"...

...*WHICH PLAYERS ACTIVATED WITH "A SERIES OF ELECTRONIC RELAY SWITCHES."

ANOTHER EXAMPLE: IN 1958, TO QUELL THE NERVES OF NEARBY RESIDENTS WARY OF *ATOMIC EXPERIMENTS IN THEIR BACKYARDS...*

...BROOKHAVEN NATIONAL LABORATORY (BNL) IN NEW YORK STATE ALSO WELCOMED THE PUBLIC.

I VISITED BNL

FORMER RAD LAB AND MANHATTAN PROJECT PHYSICIST *WILLIAM HIGINBOTHAM*, NOW WORKED THERE, SEEKING PEACEFUL USES FOR NUCLEAR ENERGY.

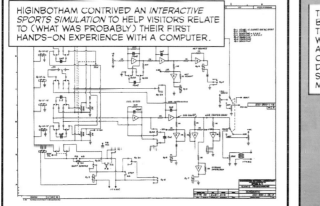

HIGINBOTHAM CONTRIVED AN *INTERACTIVE SPORTS SIMULATION* TO HELP VISITORS RELATE TO (WHAT WAS PROBABLY) THEIR FIRST HANDS-ON EXPERIENCE WITH A COMPUTER.

TECHNOLOGY BACKING THIS GAME WAS MOSTLY ANALOG: CHIEFLY, A DONNER SCIENTIFIC MODEL 30.

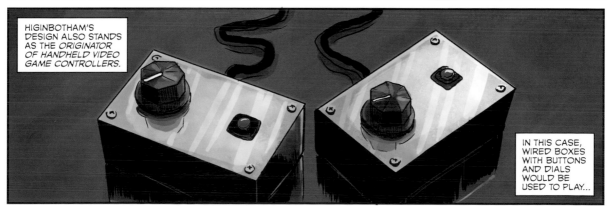

HIGINBOTHAM'S DESIGN ALSO STANDS AS THE *ORIGINATOR OF HANDHELD VIDEO GAME CONTROLLERS.*

IN THIS CASE, WIRED BOXES WITH BUTTONS AND DIALS WOULD BE USED TO PLAY...

...COMPUTER TENNIS.*

HIGINBOTHAM'S CREATION (ALSO VIEWED ON A DUMONT OSCILLOSCOPE!) SEEMS TO HAVE FEATURED TIGHT, RESPONSIVE GAMEPLAY AND EYE-CATCHING GRAPHICS.

IT COULD SUPPORT NO MUSIC OR SOUND EFFECTS, BUT CONTROLLER ACTIONS WERE ACCOMPANIED BY SATISFYING *CLICKS* FROM THE SYSTEM'S ELECTROMECHANICAL RELAYS.

*OFTEN ERRONEOUSLY CALLED *TENNIS FOR TWO*, A NAME NEITHER HIGINBOTHAM NOR BNL EVER USED.

PROPHESYING THE GLOBAL OBSESSION TO COME, THE RESPONSE TO *COMPUTER TENNIS* WAS "OVERWHELMING."

THIS WAS *PARADISE* UNTIL WE FOUND OUT *YOU* WEREN'T *DEAD!*

FOLKS LINED UP "AROUND THE GYM FLOOR AND OUT THE BUILDING" FOR 30-SECOND TURNS AT THE GAME.

BUT KEEP IN MIND: ULTIMATELY THE NUMBER OF PEOPLE TO PLAY THIS, LIKE ALL THE GAMES TO COME BEFORE IT, WOULD BE *MINUSCULE.*

ONE LOCAL BOY WAS LUCKY. HIS FATHER WAS ONE OF THE ENGINEERS WHO ACTUALLY BUILT *COMPUTER TENNIS.*

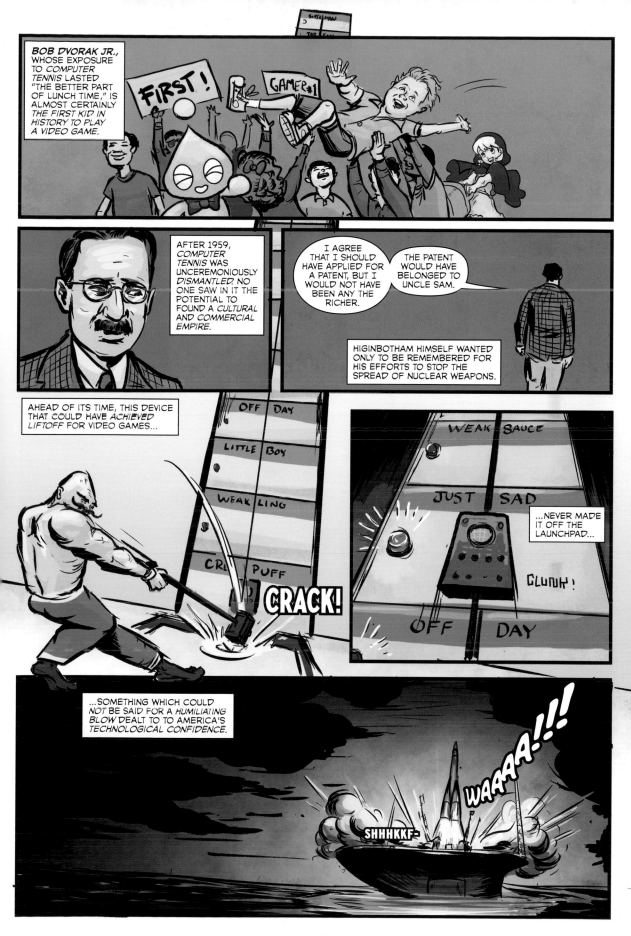

BOB DVORAK JR., WHOSE EXPOSURE TO COMPUTER TENNIS LASTED "THE BETTER PART OF LUNCH TIME," IS ALMOST CERTAINLY THE FIRST KID IN HISTORY TO PLAY A VIDEO GAME.

FIRST!

GAMER #1

AFTER 1959, COMPUTER TENNIS WAS UNCEREMONIOUSLY DISMANTLED. NO ONE SAW IN IT THE POTENTIAL TO FOUND A CULTURAL AND COMMERCIAL EMPIRE.

I AGREE THAT I SHOULD HAVE APPLIED FOR A PATENT, BUT I WOULD NOT HAVE BEEN ANY THE RICHER.

THE PATENT WOULD HAVE BELONGED TO UNCLE SAM.

HIGINBOTHAM HIMSELF WANTED ONLY TO BE REMEMBERED FOR HIS EFFORTS TO STOP THE SPREAD OF NUCLEAR WEAPONS.

AHEAD OF ITS TIME, THIS DEVICE THAT COULD HAVE ACHIEVED LIFTOFF FOR VIDEO GAMES...

OFF DAY

LITTLE BOY

WEAK LING

CREAM PUFF

WEAK SAUCE

JUST SAD

OFF DAY

...NEVER MADE IT OFF THE LAUNCHPAD...

CRACK!

CLUNK!

...SOMETHING WHICH COULD NOT BE SAID FOR A HUMILIATING BLOW DEALT TO TO AMERICA'S TECHNOLOGICAL CONFIDENCE.

WAAAA!!!

SHHHKKF-

43

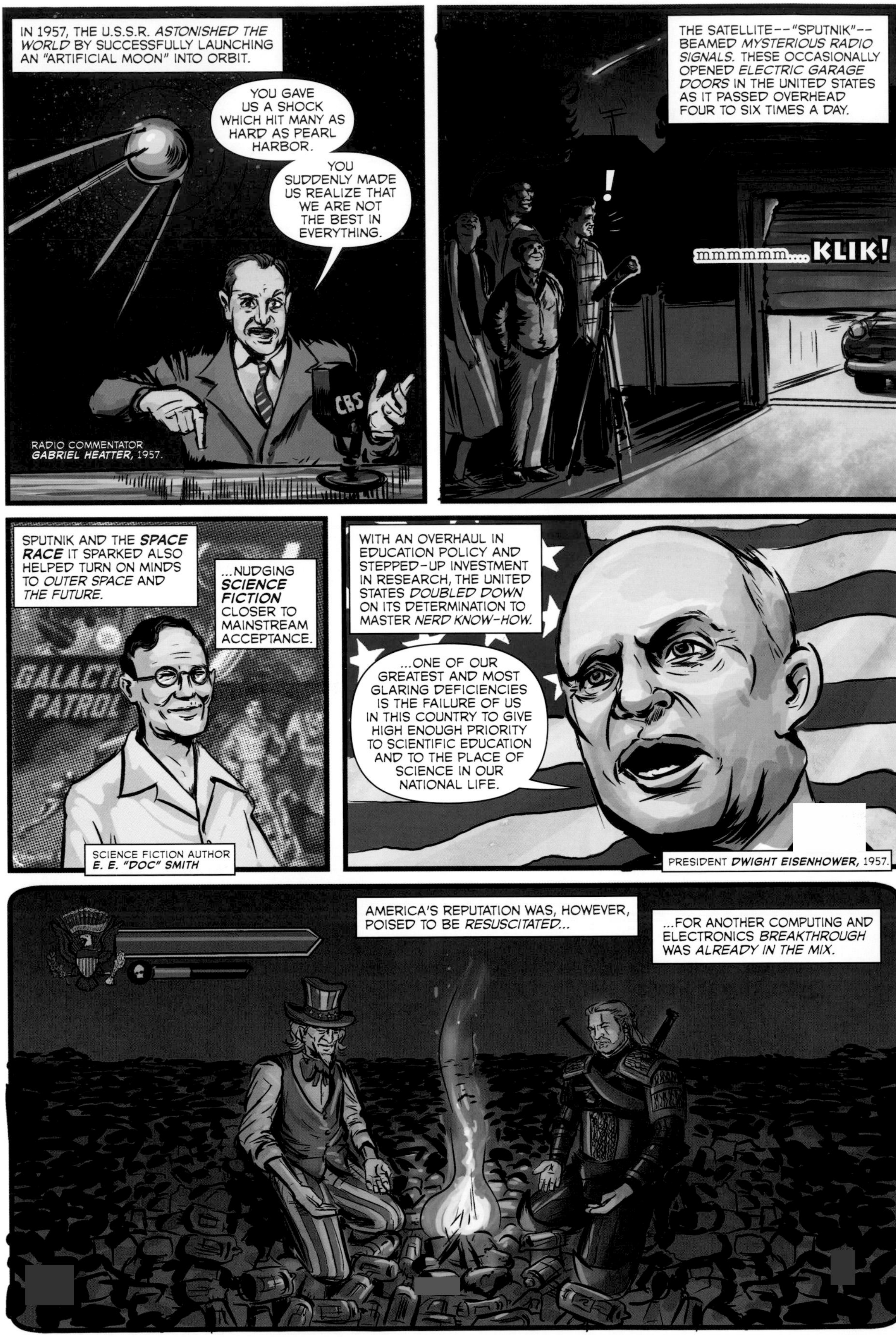
IN 1957, THE U.S.S.R. *ASTONISHED THE WORLD* BY SUCCESSFULLY LAUNCHING AN "ARTIFICIAL MOON" INTO ORBIT.
YOU GAVE US A SHOCK WHICH HIT MANY AS HARD AS PEARL HARBOR.
YOU SUDDENLY MADE US REALIZE THAT WE ARE NOT THE BEST IN EVERYTHING.
CBS
RADIO COMMENTATOR *GABRIEL HEATTER*, 1957.
THE SATELLITE--"SPUTNIK"--BEAMED *MYSTERIOUS RADIO SIGNALS.* THESE OCCASIONALLY OPENED *ELECTRIC GARAGE DOORS* IN THE UNITED STATES AS IT PASSED OVERHEAD FOUR TO SIX TIMES A DAY.
!
mmmmmm.... KLIK!
SPUTNIK AND THE ***SPACE RACE*** IT SPARKED ALSO HELPED TURN ON MINDS TO *OUTER SPACE* AND *THE FUTURE.*
...NUDGING ***SCIENCE FICTION*** CLOSER TO MAINSTREAM ACCEPTANCE.
GALACTI
PATROL
SCIENCE FICTION AUTHOR ***E. E. "DOC" SMITH***
WITH AN OVERHAUL IN EDUCATION POLICY AND STEPPED-UP INVESTMENT IN RESEARCH, THE UNITED STATES *DOUBLED DOWN* ON ITS DETERMINATION TO MASTER *NERD KNOW-HOW.*
...ONE OF OUR GREATEST AND MOST GLARING DEFICIENCIES IS THE FAILURE OF US IN THIS COUNTRY TO GIVE HIGH ENOUGH PRIORITY TO SCIENTIFIC EDUCATION AND TO THE PLACE OF SCIENCE IN OUR NATIONAL LIFE.
PRESIDENT ***DWIGHT EISENHOWER***, 1957.
AMERICA'S REPUTATION WAS, HOWEVER, POISED TO BE *RESUSCITATED...*
...FOR ANOTHER COMPUTING AND ELECTRONICS *BREAKTHROUGH* WAS *ALREADY IN THE MIX.*

THE ENIAC, FERRANTI MARK I, IBM 701, UNIVAC, AND MIDSAC COMPUTERS ALL RELIED ON VACUUM TUBES.

THEY WERE ALSO *CRUCIAL* TO THE RADIO, TELEVISION, AND TELEPHONE INDUSTRIES.

WHILE IT WAS TRUE THAT THE TECHNOLOGY HAD *MASSIVELY IMPROVED* OVER TIME...

...WHEN IT CAME TO COMPUTERS, VACUUM TUBES REMAINED *SCRUBS* OF THE HIGHEST ORDER.

REVEL IN THE VILE MUSTARD OF MY TECHNO-INSUFFICIENCY, FINK-RATS!

ESPECIALLY IN COMPUTER APPLICATIONS, THEY WERE *BULKY*––AND SUCKED UP *GOBS OF ELECTRICAL POWER.*

VACUUM TUBE COMPUTERS REQUIRED HUGE *MAINTENANCE STAFFS* TO PLAY *KEEP-AWAY* WITH UNAUTHORIZED USERS

COLOSSAL AIR CONDITIONING UNITS WERE NEEDED TO COMBAT ALL THE WASTE HEAT THEY GENERATED.

EEEYAH HA HA HA HA!

45

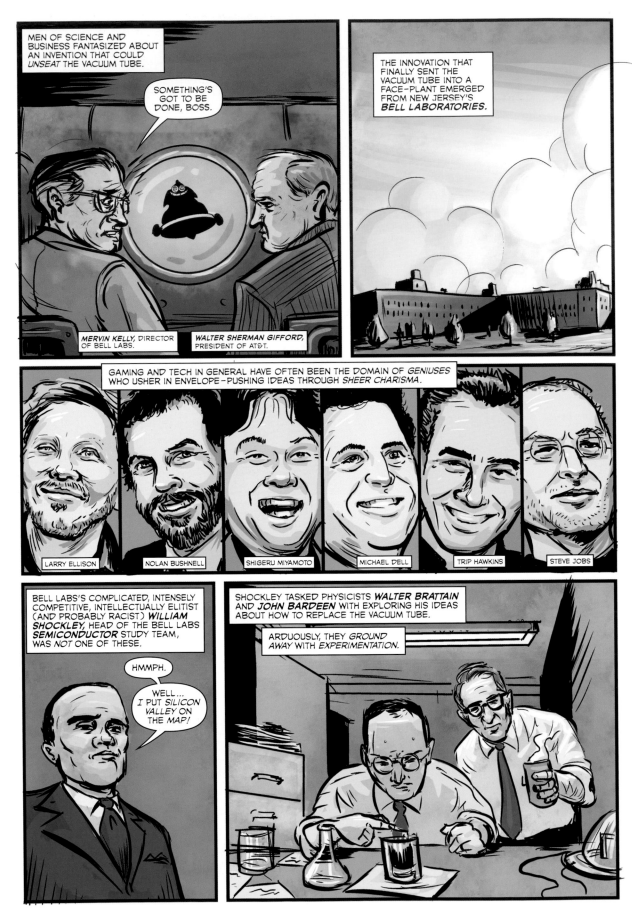

MEN OF SCIENCE AND BUSINESS FANTASIZED ABOUT AN INVENTION THAT COULD *UNSEAT* THE VACUUM TUBE.

SOMETHING'S GOT TO BE DONE, BOSS.

MERVIN KELLY, DIRECTOR OF BELL LABS.

WALTER SHERMAN GIFFORD, PRESIDENT OF AT&T.

THE INNOVATION THAT FINALLY SENT THE VACUUM TUBE INTO A FACE-PLANT EMERGED FROM NEW JERSEY'S *BELL LABORATORIES.*

GAMING AND TECH IN GENERAL HAVE OFTEN BEEN THE DOMAIN OF *GENIUSES* WHO USHER IN ENVELOPE-PUSHING IDEAS THROUGH *SHEER CHARISMA.*

LARRY ELLISON

NOLAN BUSHNELL

SHIGERU MIYAMOTO

MICHAEL DELL

TRIP HAWKINS

STEVE JOBS

BELL LABS'S COMPLICATED, INTENSELY COMPETITIVE, INTELLECTUALLY ELITIST (AND PROBABLY RACIST) *WILLIAM SHOCKLEY*, HEAD OF THE BELL LABS *SEMICONDUCTOR* STUDY TEAM, WAS *NOT* ONE OF THESE.

HMMPH.

WELL... I PUT *SILICON VALLEY* ON THE *MAP!*

SHOCKLEY TASKED PHYSICISTS *WALTER BRATTAIN* AND *JOHN BARDEEN* WITH EXPLORING HIS IDEAS ABOUT HOW TO REPLACE THE VACUUM TUBE.

ARDUOUSLY, THEY *GROUND AWAY* WITH *EXPERIMENTATION.*

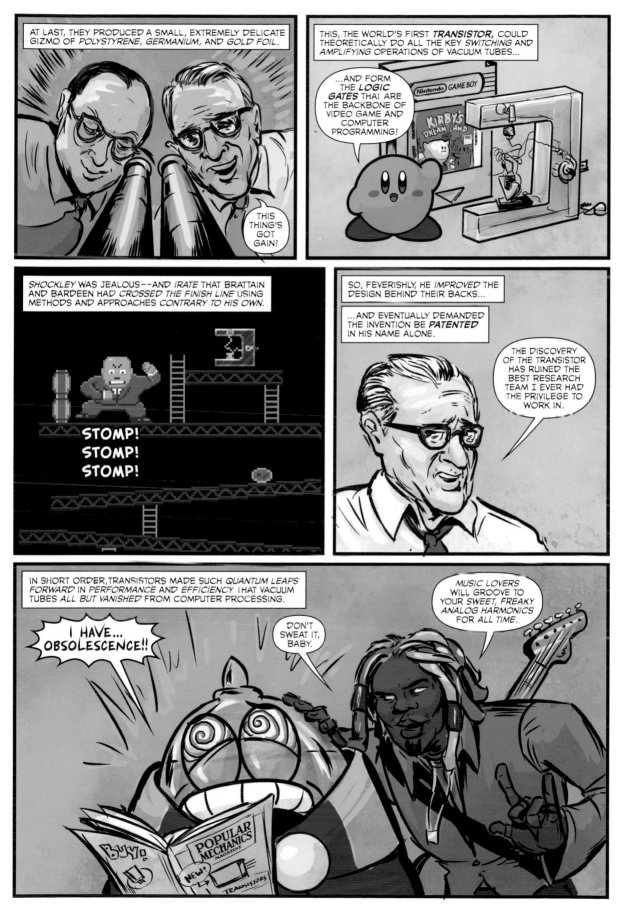

AT LAST, THEY PRODUCED A SMALL, EXTREMELY DELICATE GIZMO OF *POLYSTYRENE, GERMANIUM,* AND *GOLD FOIL.*

THIS THING'S GOT GAIN!

THIS, THE WORLD'S FIRST *TRANSISTOR,* COULD THEORETICALLY DO ALL THE KEY *SWITCHING* AND *AMPLIFYING* OPERATIONS OF VACUUM TUBES...

...AND FORM THE *LOGIC GATES* THAT ARE THE BACKBONE OF VIDEO GAME AND COMPUTER PROGRAMMING!

SHOCKLEY WAS JEALOUS—AND *IRATE* THAT BRATTAIN AND BARDEEN HAD *CROSSED THE FINISH LINE* USING METHODS AND APPROACHES *CONTRARY TO HIS OWN.*

STOMP!
STOMP!
STOMP!

SO, FEVERISHLY, HE *IMPROVED* THE DESIGN BEHIND THEIR BACKS...

...AND EVENTUALLY DEMANDED THE INVENTION BE *PATENTED* IN HIS NAME ALONE.

THE DISCOVERY OF THE TRANSISTOR HAS RUINED THE BEST RESEARCH TEAM I EVER HAD THE PRIVILEGE TO WORK IN.

IN SHORT ORDER, TRANSISTORS MADE SUCH *QUANTUM LEAPS* FORWARD IN *PERFORMANCE* AND *EFFICIENCY* THAT VACUUM TUBES *ALL BUT VANISHED* FROM COMPUTER PROCESSING.

I HAVE... OBSOLESCENCE!!

DON'T SWEAT IT, BABY.

MUSIC LOVERS WILL GROOVE TO YOUR *SWEET, FREAKY ANALOG HARMONICS* FOR ALL TIME.

POPULAR MECHANICS MAGAZINE

NEW! TRANSISTORS

CHAPTER THREE TRANSISTORS
This Means SPACEWAR!

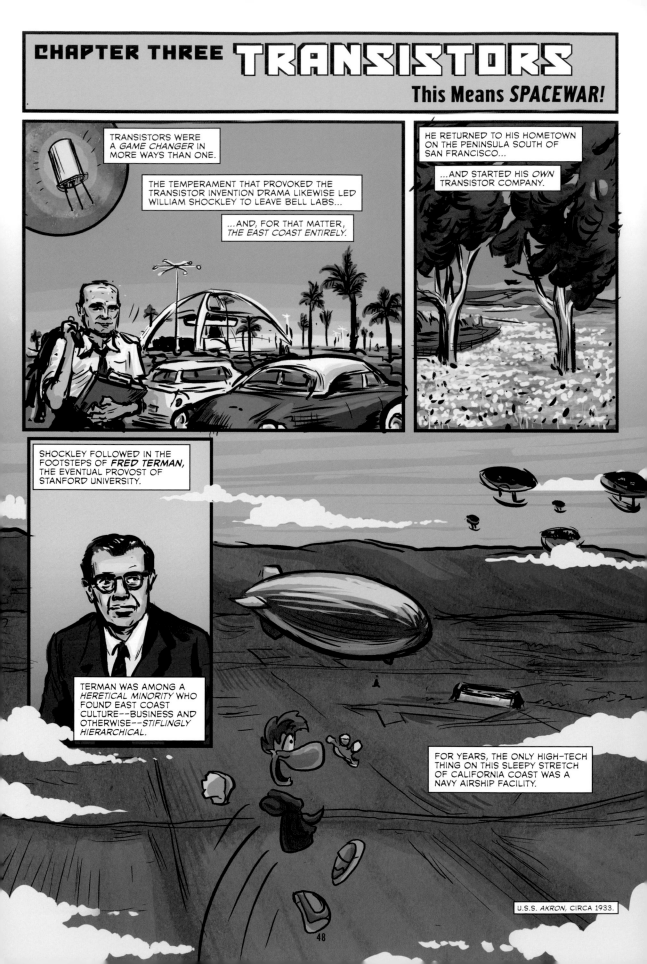

TRANSISTORS WERE A *GAME CHANGER* IN MORE WAYS THAN ONE.

THE TEMPERAMENT THAT PROVOKED THE TRANSISTOR INVENTION DRAMA LIKEWISE LED WILLIAM SHOCKLEY TO LEAVE BELL LABS...

...AND, FOR THAT MATTER, *THE EAST COAST ENTIRELY.*

HE RETURNED TO HIS HOMETOWN ON THE PENINSULA SOUTH OF SAN FRANCISCO...

...AND STARTED HIS *OWN* TRANSISTOR COMPANY.

SHOCKLEY FOLLOWED IN THE FOOTSTEPS OF *FRED TERMAN,* THE EVENTUAL PROVOST OF STANFORD UNIVERSITY.

TERMAN WAS AMONG A *HERETICAL MINORITY* WHO FOUND EAST COAST CULTURE--BUSINESS AND OTHERWISE--*STIFLINGLY HIERARCHICAL.*

FOR YEARS, THE ONLY HIGH-TECH THING ON THIS SLEEPY STRETCH OF CALIFORNIA COAST WAS A NAVY AIRSHIP FACILITY.

U.S.S. *AKRON,* CIRCA 1933.

IN THE 1950s, THOUGH, THAT CHANGED.

MENU
JUN 1950
$ 18000
37X
52

SAN JOSE . 1950

NCO 3

VIVIAN ASSOC.   SHOCKLEY   FAIRCHILD   GE LABS   IBM

FOR ONE, THE AREA HAD INEXPENSIVE LAND!

AND STANFORD WAS GENEROUS WITH ITS BIG UNIVERSITY RESOURCES!

THE DISTANCE FROM *STODGY NEW YORK* BANKS AND SPUTNIK-INSPIRED *SMALL BUSINESS LEGISLATION* DESIGNED TO *JUMPSTART* SCIENCE AND TECHNOLOGY FIRMS SPURRED CREATIVE MODES OF BUSINESS FINANCING!

CASUAL WEST COAST LIFESTYLES PROMOTED A SOCIAL LANDSCAPE WHERE EXECUTIVES AND ENGINEERS COULD MINGLE WITHOUT LAYERS OF MIDDLE MANAGEMENT GETTING IN THEIR WAY!

THE LATEST TECHNOLOGY--*AND THE NEW WAYS OF THINKING THEY INSPIRED*-- FOUND FERTILE GROUND INDEED IN WHAT WOULD BECOME *SILICON VALLEY.*

TRANSISTORS WERE ALSO MAKING WAVES THOUSANDS OF MILES ACROSS THE PACIFIC.

IN POSTWAR, JAPAN TWO AMIABLE INVENTORS--*MASARU IBUKA* AND *AKIO MORITA*--JOINED FORCES.

THEIR BUSINESS STARTED IN THE *FIREBOMBED REMAINS* OF A TOKYO DEPARTMENT STORE.

FIRST MAKING RICE COOKERS AND VOLTMETERS FROM SCAVENGED SPARE PARTS, THEY SOON LICENSED TRANSISTOR TECHNOLOGY FROM BELL LABS.

WITH IT, THEY BEGAN MANUFACTURING ALMOST *UNTHINKABLY* SMALL AND CHEAP TRANSISTOR RADIOS.

IBUKA AND MORITA'S COMPANY BECAME *SONY*...

...WHICH BEGAN RELEASING *PLAYSTATION* CONSOLES IN 1994.

THANKS TO SHOCKLEY & CO., SCRAPPY AND (COMPARATIVELY) COMPACT *TRANSISTORIZED* COMPUTERS HIT THE SCENE...

...LIKE THE EXPERIMENTAL TX-O, WHICH WENT ONLINE AT THE MIT-BASED LINCOLN LABORATORY IN 1956.

UNLIKE *EVERY COMPUTER THAT PRECEDED IT*, THE TX-O WAS DESIGNED SO *JUST ONE PERSON* COULD USE IT.

BIG WOW. HOW ABOUT ONE THAT *TRANSCENDS* YOU *IMPUDENT INSECTS* COMPLETELY?

BUT CAN YOU RUN *CRYSIS*?

THE TX-O'S CRT SCREEN COULD ALSO DISPLAY CRUDE DRAWINGS MADE BY A *LIGHT PEN.*

DOUG ROSS OF LINCOLN LABORATORY'S COMPUTER APPLICATIONS GROUP COWROTE A VIDEO GAME FOR THE TX-O CALLED *MOUSE IN THE MAZE* WITH THIS FEATURE IN MIND.

MOUSE WAS ALSO CONCEIVED AS A COMPUTING EXPERIMENT FOR OCCASIONAL PUBLIC DISPLAY.

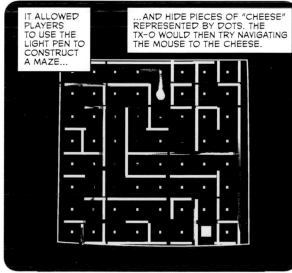

IT ALLOWED PLAYERS TO USE THE LIGHT PEN TO CONSTRUCT A MAZE...

...AND HIDE PIECES OF "CHEESE" REPRESENTED BY DOTS. THE TX-O WOULD THEN TRY NAVIGATING THE MOUSE TO THE CHEESE.

THERE WAS ALSO A PROPERLY GRAPHICAL *PLAYER VS. COMPUTER* TIC-TAC-TOE GAME FOR THE TX-O.

COMMANDS WOULD BE ENTERED WITH A *FLEXOWRITER* TYPEWRITER--THE DAY'S STANDARD-ISSUE COMPUTER KEYBOARD.

THE TX-O'S ASSOCIATION WITH *DIGITAL AGE RODENTS* DIDN'T END WITH *MOUSE IN THE MAZE.*

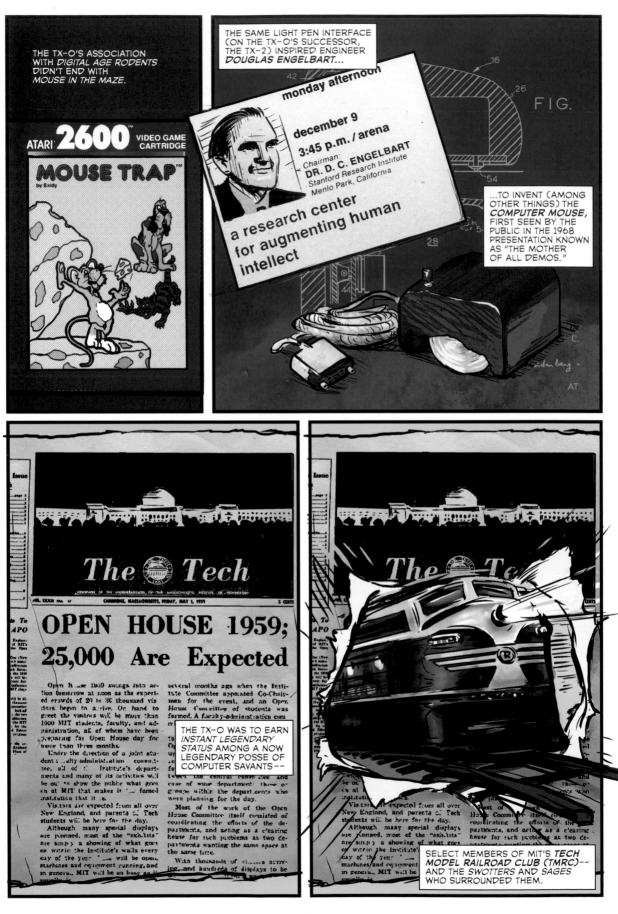

ATARI 2600 VIDEO GAME CARTRIDGE

MOUSE TRAP
by Exidy

THE SAME LIGHT PEN INTERFACE (ON THE TX-O'S SUCCESSOR, THE TX-2) INSPIRED ENGINEER *DOUGLAS ENGELBART...*

monday afternoon

december 9
3:45 p.m. / arena
Chairman:
DR. D. C. ENGELBART
Stanford Research Institute
Menlo Park, California

a research center for augmenting human intellect

FIG.

...TO INVENT (AMONG OTHER THINGS) THE *COMPUTER MOUSE*, FIRST SEEN BY THE PUBLIC IN THE 1968 PRESENTATION KNOWN AS "THE MOTHER OF ALL DEMOS."

The ☉ *Tech*
NEWSPAPER OF THE UNDERGRADUATES OF THE MASSACHUSETTS INSTITUTE OF TECHNOLOGY
CAMBRIDGE, MASSACHUSETTS, FRIDAY, MAY 1, 1959   5 CENTS

OPEN HOUSE 1959;
25,000 Are Expected

Open house 1959 swings into action tomorrow at noon as the expected crowds of 20 to 30 thousand visitors begin to arrive. On hand to greet the visitors will be more than 1600 MIT students, faculty, and administration, all of whom have been preparing for Open House day for more than three months.

Under the direction of a joint student-faculty-administration committee, all of the Institute's departments and many of its activities will be out to show the public what goes on at MIT that makes it the famed institution that it is.

Visitors are expected from all over New England, and parents of Tech students will be here for the day.

Although many special displays are planned, most of the "exhibits" are simply a showing of what goes on within the Institute's walls every day of the year — labs will be open, machines and equipment running, and in general, MIT will be as busy as it usually is.

several months ago when the Institute Committee appointed Co-Chairmen for the event, and an Open House Committee of students was formed. A faculty-administration committee...

Most of the work of the Open House Committee itself consisted of coordinating the efforts of the departments, and acting as a clearing house for tech problems as two departments wanting the same space at the same time.

With thousands of visitors arriving, and hundreds of displays to be seen...

THE TX-O WAS TO EARN *INSTANT LEGENDARY STATUS* AMONG A NOW LEGENDARY POSSE OF COMPUTER SAVANTS--

SELECT MEMBERS OF MIT'S *TECH MODEL RAILROAD CLUB (TMRC)*-- AND THE *SWOTTERS* AND *SAGES* WHO SURROUNDED THEM.

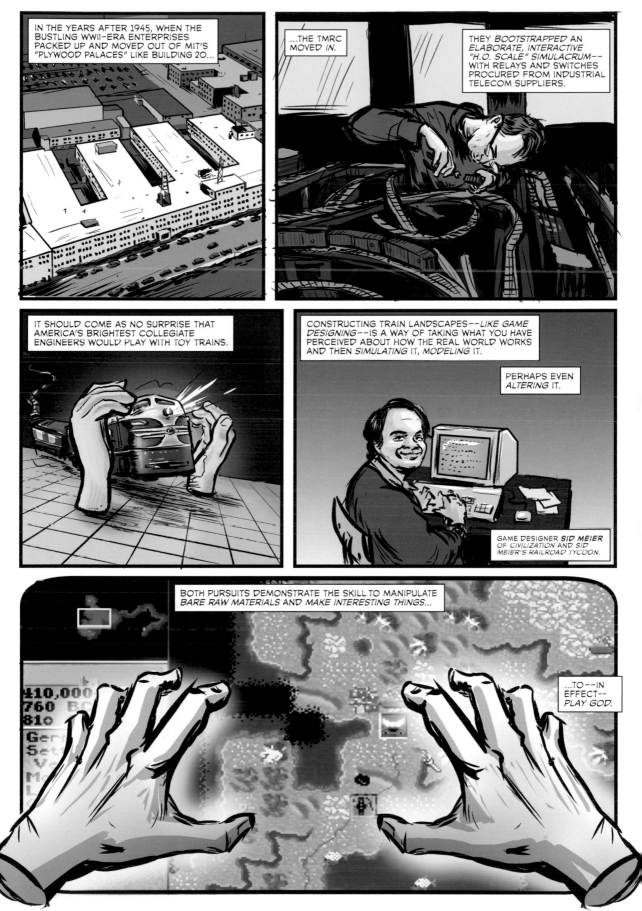

IN THE YEARS AFTER 1945, WHEN THE BUSTLING WWII-ERA ENTERPRISES PACKED UP AND MOVED OUT OF MIT'S "PLYWOOD PALACES" LIKE BUILDING 20...

...THE TMRC MOVED IN.

THEY *BOOTSTRAPPED* AN *ELABORATE, INTERACTIVE "H.O. SCALE" SIMULACRUM*-- WITH RELAYS AND SWITCHES PROCURED FROM INDUSTRIAL TELECOM SUPPLIERS.

IT SHOULD COME AS NO SURPRISE THAT AMERICA'S BRIGHTEST COLLEGIATE ENGINEERS WOULD PLAY WITH TOY TRAINS.

CONSTRUCTING TRAIN LANDSCAPES--*LIKE GAME DESIGNING*--IS A WAY OF TAKING WHAT YOU HAVE PERCEIVED ABOUT HOW THE REAL WORLD WORKS AND THEN *SIMULATING* IT, *MODELING* IT.

PERHAPS EVEN *ALTERING* IT.

GAME DESIGNER *SID MEIER* OF *CIVILIZATION* AND *SID MEIER'S RAILROAD TYCOON.*

BOTH PURSUITS DEMONSTRATE THE SKILL TO MANIPULATE *BARE RAW MATERIALS* AND *MAKE INTERESTING THINGS...*

...TO--IN EFFECT-- *PLAY GOD.*

TOO YOUNG TO HAVE BEEN IN THE WAR, THE TMRC CREW WAS OF THE FIRST GENERATION TO *GROW UP WITH* COMPUTERS.

AND THEY POSSESSED *IMAGINATIONS* AND *EXPECTATIONS PRIMED TO KEEP PACE WITH* THE TEMPO OF COMPUTING'S ADVANCES.

ALAN KOTOK ENCOUNTERING HIS FIRST "THINKING MACHINE"– AS A HIGH SCHOOL STUDENT IN NEW JERSEY, MID-1950s.

AS THE 1950s SPLASHED OVER INTO THE 1960s, CURIOUS, *INCURABLE TINKERERS*––WITH COMPULSIVE DRIVES TO *UNDERSTAND HOW THINGS WORK*––WEREN'T NECESSARILY NEW.

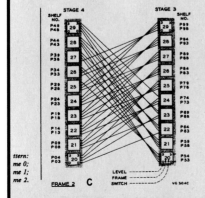

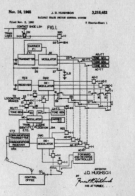

HOWEVER, BESIDES COMPUTERS, WHAT *WAS* NEW IN THE DAYS OF THESE PARTICULAR TECHIE TYPES WAS THE NEARLY GLOBAL REACH OF AND INCREDIBLE INGENUITY INVOLVED IN THE TELEPHONE AND RAILWAY SUPERSTRUCTURES.

LONG BEFORE THE INTERNET AND "THE CLOUD," THE TMRC CREW YEARNED TO *COMPREHEND, EXPERIENCE,* AND *TAP INTO THE POWER OF* THESE ENGINEERING MARVELS.

AND MORE IMPORTANTLY, THEY LEARNED THEY *COULD.*

KEEP IN MIND: THIS WAS THE *PRELAPSARIAN AGE* BEFORE THE THREATS OF *COMPUTER VIRUSES, MALWARE, CYBER-TERRORISM* AND *COMPUTER FRAUD.*

THE TELEPHONE SYSTEM WAS GUARDED ONLY BY WHAT ALAN KOTOK DESCRIBES AS...

..."SECURITY BY OBSCURITY."

THIS MEANT THAT ADMINISTRATORS ASSUMED IT WAS SIMPLY *IMPOSSIBLE* FOR OUTSIDERS TO ACCRUE THE TECHNICAL EXPERTISE REQUIRED TO *PENETRATE* AND *EXPLOIT* THEIR SYSTEM.

ALAN KOTOK IN 2000.

BUT ENGINEERING STUDENTS-- ONES WHO HAD *"MODDED"* (MODIFIED) TELEPHONE GEAR TO CONTROL TOY TRAINS--HAD *THAT* EXPERTISE IN *SPADES!*

beep boop meep mip

AND THEY COULD DO ALL SORTS OF FUN THINGS WITH IT.

THIS IS THE PENTAGON!

WHAT IS YOUR SECURITY CLEARANCE?!

SO THE TMRC WERE THE WORLD'S ORIGINAL *HACKERS.*

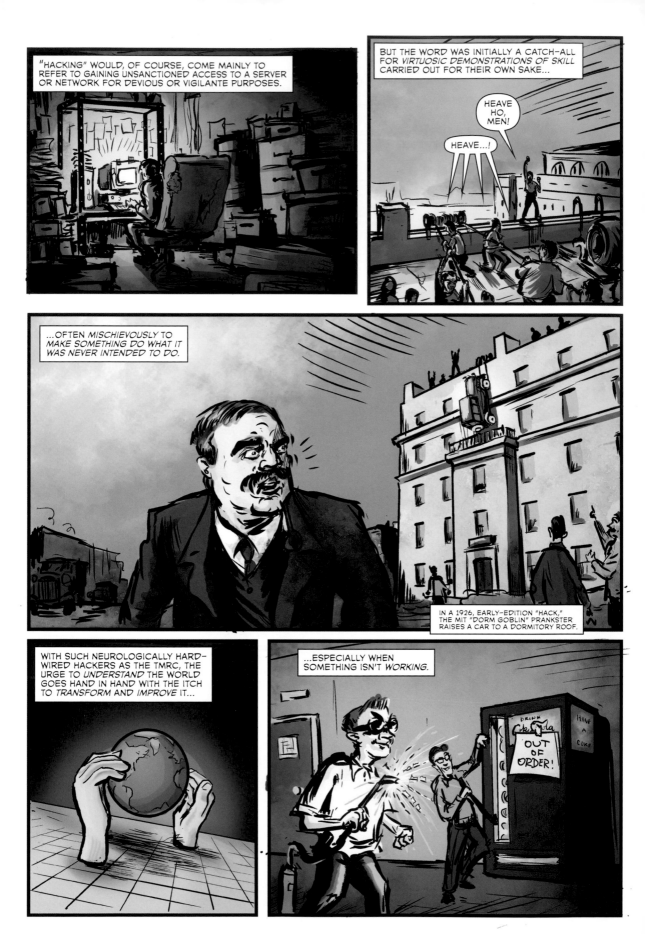

"HACKING" WOULD, OF COURSE, COME MAINLY TO REFER TO GAINING UNSANCTIONED ACCESS TO A SERVER OR NETWORK FOR DEVIOUS OR VIGILANTE PURPOSES.

BUT THE WORD WAS INITIALLY A CATCH-ALL FOR *VIRTUOSIC DEMONSTRATIONS OF SKILL* CARRIED OUT FOR THEIR OWN SAKE...

HEAVE HO, MEN!

HEAVE...!

...OFTEN *MISCHIEVOUSLY* TO *MAKE SOMETHING DO WHAT IT WAS NEVER INTENDED TO DO.*

IN A 1926, EARLY-EDITION "HACK," THE MIT "DORM GOBLIN" PRANKSTER RAISES A CAR TO A DORMITORY ROOF.

WITH SUCH NEUROLOGICALLY HARD-WIRED HACKERS AS THE TMRC, THE URGE TO *UNDERSTAND* THE WORLD GOES HAND IN HAND WITH THE ITCH TO *TRANSFORM* AND *IMPROVE* IT...

...ESPECIALLY WHEN SOMETHING ISN'T *WORKING.*

DRINK Coca Cola

OUT OF ORDER!

HAVE A COKE

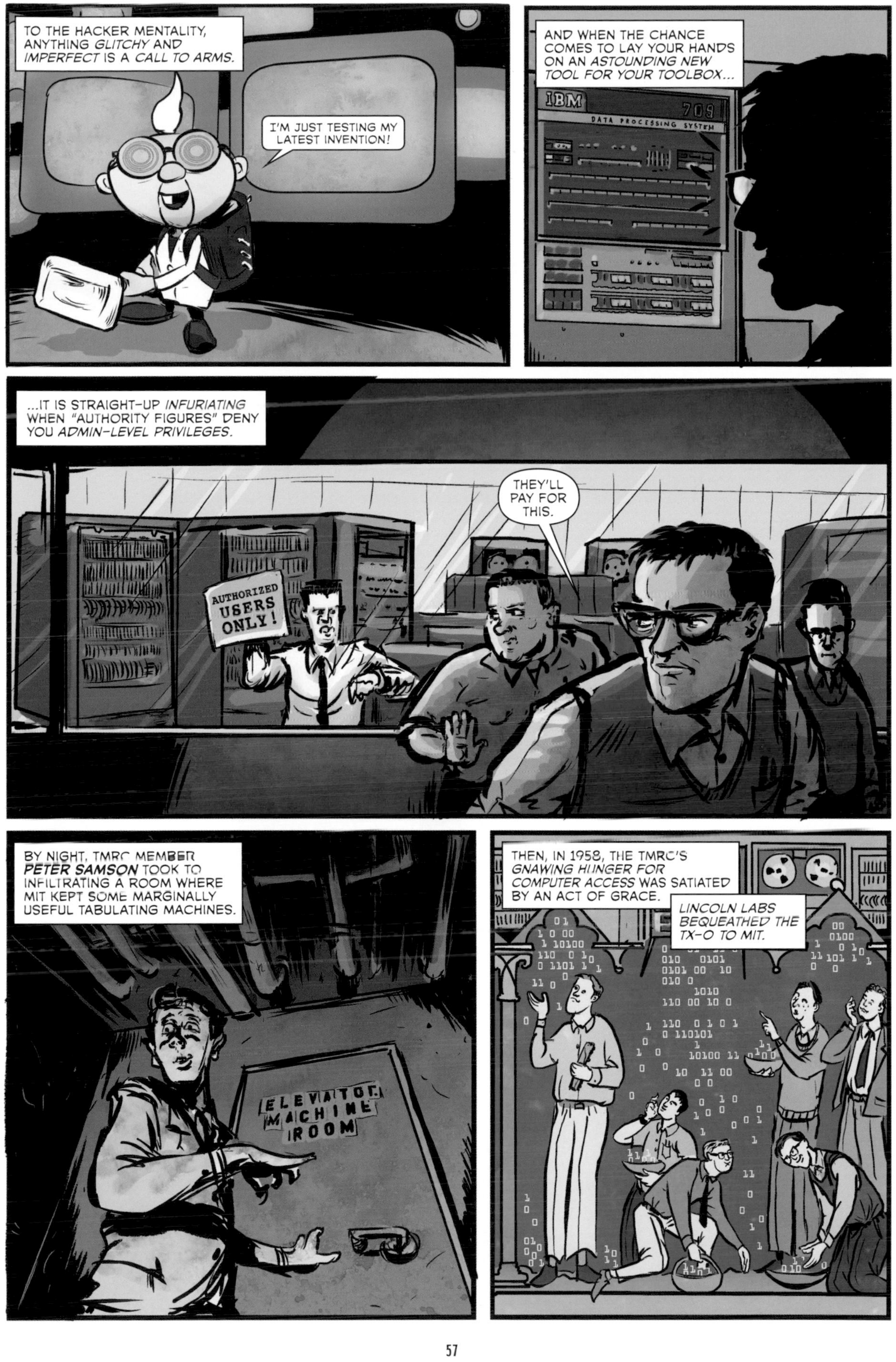
TO THE HACKER MENTALITY, ANYTHING *GLITCHY* AND *IMPERFECT* IS A *CALL TO ARMS.*
I'M JUST TESTING MY LATEST INVENTION!
AND WHEN THE CHANCE COMES TO LAY YOUR HANDS ON AN *ASTOUNDING NEW TOOL FOR YOUR TOOLBOX...*
IBM
709
DATA PROCESSING SYSTEM
...IT IS STRAIGHT-UP *INFURIATING* WHEN "AUTHORITY FIGURES" DENY YOU *ADMIN-LEVEL PRIVILEGES.*
AUTHORIZED USERS ONLY!
THEY'LL PAY FOR THIS.
BY NIGHT, TMRC MEMBER ***PETER SAMSON*** TOOK TO INFILTRATING A ROOM WHERE MIT KEPT SOME MARGINALLY USEFUL TABULATING MACHINES.
ELEVATOR MACHINE ROOM
THEN, IN 1958, THE TMRC'S *GNAWING HUNGER FOR COMPUTER ACCESS* WAS SATIATED BY AN ACT OF GRACE.
LINCOLN LABS BEQUEATHED THE TX-O TO MIT.

TO COLLEGE KIDS ALREADY FAIRLY JAZZED BY VACUUM TUBE-BASED, PUNCH-CARD UNITS--WITH *NO* GRAPHIC DISPLAYS--THE "TIXO" WAS A DIZZYING *POWER-UP.*

THE HACKERS ATTACKED IT ON EVERY FRONT, CONTRIVING ACCESS IN THE WEE HOURS WHEN PROFESSORS AND ADMINISTRATORS WERE SLEEPING.

ASSAULT

◄ Ⓐ ►

42 m
MIT BUILDING 26

tmrcGo

GO! GO! GO! GO!
GO!

b.saunders

US 234 MIT 120

b.saunders
tmrcGOAT

40 /120
[AUTO]
● 0 +100

THE TX-O THRUST THE HACKERS' IMAGINATIONS INTO *HIGH ORBIT.*

AND ORBIT WAS PRECISELY WHERE THE U.S.S.R. HAD JUST SENT COSMONAUT *YURI ALEKSEYEVICH GAGARIN* IN APRIL 1961.

THIS RESPONSIBILITY IS NOT TOWARD ONE PERSON, NOT TOWARD A FEW DOZEN, NOT TOWARD A GROUP.

IT IS A RESPONSIBILITY TOWARD ALL MANKIND-- TOWARD ITS PRESENT AND ITS FUTURE.

GAGARIN WAS THE FIRST HUMAN BEING IN SPACE.

AGAIN, THE "RED COMMIES" HAD BEATEN AMERICA.

58

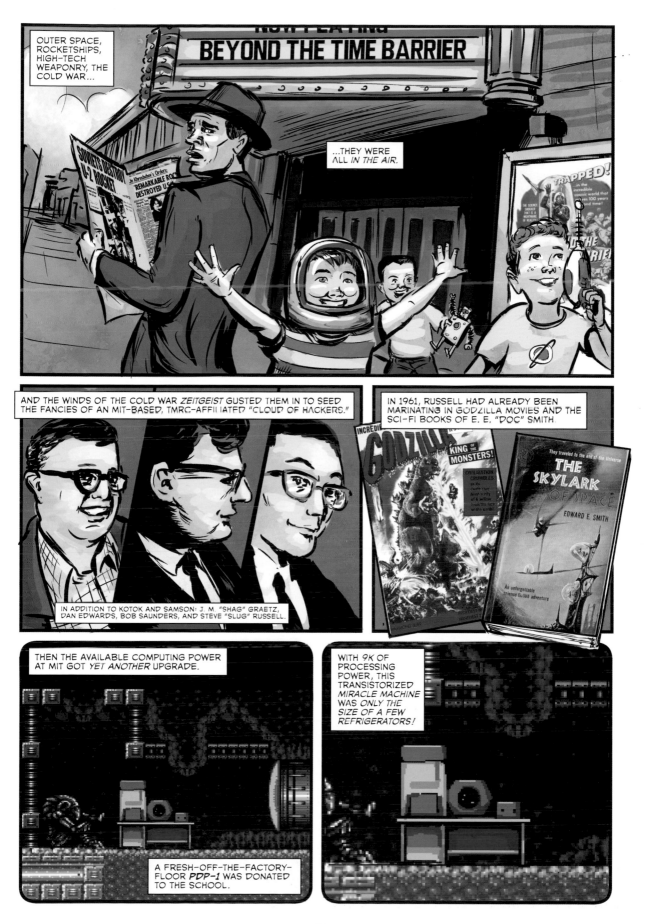

OUTER SPACE, ROCKETSHIPS, HIGH-TECH WEAPONRY, THE COLD WAR...

NOW PLAYING
BEYOND THE TIME BARRIER

...THEY WERE ALL *IN THE AIR.*

AND THE WINDS OF THE COLD WAR *ZEITGEIST* GUSTED THEM IN TO SEED THE FANCIES OF AN MIT-BASED, TMRC-AFFILIATED "CLOUD OF HACKERS."

IN 1961, RUSSELL HAD ALREADY BEEN MARINATING IN GODZILLA MOVIES AND THE SCI-FI BOOKS OF E. E. "DOC" SMITH.

IN ADDITION TO KOTOK AND SAMSON: J. M. "SHAG" GRAETZ, DAN EDWARDS, BOB SAUNDERS, AND STEVE "SLUG" RUSSELL.

THEN THE AVAILABLE COMPUTING POWER AT MIT GOT *YET ANOTHER* UPGRADE.

A FRESH-OFF-THE-FACTORY-FLOOR *PDP-1* WAS DONATED TO THE SCHOOL.

WITH 9K OF PROCESSING POWER, THIS TRANSISTORIZED *MIRACLE MACHINE* WAS *ONLY* THE SIZE OF A FEW *REFRIGERATORS!*

FOR HACKERS WITH A JONES TO REACH INTO THE *DIGITAL VOID* AND CREATE *SOMETHING* FROM *NOTHING*, THERE WAS NO BETTER INSTRUMENT WITH WHICH TO *PLAY GOD.*

AND WE *DO* MEAN "DIGITAL VOID"...

...BECAUSE LIKE *ALL* PREVIOUSLY MENTIONED COMPUTERS, THE PDP-1 ESSENTIALLY CAME WITH *NO SOFTWARE*-- AND *NO OPERATING SYSTEM.*

A COUPLE OF INTERESTING PROGRAMS HAD BEEN WRITTEN TO SHOW OFF THE PDP-1'S POWER AND GRAPHICS.

BUT STEVE RUSSELL THOUGHT SOMEONE COULD DO A WHOLE LOT BETTER.

GETS BORING AFTER A WHILE.

AND THAT PERHAPS SOME KIND OF *GAME* WOULD DO THE TRICK.

...MAYBE SOMETHING THAT TEACHES PEOPLE HOW TO FLY A SPACESHIP...

RUSSELL SPOUTED OFF ABOUT THIS OFTEN ENOUGH TO MAKE HIS FRIENDS FINALLY *SHAME HIM INTO MAKING THE GAME.*

ALL RIGHT, RUSSELL, HERE'S A SINE-COSINE ROUTINE. *NOW* WHAT'S YOUR EXCUSE?

RECALL THAT THE *NE PLUS ULTRA* OF HACKING IS TO DEMONSTRATE ENOUGH *MASTERY* OVER SOMETHING...

DUDE!

IS THAT WHAT I THINK IT IS...?

...TO MAKE IT DO SOMETHING *COOL*--WHICH IT WAS NEVER INTENDED TO DO.

SURE IS!

TETRIS ON A *BUILDING.* COURTESY OF 153 *WIRELESS LED* MODULES IN A 9x17 ARRAY!!

APRIL 20, 2012: HACKERS TAKING A CUE FROM POLAND'S *PROJEKT P.I.W.O.* ET AL. TRANSFORM THE MIT GREEN BUILDING INTO A GIANT GAMING SCREEN.

AND REMEMBER HOW *EVEN IN ALAN TURING'S* DAY THE IDEA OF USING COMPUTERS FOR *GAMES* WAS CONSIDERED ALL BUT *HERETICAL.*

THE TECHNOLOGY WAS CONCEIVED AND INTENDED ONLY FOR MILITARY, SCIENTIFIC, GOVERNMENT, AND INDUSTRY USE.

SO VIDEO GAMES ARE THEMSELVES A "HACK!"

RUSSELL AND COMPANY HAD THE PROGRAMMING CHOPS. THEIR GROUP DYNAMIC WAS BOTH COLLABORATIVE AND COMPETITIVE-- PERFECT FOR MAKING AND PLAYING GAMES. THEY WERE SENSITIVE TO THE PROMISES OF A HIGH-TECH FUTURE--AND THE SPECTER OF ARMED CONFLICT BETWEEN THE GLOBE'S SUPERPOWERS.

THE MAKERS OF THE PDP-1 WERE HOPING THEY WOULD DO SOMETHING WITH THE COMPUTER THAT WOULD BE INTERESTING AND MEMORABLE-- "VIRAL" IF YOU WILL.

AND THEY DID. FOR AFTER CRAFTING ABOUT 2,000 LINES OF ASSEMBLY LANGUAGE CODE, THE HACKERS GAVE US...

SPACEWAR!

SPACEWAR!

YEAR OF RELEASE: 1962

COUNTRY OF ORIGIN: UNITED STATES

GRAPHICS: X-Y DISPLAY AT 20 KILOCYCLE RATE

PLATFORMS: ORIGINALLY PDP-1 ONLY; PORTED TO MANY

DEVELOPER: STEVE RUSSELL, ET AL.

PUBLISHER: SELF-PUBLISHED

A LONG WAY FROM *CYBERPUNK 2077*, MAYBE THIS ARENA SHOOTER WASN'T THE VIDEO GAME TO END ALL VIDEO GAMES.

BUT YOU CAN MAKE A STRONG CASE THAT *SPACEWAR!* WAS THE ONE TO *BEGIN* THEM ALL.

GAMEPLAY CONSISTED OF SPACESHIPS DUELING WITH DEADLY *PHOTON TORPEDOES*. MEANWHILE, A NEARBY STAR TWINKLES, READY TO *GRAVITATIONALLY SUCK* SHIPS INTO *FUSION-HOT GRAVES*.

RUSSELL & CO. GRAPPLED WITH THE PDP-1'S LACK OF MEMORY, EMPLOYING PROGRAMMING TRICKS LIKE AN "OUTLINE COMPILER" TO MORE EASILY REDRAW THE SHIPS AT VARIOUS ROTATIONAL ANGLES.

SYSTEM LIMITATIONS, HOWEVER, PRECLUDED THE POSSIBILITY OF COLOR, MUSIC, OR SOUND EFFECTS.

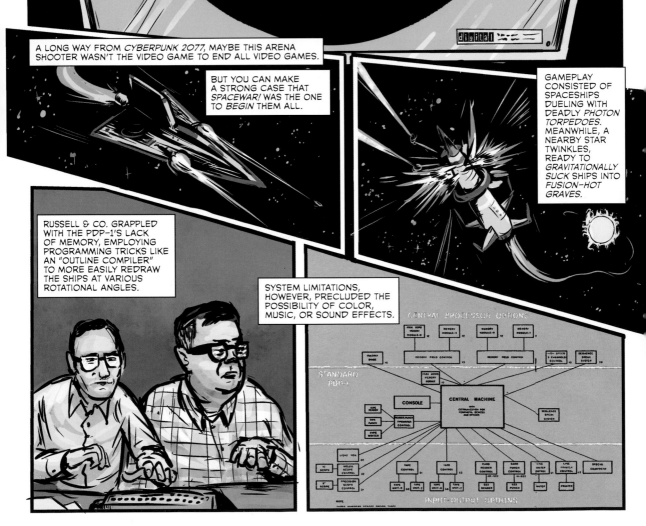

FROM THE DAY IT DEBUTED TO THE PUBLIC AT AN MIT SCIENCE OPEN HOUSE IN MAY 1962, *SPACEWAR!* WAS A *SMASH HIT...*

...THAT IS, WITH THE *SLIVER* OF A *SLIVER* OF THE PUBLIC WHO GOT TO PLAY IT. COMPUTERS SMALL AND CHEAP ENOUGH TO EXIST OUTSIDE OF *INSTITUTIONS* WERE STILL A WAYS AWAY.

BUT, AS WE'LL SEE, THOSE WHO EXPERIENCED *SPACEWAR!* (AND IN PARTICULAR ITS CLONES) WOULD AMOUNT TO A VERITABLE *WHO'S WHO* OF GAMING HEAVYWEIGHTS.

TIME PASSED. THE HACKERS DRIFTED OFF TO OTHER JOBS AND RESEARCH ASSIGNMENTS.

PANT PANT SAN FRANCISCO...?

HURRY.

BUT EVEN IN 1966, THE GAME THEY LEFT BEHIND REMAINED SO *ADDICTIVE*—AND SPONGED UP SO MUCH *PRECIOUS COMPUTER TIME*—THAT MIT WAS FORCED TO "CONFISCATE" THE CONTROL CONSOLE.

ZBT
Zeta Beta Toento

SPACEWA

WAR!

Phi Kappa SIGMA

GIVEN THE STATE OF *INFANCY* THAT VIDEO GAMES—AND SOFTWARE IN GENERAL—WERE IN 1962, THERE WAS NO METHOD OF COPYRIGHTING THEM.

DEC INCLUDED *SPACEWAR!* ON EVERY PDP-1 SOLD. THIS WAS ALMOST EXCLUSIVELY TO UNIVERSITIES AND THINK TANKS. THERE, IN SNOWBALLING NUMBERS, STUDENTS AND STAFFERS HYPED IT AND SHARED IT WITH FRIENDS.

THE GAME WAS REPEATEDLY PORTED TO NEW SYSTEMS, MODDED TO INCORPORATE NEW FEATURES, AND REVERSE ENGINEERED.

WINNER OF THE "FIRST INTERGALACTIC SPACEWAR OLYMPICS"--STANFORD UNIVERSITY, 1972.

SPACEWAR! HELPED SPREAD THE REVOLUTIONARY MESSAGE THAT COMPUTERS COULD BE USED FOR FUN.

I'd rather be playing spacewar!

MORE THAN THAT, IT MADE PEOPLE FEEL EMPOWERED AND ENCOURAGED TO MAKE THEIR OWN SOFTWARE--OR PUT THEIR PERSONAL STAMP ON SOMEONE ELSE'S.

COMPUTERS ARE MOSTLY USED AGAINST PEOPLE INSTEAD OF FOR PEOPLE; USED TO CONTROL PEOPLE INSTEAD OF TO FREE THEM; TIME TO CHANGE ALL THAT...

IT MAY NOT HAVE BEEN THE HACKERS' INTENTION, BUT THE COST-FREE, FREE-FORM NATURE OF SPACEWAR! CAME ALONG AT A TIME WHEN...

...A HIGHLY VISIBLE, HIGHLY VOCAL, AND INFLUENTIAL MINORITY WAS DETERMINED TO REVISE THE SOURCE CODE OF CIVILIZATION ITSELF.

WE MUST GUARD AGAINST MILITARY INDUSTRIAL COMPLEX !

PEOPLE'S PARK

AGAINST VIETNAM WAR

CHAPTER FOUR
COLD ON THE COLD WAR
GAMING HEATS UP!

TO *DISCREDIT* AND *DISSOLVE* THEIR *INTERNATIONAL RIVALS*, WESTERN LEADERS SET OUT TO PROVE THAT *THEIR* SYSTEM PRODUCED THE BETTER, FREER SOCIETY.

THREAT TO FREEDOM

A PICTURE STORY EXPOSING COMMUNISM

TO MAKE THIS CASE, THEY STROVE TO ATTAIN THE *HIGHEST-CALIBER CAPACITY TO WAGE WAR* ON THE ONE HAND...

US NAVY

...AND TO DISPLAY *CONSPICUOUS MATERIAL PROSPERITY* ON THE OTHER.

BUT INCREASINGLY, MORE PEOPLE BECAME *CONVINCED* THAT THIS *RIGID COLD WAR VISION* OF WHAT *LIFE SHOULD BE ABOUT*...

BUS

GREYHOUND

...HAD *UNACCEPTABLE FLAWS.*

THE STANDARD THING IS TO FEEL IN THE GUT THAT MIDDLE-CLASS VALUES ARE ALL WRONG.

ARGUMENTS COMMONLY WENT:

THE SYSTEM DIDN'T ACCOMMODATE INDIVIDUALISM. IT *DEHUMANIZED* WOMEN AND NONWHITES. IT PRODUCED A *MATERIALISTIC, ONE DIMENSIONAL CULTURE.*

IT CONTRIBUTED TO *LOCKING THE GLOBE* IN A PERMANENT STATE WHERE THE *FLASHPOINT OF ATOMIC ARMAGEDDON* COULD COME AT ANY MOMENT.

AND IT MEANT LIVING IN A NATION-STATE THAT WAS *TRIGGER-HAPPY FOR ARMED CONFLICT...*

KAK KOOMM!!

Ssshhhhfffff!!!

...SUCH AS WHEN THE NEXT COLD WAR BATTLEFRONT OPENED IN *VIETNAM AND SOUTHEAST ASIA.*

THE NUMBER OF AMERICAN MEN DRAFTED INTO THE MILITARY ESCALATED. PROTESTS ERUPTED ON COLLEGE CAMPUSES NATIONWIDE.

4 DEAD, 10 HURT AT KSU

United Press International
William K. Schroeder

Associated Press
Allison Krause

Novostov
Jeffrey Glenn Miller

Associated Press
Sandra Lee Scheuer

KENT STATE MASSACRE, MAY 4, 1970.

IN NUMBERS TOO HIGH TO OVERLOOK, PEOPLE (ESPECIALLY YOUNG PEOPLE) QUESTIONED TRADITIONAL IDEAS. SOME WANTED TO GO BACK TO NATURE.

FREE KITTENS!

DROP CITY
SONS AND DAUGHTERS
OF LIFE'S
LONGING FOR ITSELF

SOME BELIEVED *REALITY ITSELF* TO BE *DEFICIENT...*

...AND STROVE TO EXPAND *CONSCIOUSNESS* WITH *MIND-ALTERING DRUGS.*

THE POINT IS, MANY WANTED TO CHANGE THE WORLD.

MORE IMPORTANTLY, MANY BELIEVED THEY *REALLY COULD.*

TO ONE SUBSET OF THE COUNTERCULTURE, COMPUTERS EMERGED AS PREEMINENT TOOLS FOR ACHIEVING PERSONAL OR GLOBAL REVOLUTION.

CALIFORNIA'S EASIER EMBRACE OF *IDEALISM* AND *ALTERNATE LIFESTYLES* SUITED THESE *TECHNO-UTOPIANISTS...*

...WHO ALSO HAD THE ADVANTAGE OF CLOSENESS TO SILICON VALLEY JUST AS IT WAS ABSORBING ITS LATEST TECHNOLOGICAL MILESTONES.

TRANSISTOR INVENTOR WILLIAM SHOCKLEY WAS SCANDALIZED IN 1958 WHEN A HANDFUL OF HIS PROTÉGÉS LEFT HIS COMPANY TO FORM THEIR OWN.

THE TRAITOROUS 8 [BIT]

ONE, **ROBERT NOYCE,** COINVENTED THE **MICROCHIP,** PACKING MANY ELECTRONIC COMPONENTS ON ONE PIECE OF SILICON-- AN IMPROVEMENT ON THE TRANSISTOR THAT MADE COMPUTERS EVEN SMALLER AND MORE POWERFUL.

INTEL, THE COMPANY NOYCE WOULD LATER FORM, WENT ON TO CREATE THE **MICROPROCESSOR--** ESSENTIALLY A COMPUTER ON A SINGLE CHIP.

AT LAST THE GROUNDWORK WAS LAID FOR COMPUTERS--*AND VIDEO GAMES*--TO TRANSITION FROM THE BIG INSTITUTIONS OF *"THE MAN"* TO THE EVERYDAY SPACES OF *"THE PEOPLE."*

DEMYSTIFY COMPUTERS!

COMPUTERS BELONG TO ALL MANKIND!

COMPUTER LIB

WHAT IN SHORTHAND WE REFER TO AS "THE SIXTIES" WAS A COMPLICATED TIME. URGES TO SIMPLIFY AND REDUCE THEM TO A THUMBNAIL SKETCH OUGHT TO BE RESISTED.

GAME OVER?

BETWEEN THE ANTIWAR MOVEMENT'S INFLUENCE, ANGER THAT THE GOVERNMENT HAD MISLED THEM FOR YEARS, AND THE EMERGING CLARITY THAT THERE WAS NO REAL WAY TO "WIN" IN SOUTHEAST ASIA...

EACH DAY... SOMEONE HAS TO DIE SO THAT PRESIDENT NIXON WON'T BE--AND THESE ARE HIS WORDS-- THE FIRST PRESIDENT TO LOSE A WAR.

HOW DO YOU ASK A MAN TO BE THE LAST MAN TO DIE FOR A MISTAKE?

...THE VIETNAM CONFLICT WOUND DOWN TO A SPUTTERING, IGNOBLE END.

BIỆT-ĐỘNG-QUÂN

VÌ DÂN QUYẾT CHIẾN

THIS LEFT MUCH OF THE COLD WAR "MILITARY-INDUSTRIAL COMPLEX" REELING. ELECTRONICS FIRMS EXPECTING AN UNABATED BUFFET OF MILITARY CONTRACTS WENT HUNGRY...

Down and Out Along Route 128

By BERKELEY RICE

Like the massive layoffs in the W Coast aerospace industry, mo those in this area have been by cutbacks in Federal spendi defense and space. But unli

...WHICH MAY SHED LIGHT ON WHY ONE OF THEM TOOK A GAMBLE ON AN OUT-OF-LEFT-FIELD PROPOSITION FROM ONE OF ITS OWN DIVISION MANAGERS...

SA

SANDERS ASSOCIATES, INC.

...THE IDEA THAT THEY MIGHT MAKE BIG BUCKS HELPING PEOPLE PLAY GAMES ON THEIR TVs.

SPOTLIGHT: RALPH BAER

AT AGE 14 IN PREWAR COLOGNE, GERMANY, *RALPH BAER* WAS EJECTED FROM SCHOOL FOR BEING JEWISH.

SEEING EVEN DARKER DAYS AHEAD, IN 1938 HIS FAMILY ESCAPED TO AMERICA. HE LEARNED TO FIX RADIOS.

DRAFTED INTO THE U.S. MILITARY IN 1943, HE BECAME AN INTELLIGENCE EXPERT IN THE SMALL ARMS OF FOREIGN ARMIES.

MOST OF THE FAMILY ON MY FATHER'S SIDE...ALL WOUND UP IN THE CONCENTRATION CAMPS.

AFTER THE WAR, HE LIVED WITH HIS PARENTS IN BLUE-COLLAR WASHINGTON HEIGHTS, NYC, AND SPENT EVERY DAY AT THE LIBRARY STUDYING ELECTRONICS.

WITH DECADES OF HANDS-ON TRAINING AND A NATURAL ENGINEER'S IMPULSE TO "FIX EVERYTHING," ONE THING ABOUT TVs HAD LONG IRKED BAER.

WHAT THE HELL CAN YOU DO WITH A TV SET BESIDES TURN IT ON AND CHANGE CHANNELS?

BEFORE CABLE, SATELLITE, AND INTERNET SERVICES, TV BROADCASTERS-- LIMITED BY THE RANGE OF *VHF* OR *UHF WAVES*-- SERVED MOSTLY BIG POPULATION CENTERS. BAER (WHO HAD MOVED TO NEW HAMPSHIRE) COULD GET JUST *ONE STATION.* YOU CAN SEE WHY HE WANTED TVs TO HAVE A FEW MORE TRICKS IN THEIR REPETOIRE!

AN ITCH TO OUTFIT TVs WITH A *GAME-PLAYING PLATFORM* REPORTEDLY HAD OCCURRED TO HIM BEFORE. BUT IN 1966, A FLASH OF INSPIRATION WHILE AT A MANHATTAN BUS STATION BROUGHT IT BACK.

A PERTINENT ASIDE: BAER WAS *SELF-MADE*--WITH NO TIES TO UNIVERSITIES OR RESEARCH CENTERS.

IN 1966, HE PROBABLY HAD NEVER *HEARD OF* (LET ALONE *PLAYED*) SPACEWAR! COMPUTER TENNIS, OXO, AND SO ON.

NATURALLY, THIS WAS PRE-INTERNET. NEWS FROM THE *TECHNO-CULTURAL FRINGE* TRAVELED SLOWLY-- AND MAINSTREAM MINDS WERE FAR LESS OPEN TO IT.

SINCE THE TECHNOLOGICAL TOOLS HAD BECOME AVAILABLE, SOMEONE, SOONER OR LATER, WAS GOING TO HATCH A SIMILAR SCHEME TO USE TVs FOR INTERACTIVE PLAY.

BAER'S 1966 EPIPHANY ULTIMATELY DROVE THE INVENTION OF THE WORLD'S FIRST *HOME VIDEO GAME CONSOLE.*

UNDER LOCK AND KEY AT SANDERS ASSOCIATES, BAER HAD GOTTEN AS FAR AS A UNIT THAT COULD PUT TWO PLAYER-CONTROLLED SPOTS ON THE SCREEN.

THAT'S PRETTY MUCH IT.

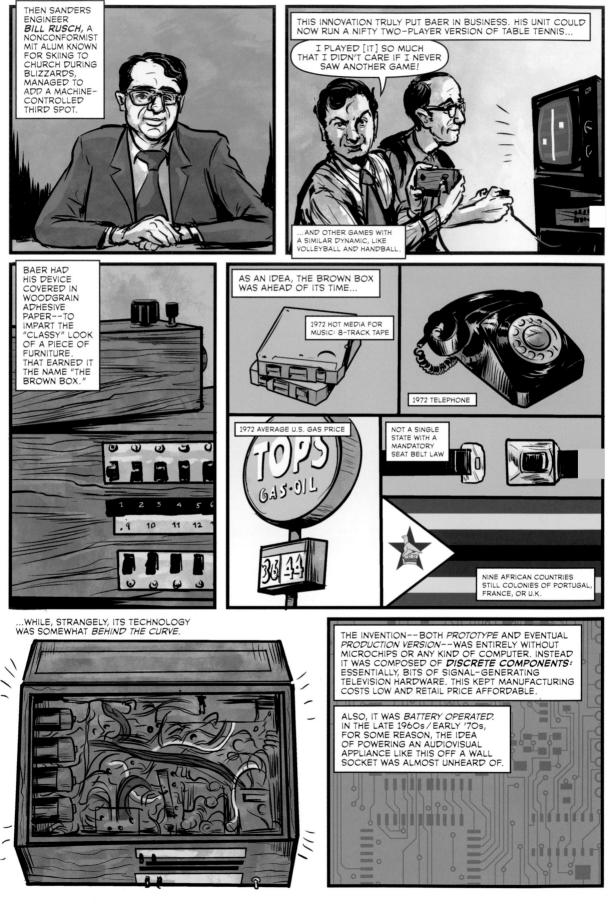

THEN SANDERS ENGINEER **BILL RUSCH**, A NONCONFORMIST MIT ALUM KNOWN FOR SKIING TO CHURCH DURING BLIZZARDS, MANAGED TO ADD A MACHINE-CONTROLLED THIRD SPOT.

THIS INNOVATION TRULY PUT BAER IN BUSINESS. HIS UNIT COULD NOW RUN A NIFTY TWO-PLAYER VERSION OF TABLE TENNIS...

I PLAYED [IT] SO MUCH THAT I DIDN'T CARE IF I NEVER SAW ANOTHER GAME!

...AND OTHER GAMES WITH A SIMILAR DYNAMIC, LIKE VOLLEYBALL AND HANDBALL.

BAER HAD HIS DEVICE COVERED IN WOODGRAIN ADHESIVE PAPER--TO IMPART THE "CLASSY" LOOK OF A PIECE OF FURNITURE. THAT EARNED IT THE NAME "THE BROWN BOX."

AS AN IDEA, THE BROWN BOX WAS AHEAD OF ITS TIME...

1972 HOT MEDIA FOR MUSIC: 8-TRACK TAPE

1972 TELEPHONE

1972 AVERAGE U.S. GAS PRICE

TOPS GAS·OIL

36 44

NOT A SINGLE STATE WITH A MANDATORY SEAT BELT LAW

NINE AFRICAN COUNTRIES STILL COLONIES OF PORTUGAL, FRANCE, OR U.K.

...WHILE, STRANGELY, ITS TECHNOLOGY WAS SOMEWHAT *BEHIND THE CURVE.*

THE INVENTION--BOTH *PROTOTYPE* AND EVENTUAL *PRODUCTION VERSION*--WAS ENTIRELY WITHOUT MICROCHIPS OR ANY KIND OF COMPUTER. INSTEAD IT WAS COMPOSED OF *DISCRETE COMPONENTS:* ESSENTIALLY, BITS OF SIGNAL-GENERATING TELEVISION HARDWARE. THIS KEPT MANUFACTURING COSTS LOW AND RETAIL PRICE AFFORDABLE.

ALSO, IT WAS *BATTERY OPERATED.* IN THE LATE 1960s / EARLY '70s, FOR SOME REASON, THE IDEA OF POWERING AN AUDIOVISUAL APPLIANCE LIKE THIS OFF A WALL SOCKET WAS ALMOST UNHEARD OF.

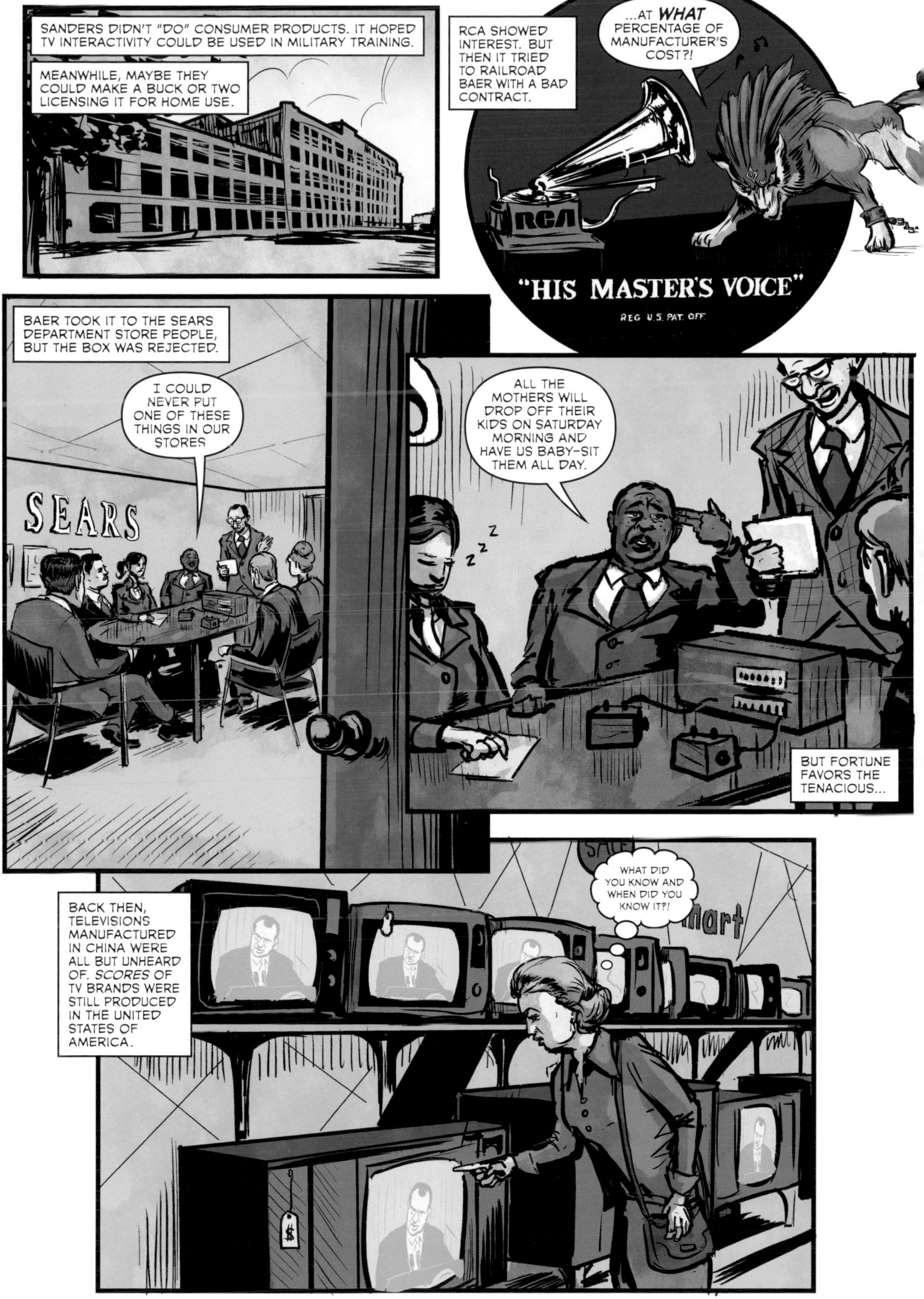
SANDERS DIDN'T "DO" CONSUMER PRODUCTS. IT HOPED TV INTERACTIVITY COULD BE USED IN MILITARY TRAINING.
MEANWHILE, MAYBE THEY COULD MAKE A BUCK OR TWO LICENSING IT FOR HOME USE.
RCA SHOWED INTEREST. BUT THEN IT TRIED TO RAILROAD BAER WITH A BAD CONTRACT.
...AT *WHAT* PERCENTAGE OF MANUFACTURER'S COST?!
RCA
"HIS MASTER'S VOICE"
REG U.S. PAT. OFF.
BAER TOOK IT TO THE SEARS DEPARTMENT STORE PEOPLE, BUT THE BOX WAS REJECTED.
I COULD NEVER PUT ONE OF THESE THINGS IN OUR STORES.
SEARS
ALL THE MOTHERS WILL DROP OFF THEIR KIDS ON SATURDAY MORNING AND HAVE US BABY-SIT THEM ALL DAY.
Z Z Z
BUT FORTUNE FAVORS THE TENACIOUS...
BACK THEN, TELEVISIONS MANUFACTURED IN CHINA WERE ALL BUT UNHEARD OF. *SCORES* OF TV BRANDS WERE STILL PRODUCED IN THE UNITED STATES OF AMERICA.
WHAT DID YOU KNOW AND WHEN DID YOU KNOW IT?!

AND IN FORT WAYNE, INDIANA, THE BROWN BOX FOUND A BUYER AT MAGNAVOX.

WE'RE GOING WITH THIS!

AFTER LENGTHY NEGOTIATIONS AND A *FEATURE-SLASHING PRODUCT DEVELOPMENT PROCESS,* AT LAST IN 1972 THEY PUT BAER'S "BABY" ON THE MARKET.

FIRST CHRISTENED THE "SKILL-O-VISION" BUT LATER RENAMED, THE *MAGNAVOX ODYSSEY* SHIPPED WITH TABLE TENNIS AND ELEVEN OTHER BUILT-IN GAMES.

THE PUBLIC AT THE TIME WAS ALMOST WHOLLY UNEXPOSED TO VIDEO GAMES-- EVEN AS A CONCEPT.

(SOME REQUIRED MORE IMAGINATION TO ENJOY THAN OTHERS. MANY ODYSSEY GAMES WERE DESIGNED TO BE PLAYED BY STICKING A PLASTIC OVERLAY ON THE OTHERWISE "BARREN" SCREEN.)

MAGNAVOX ODYSSEY

YEAR OF RELEASE: 1972

COUNTRY OF ORIGIN: UNITED STATES

CPU BITS: [NO PROCESSOR]

RAM: N/A

CPU SPEED: N/A

MAX. DISPLAY RESOLUTION:
COULD GENERATE 4 SPOTS OR LINES ONLY

COLORS: 1

AUDIO: NONE

MEDIA: NONE. "GAME CARDS" SERVED AS JUMPERS TO SELECT SELECT ON-BOARD GAMES.

THE ODYSSEY HAD ONLY BLACK AND GRAPHICS. AND *NO SOUND* AT ALL.

MAGNAVOX WAS CONCERNED CUSTOMERS WOULDN'T "GET" THIS INTERACTIVE ACCESSORY MEANT TO TRANSFORM A TV INTO A "CHALLENGING ELECTRONIC PLAY-GROUND OF FUN AND LEARNING FOR THE ENTIRE FAMILY."

THIS WAS NOT A SOFTWARE-BASED SYSTEM. ONLY NEW HARDWARE COULD ADD NEW GAMES.

SO THEY MADE SURE TO INCLUDE BOARD GAME ELEMENTS LIKE CHIPS AND PLAYING CARDS.

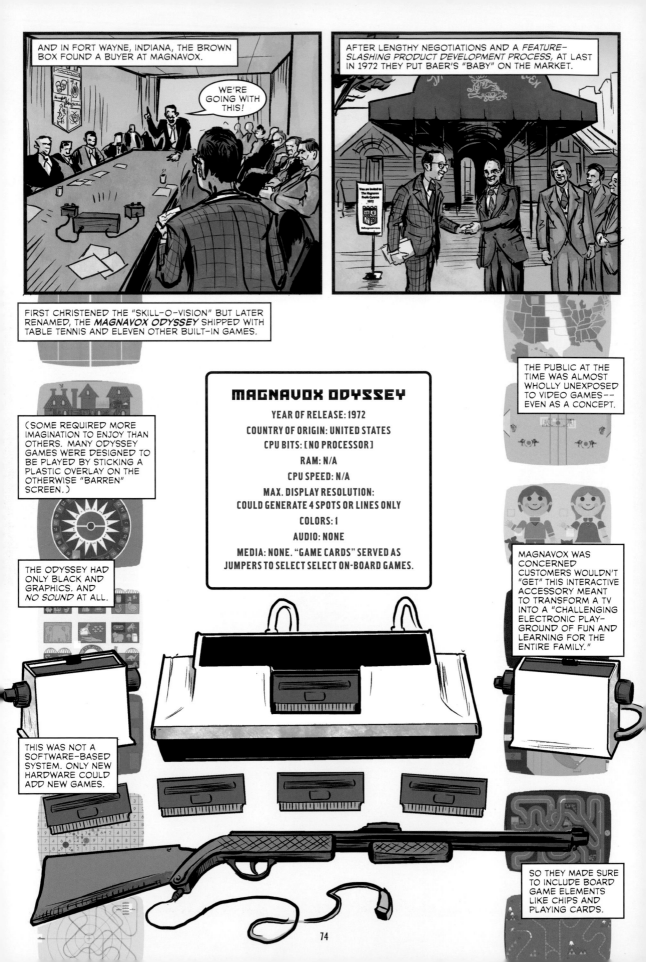

THE ODYSSEY WOULD SELL REASONABLY WELL, ONE ASSESSMENT CLAIMING 200,000 UNITS BY THE FALL OF 1974.

BUT IT WAS NOT DESTINED TO BE AN *INDUSTRY-MAKING PARADIGM SHIFT.*

AND SINCE THE RIGHTS BELONGED TO SANDERS, IT DIDN'T MAKE BAER A MILLIONAIRE.

PLUS, MAGNAVOX FIRST RELEASED IT ONLY IN MAGNAVOX *STORES*-- AND DIDN'T MAKE *EXPLICIT* THAT IT WAS COMPATIBLE WITH *ANY* BRAND TELEVISION!

YET THERE WAS A CERTAIN SOMEONE THOUSANDS OF MILES AWAY...

...WHO HAD *MORE* THAN ENOUGH *ENTERPRISE* AND *PANACHE* TO MAKE VIDEO GAMES A *SENSATION*...

WHEEEEEE!!!

...AND BECOME VIDEO GAMES' FIRST *MULTIMILLIONAIRE.*

SOLD

EVIDENTLY, THIS MAN KNEW *BETTER THAN ANYONE ELSE* WHAT TO DO WITH BAER AND RUSCH'S BRAINCHILD.

THE RESULTING ACT OF *BRAINCHILD ABDUCTION* WOULD LEAVE BAER'S EGO BRUISED IN A WAY HE WOULD NEVER FORGET...*OR FORGIVE.*

BUT WE CAN'T CONTINUE WITHOUT A BRIEF RETURNING INTERLUDE WITH *SPACEWAR!*

PDP-1 COMPUTER and

SPACE WAR

MOST WERE CONTENT TO ALLOW THE MIT HACKERS' HABIT-FORMING *GEM* TO SPREAD ON A *GROOVY OPEN-SOURCE BASIS.*

THE GAME OF *SPACEWAR!* BLOSSOMS SPONTANEOUSLY WHEREVER THERE IS A GRAPHICS DISPLAY CONNECTED TO A COMPUTER.

COMPUTER SCIENTIST *ALAN KAY.*

BUT THERE WERE ALSO *ENTREPRENEURS* LOOKING TO *MONETIZE.*

INSERT COIN

BILL PITTS WAS A STANFORD STUDENT WITH A HACKER'S PENCHANT FOR CREATIVE TRESPASSING.

IN 1966, HE INFILTRATED THE OFF-CAMPUS BUILDING THAT HOUSED S.A.I.L.: THE STANFORD ARTIFICIAL INTELLIGENCE LAB.

SPACEWAR! CREATOR STEVE RUSSELL HAD JUST BEEN ON THE S.A.I.L STAFF. THE GAME PIERCED HIM LIKE CUPID'S AAROW.

PITTS BECAME A *CONVERT.* HE WANTED TO BRING *SPACEWAR!* TO THE MASSES.

THE BUSINESS OF *COIN-OPERATED AMUSEMENTS* IS ROOTED IN THE 19TH CENTURY, WHEN FAR MORE FORMS OF ENTERTAINMENT WERE *LIVE*.

AS THE 20TH CENTURY NEARED, ADVANCES IN TECHNOLOGY HAD MADE POSSIBLE *NOVELTY DEVICES* LIKE MUSIC-PLAYING *PHONOGRAPHS*...

...AND MOVIE-PLAYING *KINETOSCOPES* AND *MUTOSCOPES*.

BRONCHO BUSTERS & INDIAN WARRIORS!!

1¢

IN THIS ERA, THE POOR COULD ONLY AFFORD TO EXPERIENCE THESE PRICEY NEW MACHINES A PENNY OR NICKEL AT A TIME.

BUT THOSE WITH CAPITAL--IN THIS CASE MOSTLY IMMIGRANT SHOWMEN IN CITIES LIKE NEW YORK AND CINCINATTI--COULD PURCHASE THEM IN *BULK* AND MAKE *HIGH PROFIT MARGINS*...

COIN-OP MAGNATES *MARCUS LOEW, ADOLPHUS ZUKOR,* AND *CARL LAEMMLE* LATER BECAME MOVIE STUDIO MOGULS--ANOTHER EARLY CONNECTION BETWEEN VIDEO GAMES AND HOLLYWOOD.

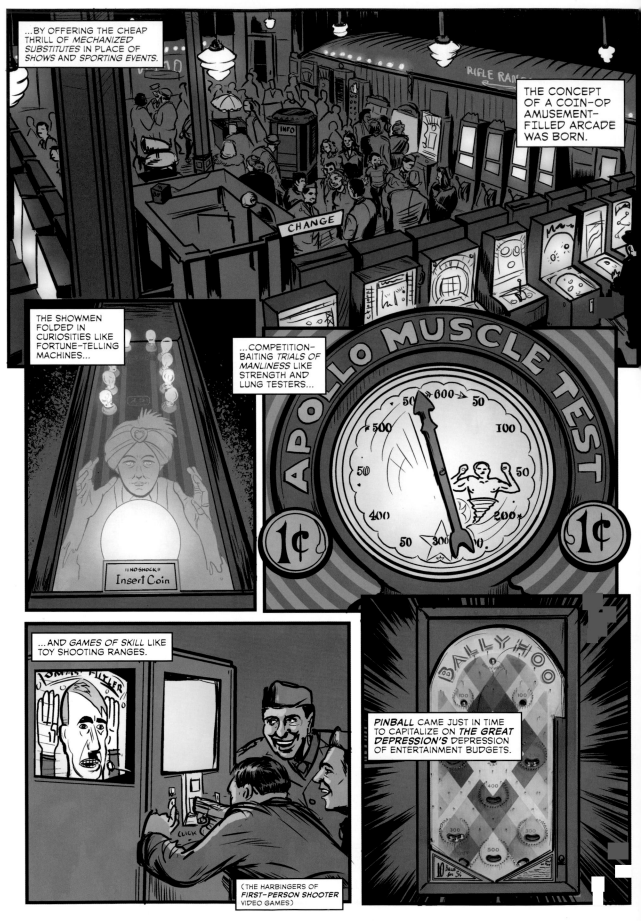

...BY OFFERING THE CHEAP THRILL OF *MECHANIZED SUBSTITUTES* IN PLACE OF *SHOWS* AND *SPORTING EVENTS.*

THE CONCEPT OF A COIN-OP AMUSEMENT-FILLED ARCADE WAS BORN.

THE SHOWMEN FOLDED IN CURIOSITIES LIKE FORTUNE-TELLING MACHINES...

...COMPETITION-BAITING *TRIALS OF MANLINESS* LIKE STRENGTH AND LUNG TESTERS...

...AND *GAMES OF SKILL* LIKE TOY SHOOTING RANGES.

PINBALL CAME JUST IN TIME TO CAPITALIZE ON *THE GREAT DEPRESSION'S* DEPRESSION OF ENTERTAINMENT BUDGETS.

(THE HARBINGERS OF *FIRST-PERSON SHOOTER* VIDEO GAMES)

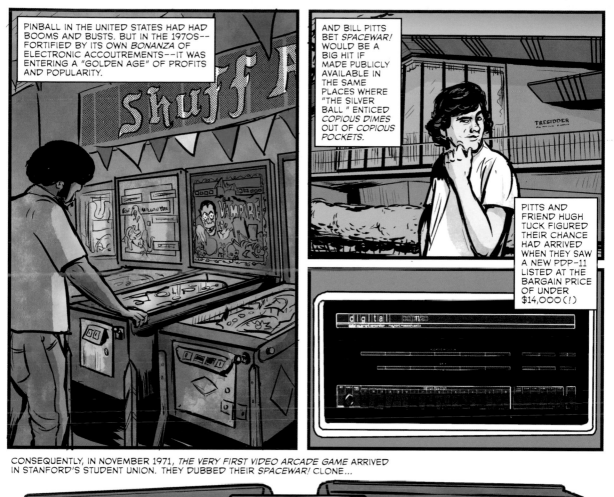

PINBALL IN THE UNITED STATES HAD HAD BOOMS AND BUSTS. BUT IN THE 1970S-- FORTIFIED BY ITS OWN *BONANZA* OF ELECTRONIC ACCOUTREMENTS--IT WAS ENTERING A "GOLDEN AGE" OF PROFITS AND POPULARITY.

AND BILL PITTS BET *SPACEWAR!* WOULD BE A BIG HIT IF MADE PUBLICLY AVAILABLE IN THE SAME PLACES WHERE "THE SILVER BALL" ENTICED *COPIOUS DIMES* OUT OF *COPIOUS POCKETS.*

PITTS AND FRIEND HUGH TUCK FIGURED THEIR CHANCE HAD ARRIVED WHEN THEY SAW A NEW PDP-11 LISTED AT THE BARGAIN PRICE OF UNDER $14,000 (!)

CONSEQUENTLY, IN NOVEMBER 1971, *THE VERY FIRST VIDEO ARCADE GAME* ARRIVED IN STANFORD'S STUDENT UNION. THEY DUBBED THEIR *SPACEWAR!* CLONE...

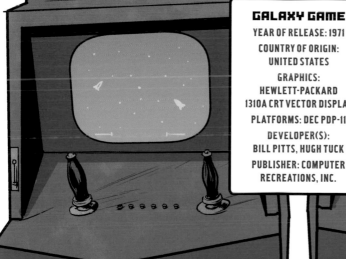
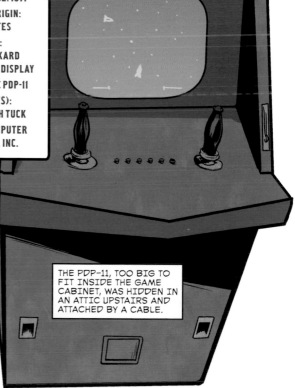

GALAXY GAME

YEAR OF RELEASE: 1971

COUNTRY OF ORIGIN:
UNITED STATES

GRAPHICS:
HEWLETT-PACKARD
1310A CRT VECTOR DISPLAY

PLATFORMS: DEC PDP-11

DEVELOPER(S):
BILL PITTS, HUGH TUCK

PUBLISHER: COMPUTER
RECREATIONS, INC.

THE PDP-11, TOO BIG TO FIT INSIDE THE GAME CABINET, WAS HIDDEN IN AN ATTIC UPSTAIRS AND ATTACHED BY A CABLE.

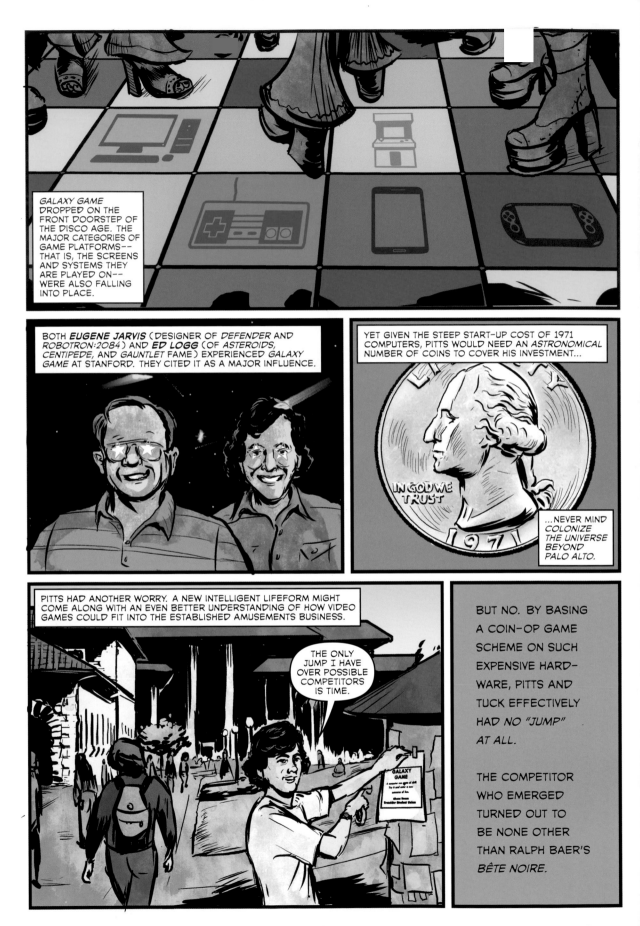

GALAXY GAME DROPPED ON THE FRONT DOORSTEP OF THE DISCO AGE. THE MAJOR CATEGORIES OF GAME PLATFORMS-- THAT IS, THE SCREENS AND SYSTEMS THEY ARE PLAYED ON-- WERE ALSO FALLING INTO PLACE.

BOTH *EUGENE JARVIS* (DESIGNER OF *DEFENDER* AND *ROBOTRON:2084*) AND *ED LOGG* (OF *ASTEROIDS, CENTIPEDE,* AND *GAUNTLET* FAME) EXPERIENCED *GALAXY GAME* AT STANFORD. THEY CITED IT AS A MAJOR INFLUENCE.

YET GIVEN THE STEEP START-UP COST OF 1971 COMPUTERS, PITTS WOULD NEED AN *ASTRONOMICAL* NUMBER OF COINS TO COVER HIS INVESTMENT...

...NEVER MIND *COLONIZE THE UNIVERSE BEYOND PALO ALTO.*

PITTS HAD ANOTHER WORRY. A NEW INTELLIGENT LIFEFORM MIGHT COME ALONG WITH AN EVEN BETTER UNDERSTANDING OF HOW VIDEO GAMES COULD FIT INTO THE ESTABLISHED AMUSEMENTS BUSINESS.

THE ONLY JUMP I HAVE OVER POSSIBLE COMPETITORS IS TIME.

BUT NO. BY BASING A COIN-OP GAME SCHEME ON SUCH EXPENSIVE HARD-WARE, PITTS AND TUCK EFFECTIVELY HAD *NO "JUMP"* AT ALL.

THE COMPETITOR WHO EMERGED TURNED OUT TO BE NONE OTHER THAN RALPH BAER'S *BÊTE NOIRE.*

SPOTLIGHT: NOLAN BUSHNELL

"HE LOOKS LIKE SOMEONE, AND HE IS," WROTE JOURNALIST HERB CAEN OF NOLAN BUSHNELL IN A 1983 PROFILE.

HE HAS ALSO BEEN CALLED "THE P. T. BARNUM OF SILICON VALLEY."

THE HANDY, TINKERING SON OF A CEMENT CONTRACTOR, BUSHNELL HAILED FROM UTAH.

CLEARFIELD, UTAH
Clearfield
NAVAL SUPPLY DEPOT

IN THE 1960s, HE HELPED PAY FOR HIS EDUCATION BY WORKING AT LAGOON AMUSEMENT PARK, NORTH OF SALT LAKE CITY.

THEATRICAL, COMIC BUSHNELL WAS A *NATURAL*. HE SOON MANAGED THE PARK'S WHOLE GAMES DEPARTMENT, LEARNING HOW TO MAKE MONEY WITH ARCADE ATTRACTIONS LIKE SKEE-BALL (AND SOMETHING CALLED "BINGORING.")

STEP RIGHT UP, SIR! KNOCK 'EM DOWN, WIN A STUFFED ANIMAL FOR THAT *LOVELY SISTER OF YOURS!*

SPILL the MILK

EVER ON ACADEMIC PROBATION, BUSHNELL SECURED AN ENGINEERING DEGREE BY THE SKIN OF HIS TEETH.

CAN I BE INTERVIEWED *NOW* PLEASE?

A TECH COMPANY WITH A JOB OPENING PROMISED TO CALL HIM BACK "IN A FEW WEEKS." BUT BUSHNELL FLEW TO SILICON VALLEY *THE VERY NEXT DAY*, ON HIS OWN DIME.

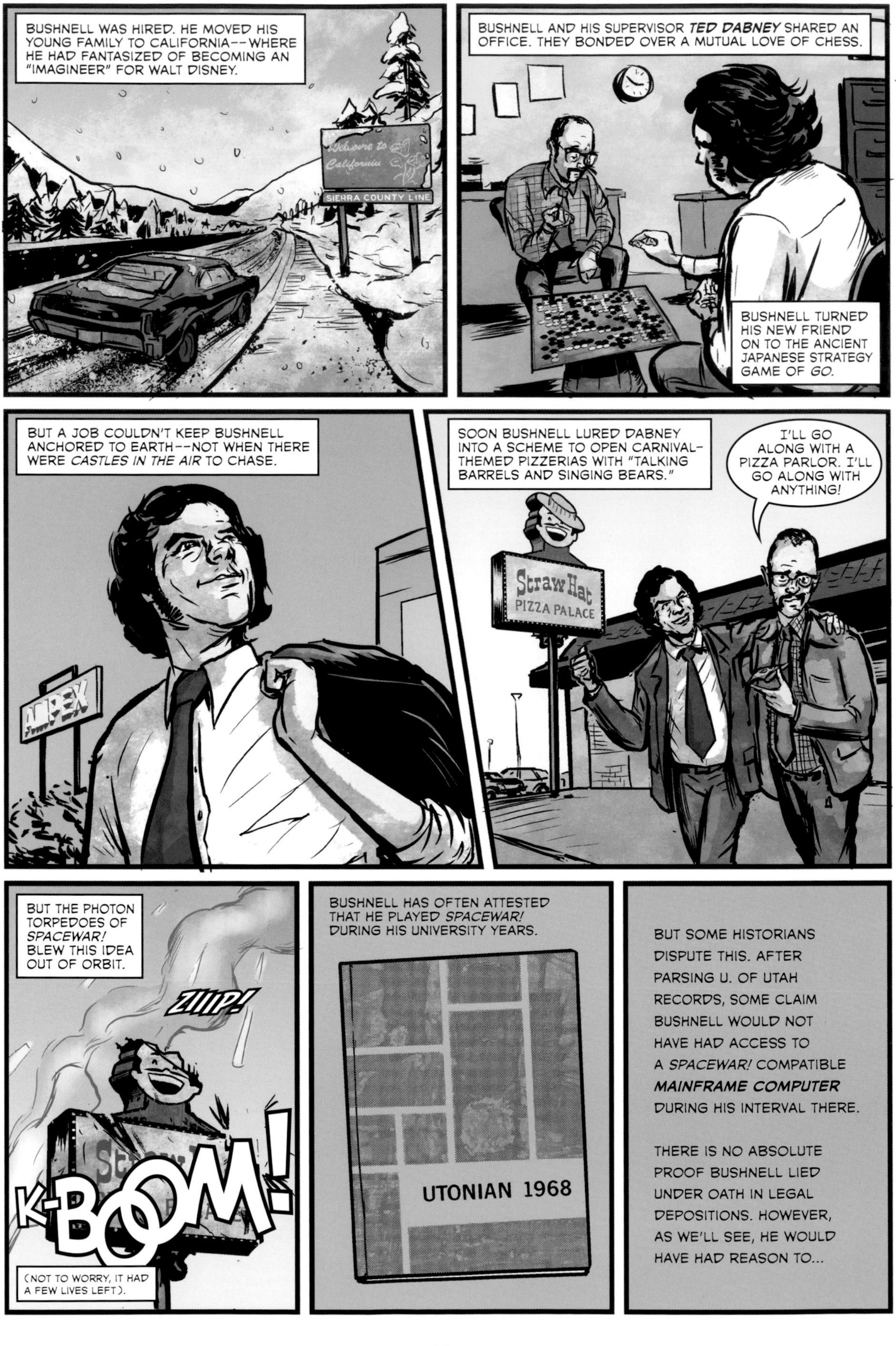
BUSHNELL WAS HIRED. HE MOVED HIS YOUNG FAMILY TO CALIFORNIA--WHERE HE HAD FANTASIZED OF BECOMING AN "IMAGINEER" FOR WALT DISNEY.
SIERRA COUNTY LINE
BUSHNELL AND HIS SUPERVISOR *TED DABNEY* SHARED AN OFFICE. THEY BONDED OVER A MUTUAL LOVE OF CHESS.
BUSHNELL TURNED HIS NEW FRIEND ON TO THE ANCIENT JAPANESE STRATEGY GAME OF *GO.*
BUT A JOB COULDN'T KEEP BUSHNELL ANCHORED TO EARTH--NOT WHEN THERE WERE *CASTLES IN THE AIR* TO CHASE.
SOON BUSHNELL LURED DABNEY INTO A SCHEME TO OPEN CARNIVAL-THEMED PIZZERIAS WITH "TALKING BARRELS AND SINGING BEARS."
I'LL GO ALONG WITH A PIZZA PARLOR. I'LL GO ALONG WITH ANYTHING!
Straw Hat
PIZZA PALACE
BUT THE PHOTON TORPEDOES OF *SPACEWAR!* BLEW THIS IDEA OUT OF ORBIT.
ZIIIP!
K-BOOM!
(NOT TO WORRY, IT HAD A FEW LIVES LEFT).
BUSHNELL HAS OFTEN ATTESTED THAT HE PLAYED *SPACEWAR!* DURING HIS UNIVERSITY YEARS.
UTONIAN 1968
BUT SOME HISTORIANS DISPUTE THIS. AFTER PARSING U. OF UTAH RECORDS, SOME CLAIM BUSHNELL WOULD NOT HAVE HAD ACCESS TO A *SPACEWAR!* COMPATIBLE ***MAINFRAME COMPUTER*** DURING HIS INTERVAL THERE.
THERE IS NO ABSOLUTE PROOF BUSHNELL LIED UNDER OATH IN LEGAL DEPOSITIONS. HOWEVER, AS WE'LL SEE, HE WOULD HAVE HAD REASON TO...

WHAT'S INDISPUTABLE IS THAT BUSHNELL *DID* FIND HIS WAY INTO THE SAME STANFORD AI LAB AS BILL PITTS.

BUSHNELL TOO SAW *SPACEWAR!* THERE AND FELT IT WOULD *BLOW UP* IN COIN-OP. BUT UNLIKE PITTS...

...THE BUSINESSMAN IN HIM DEDUCED THERE WAS *NO COST-EFFECTIVE WAY* TO REPRODUCE THE GAME ON A COMPUTER.

SPACEWAR! NEEDED SOME VERY COMPLEX CALCULATIONS... AND THAT PUSHED ME INTO THE THINKING OF JUST DOING IT ALL [WITH] HARDWARE AND NOT [WITH] SOFTWARE...

INSTEAD, BUSHNELL CONSOLIDATED HIS VISION AND DABNEY'S ENGINEERING ACUMEN BY MAKING A DEAL WITH *NUTTING ASSOCIATES*...

Big Profits

COMPUTER QUIZ

...A LOCAL COIN-OP MANUFACTURER.

STRUGGLING, BUT STILL WITH SOME SALES MOJO.

NUTTING ALSO CONTROLLED A DISTRIBUTION TERRITORY FOR PINBALL AND OTHER MACHINES WHICH, LATER, BUSHNELL PURCHASED.

AND TO SLASH PRODUCTION COSTS, DABNEY AND BUSHNELL USED *ONLY* "COUNTERS AND GATES" TO CREATE THEIR GAME.

THE RESULT, WHICH SAW THE LIGHT OF DAY *SCANT MONTHS* AFTER *GALAXY GAME,* WAS A VIDEO ARCADE MACHINE CALLED...

NUTTING ASSOCIATES
of California
HAS DONE IT AGAIN!

...MEN, BROTHER! THE ONLY INNOVA-
TIVE IDEA AN... ...THE ENTIRE
INDUSTRY... ...GAMES?
TIRED OF... ...ABINET
STYLING... ...LAYERS!

NUTTIN... ...ES, I...
Mo... ...94040

START... ...WITH
...L N...

THE O...

COM...

COMPUTER SPACE
YEAR OF RELEASE: 1971
COUNTRY OF ORIGIN: UNITED STATES
GRAPHICS: BLACK AND WHITE RASTER,
256X256 PIXELS
PLATFORMS: DEDICATED CIRCUITS
DEVELOPER: NOLAN BUSHNELL, ET AL.
PUBLISHER: NUTTING ASSOCIATES

BUSHNELL AND DABNEY'S *SPACEWAR!* ADAPTATION WAS BROUGHT TO MARKET IN NOVEMBER 1971. EVIDENTLY, ABOUT 1,500 WERE SOLD.

ALTHOUGH NOT A HUGE NUMBER, THIS WAS ENOUGH TO BLAST *GALAXY GAME* INTO A BLACK HOLE.

IN GAMEPLAY, A PLAYER-CONTROLLED SHIP BATTLES TWO MACHINE-CONTROLLED FLYING SAUCERS.

ALL ARE RASTERIZED DOT OUTLINES, LACKING THE DRAMATIC, SHARP GLOW OF *SPACEWAR!* AND *GALAXY GAME* GRAPHICS.

THE CONTROL PANEL CONSISTED OF FOUR BUTTONS: TWO FOR ROTATION, ONE FOR THRUST, ONE FOR SHOOTING.

COMPUTER SPACE

25¢ QUARTER

FIRE MISSILES   THRUST   ROTATE   ROTATE

COIN RETURN

START GAME

NUTTING ASSOCIATES MT. VIEW, CALIF.

"SYZYGY" WAS THE NAME OF THE SHORT-LIVED COMPANY BUSHNELL FORMED WITH DABNEY.

SEEMS LIKE A NO-BRAINER NOW, RIGHT? BUT IN THE EARLY 1970S, THIS WAS *DEEMED COMPLICATED.*

NINETY PERCENT OF THE PEOPLE WHO PUT THEIR QUARTER IN *COMPUTER SPACE* NEVER PLAY AGAIN BECAUSE THEY DON'T UNDERSTAND IT.

BUSHNELL AND HIS TEAM HAD TWO TAKE-AWAYS: (1) A LESS-THAN-SEAMLESS *USER INTERFACE* MIGHT TURN PEOPLE AWAY...

A NERDY CONCEPT LIKE *UFO DOGFIGHTS* MIGHT APPEAL TO A NICHE COLLEGE CROWD...

...BUT NOT A WIDER MARKET OF PLUMBERS, FORKLIFT OPERATORS, AND STEVEDORES.

CHICAGO COIN
THE ONLY COMPLETE LINE OF ARCADE GAMES!

CASINO
4-PLAYER
with
TWIN
SPINNERS!

MINI-BASEBALL
THE
DOOR OPENER!

PROVEN
PROFIT MAKERS

STILL, BUSHNELL HAD ENOUGH "JUICE" TO QUIT NUTTING ASSOCIATES AND GO OUT ON HIS OWN.

THESE GUYS COULDN'T FIND THEIR BUTTS WITH BOTH HANDS.

HE SET HIS SIGHTS INSTEAD ON CHICAGO'S BALLY CORPORATION: AN *INDUSTRIAL TITAN* MANUFACTURING PINBALL AND SLOT MACHINES.

BUSHNELL MADE A DEAL TO DEVELOP A VIDEO GAME FOR THEM.

Bally

HE WAS CONVINCED A *DRIVING GAME* WOULD BE THE SPORTS-FRIENDLY *HOME RUN* TO *COMPUTER SPACE'S BLOOP* SINGLE.

TO GROW HIS COMPANY, BUSHNELL *REWOUND* BACK TO AMPEX AND TALKED A CAPABLE JUNIOR STAFFER INTO QUITTING.

AL ALCORN WAS THE FIRST ENGINEER HIRED BY *ATARI*-- THE NAME BUSHNELL GAVE HIS NEW COMPANY. IN THE JAPANESE GAME *GO*, IT MEANS "I AM ABOUT TO ENGULF YOU."

BUSHNELL FOUND THIS "SUITABLY AGGRESSIVE."

ATARI INC.

employee no. 003

name Allan Alcorn

YZYGY CO.
ENTERTAINMENT ELECTRONICS DEVELOPMENT

ALLAN E. ALCORN
SENIOR STAFF ENGINEER

ALCORN'S STATED REASONS FOR THROWING IN WITH BUSHNELL SPEAK VOLUMES ABOUT THE TIME.

THERE WAS A COLD WAR... WE WERE BUILDING FALLOUT SHELTERS...

THERE WAS THIS SENSE THAT WE COULD BE DEAD AT ANY MINUTE FROM NUCLEAR ANNIHILATION...

...AND YOU HAD PEOPLE COMING BACK FROM VIETNAM IN A BOX, DEAD.

WE LEARNED NOT TO TRUST THE GOVERNMENT ANYMORE...

...WE WERE YOUNG AND ADVENTUROUS AND CRAZY RISK TAKING.

THERE WAS THIS FEELING OF LET'S DO SOMETHING BECAUSE, YOU KNOW, LIFE IS SHORT.

ON MAY 24, 1972, THE MAGNAVOX ODYSSEY WAS EXHIBITING AT A TRADE SHOW NEAR SAN FRANCISCO.

BUSHNELL ATTENDED. HE SAW THE TABLE TENNIS GAME DESIGNED BY RALPH BAER AND BILL RUSCH.

You are invited to The Magnavox Profit Caravan 1972

BURLINGAME, CA

Magnavox

SOON AFTER THAT, BUSHNELL GAVE ALCORN AN ASSIGNMENT.

LIKE PENNIES IN A PIGGY BANK, ALCORN HAD AMASSED A SMALL FORTUNE IN ENGINEERING HACKS, WORKAROUNDS, AND "DIRTY TRICKS."

WRAUCK!

IN RESPONSE TO BUSHNELL'S CHALLENGE, *HE SMASHED THAT PIGGY BANK TO THE FLOOR.*

AND CASHED THOSE IDEAS IN.

THE PROTOTYPE WAS A LITTLE ROUGH-- WHAT WITH ITS OFF-THE-SHELF WALGREEN'S BLACK-AND-WHITE TV MONITOR AND LAUNDROMAT COIN BOX WITH BREAD PAN TO HOLD QUARTERS.

Shhhh--!!!

THE EDITORS OF THE MUSIC, JUKEBOX, AND COIN-OP INDUSTRY MAGAZINE *CASH BOX*--AROUND SINCE 1946--HARDLY SEEMED TO KNOW WHAT WAS HAPPENING BY THE SPRING OF 1973.

"FOUR OR FIVE YEARS AGO, THE [COIN-OP] TRADE LARGELY DEPENDED UPON THE STAPLE GAMES TO MAKE ITS BUCK," THEY WROTE. "PIN[BALL], SHUFFLES, TABLES, AND THE LIKE WERE *IT.*"

THEN CAME-- WHAT DO YOU CALL THEM?-- "VIDEO GAMES."

PONG

PLAYER 1   PLAYER 2

ATARI

PONG WAS POISED TO DELIVER A BLISTERING SERVE.

CHAPTER FIVE
THE HEYDAY OF ATARI
Video Games' First Dynasty

ABOUT TEN DAYS AFTER ENSCONCING THE PROTOTYPE *PONG* CONSOLE AT ANDY CAPP'S, A SUNNYVALE, CA, BEER, BURGERS, AND BAR BANDS JOINT...

...ATARI ENGINEER AL ALCORN WENT TO SERVICE THE MACHINE.

ANDY CAPP'S

HE FOUND ITS BREAD PAN *JAMMED SOLID.* COINS SPILLED OUT INDISCRIMINATELY.

the BEER & BEERS

*ting ting
p-ping
ting!*

THOSE QUARTERS CHIMED OUT WITH THE SWEET REFRAIN OF *OPPORTUNITY.*

AN OPPORTUNITY THAT COULD MAYBE BE *ATARI'S.*

NOT SOMEONE ELSE'S.

Bally

WHY DID *PONG* SO HYPNOTIZE ITS PLAYERS?

THE SPORTS CONCEPT HAD A WIDE APPEAL. AND ITS GAME-PLAY WAS FAR MORE SIMPLE AND REWARDING THAN *COMPUTER SPACE'S* WAS.

CRAFTILY, DABNEY AND BUSHNELL CONVINCED BALLY NOT TO ACCEPT *PONG* AS FULFILLMENT OF ATARI'S CONTRACT.

YOU DON'T WANT THIS GAME...

YOU DON'T WANT THIS GAME...

THE ATARI FRONTMEN PUT THEIR MODEST NET WORTHS ON THE LINE AND DECIDED TO PRODUCE AND DISTRIBUTE *PONG* ON THEIR OWN.

I—I'D LIKE TO MAKE A W—W—WITH— DRAWAL, PLEASE.

PONG

YEAR OF RELEASE: 1972

COUNTRY OF ORIGIN: UNITED STATES

GRAPHICS: BLACK & WHITE NTSC TV

SPECS: 525 SCAN LINES AT 29.97 FRAMES/SEC

PLATFORMS: ARCADE

DEVELOPER: ATARI

PUBLISHER: ATARI

BUSHNELL AND DABNEY SNAPPED UP THE LEASE OF A SKETCHY ROLLER RINK.

TO PERFORM THE GRUNT WORK OF MANUFACTURING *PONG* MACHINES, THEY STAFFED UP WITH BIKERS, HITCHHIKERS, HIPPIE STONERS, AND UNSHAVEN LAYABOUTS PLUCKED FROM UNEMPLOYMENT LINES.

WITH ITS *PARTY ATMOSPHERE* AND *LOOSEY–GOOSEY MANAGEMENT*, ATARI WAS, AT FIRST, THE VERY MODEL OF AN *INSURGENT SILICON VALLEY SPARK PLUG.*

Bushnell's gamble paid off

How Atari's founder played games with the competition

BUSHNELL'S VISION OF THE FUTURE DID NOT, HOWEVER, INCLUDE TED DABNEY.

ATARI'S COFOUNDER WAS PUSHED OUT OF THE COMPANY.

NOLAN WAS NOT BEING THE KIND OF PERSON THAT I ENJOYED BEING AROUND ANYMORE...

...HE HAD A THING ABOUT MONEY.

ORDERS FOR *PONG* CAME IN BY THE HUNDREDS. THEN BY THE THOUSANDS.

WHEN I FIRST SAW *PONG* IN A BOWLING ALLEY, I THOUGHT, "OH MY GOD, YOU COULD DO A GAME ON TV!"

STEVE WOZNIAK, DEVELOPER OF THE APPLE II, IN 2013.

IT WAS TRULY A *BREAKOUT* PERFORMANCE.

BUT MEANWHILE...

RALPH BAER WAS LIVID.

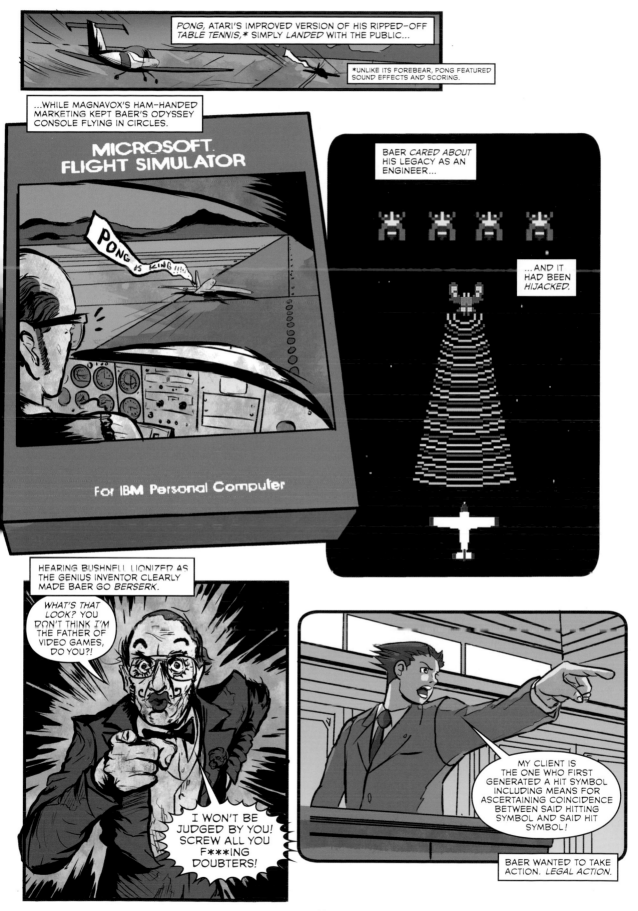

PONG, ATARI'S IMPROVED VERSION OF HIS RIPPED-OFF *TABLE TENNIS,** SIMPLY *LANDED* WITH THE PUBLIC...

*UNLIKE ITS FOREBEAR, PONG FEATURED SOUND EFFECTS AND SCORING.

...WHILE MAGNAVOX'S HAM-HANDED MARKETING KEPT BAER'S ODYSSEY CONSOLE FLYING IN CIRCLES.

MICROSOFT. FLIGHT SIMULATOR

PONG IS KING!!!

For IBM Personal Computer

BAER *CARED ABOUT* HIS LEGACY AS AN ENGINEER...

...AND IT HAD BEEN *HIJACKED.*

HEARING BUSHNELL LIONIZED AS THE GENIUS INVENTOR CLEARLY MADE BAER GO *BERSERK.*

WHAT'S THAT LOOK? YOU DON'T THINK *I'M* THE FATHER OF VIDEO GAMES, DO YOU?!

I WON'T BE JUDGED BY YOU! SCREW ALL YOU F***ING DOUBTERS!

MY CLIENT IS THE ONE WHO FIRST GENERATED A HIT SYMBOL INCLUDING MEANS FOR ASCERTAINING COINCIDENCE BETWEEN SAID HITTING SYMBOL AND SAID HIT SYMBOL!

BAER WANTED TO TAKE ACTION. *LEGAL ACTION.*

ATARI SETTLED MAGNAVOX'S LAWSUIT OUT OF COURT.

AGAIN, THE COMPANY SHOWED IMPECCABLE TIMING.

THE INK DRIED ON THE DEAL WELL BEFORE *TIDAL WAVES OF VIDEO GAME INDUSTRY PROFITS* PROVED HOW VALUABLE MAGNAVOX'S PATENTS COULD BECOME.

THERE'S NO TELLING HOW MUCH MONEY ATARI SAVED BY GETTING OUT IN FRONT OF LEGAL PROBLEMS.

BAER WOULD GROUSE...

...[BUSHNELL] GOT AWAY WITH A VERY, VERY SMALL LICENSING UP FRONT... SOME RIDICULOUS NUMBER LIKE A FEW HUNDRED GRAND.

RALPH BAER WAS A VISIONARY. BUT HISTORY KNOWS NOW THAT OTHERS WITH SIMILAR IMPULSES AND "PRIOR ART" CAME BEFORE HIM.

THE PATENTS ON WHICH BAER HUNG HIS REPUTATION REALLY HAVE NOTHING TO DO WITH HOW VIDEO GAMES WORK IN 2017 AND BEYOND.

EVEN IN HIS DAY (BAER DIED IN 2014), IT IS HARD TO IMAGINE BAER MAKING THE MANTLE OF "THE FATHER OF VIDEO GAMES" *STICK*.

NOLAN BUSHNELL HAD GAMES IN HIS HEART...

...WHILE BAER'S EMBRACE OF THE GAMING SPIRIT WAS NEVER A SINCERELY NURTURING ONE.

I WASN'T REALLY A GAME PERSON, EVER.

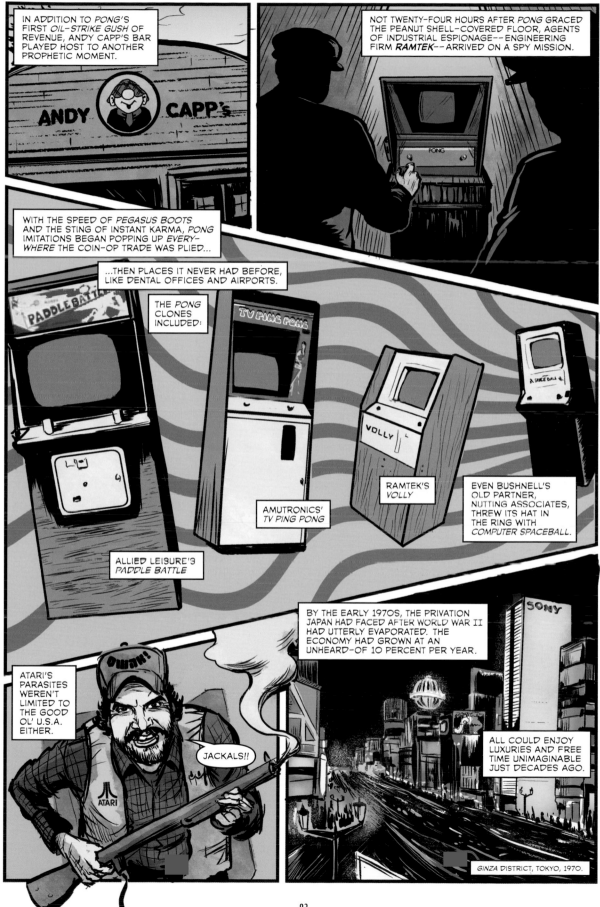

IN ADDITION TO *PONG'S* FIRST *OIL-STRIKE GUSH* OF REVENUE, ANDY CAPP'S BAR PLAYED HOST TO ANOTHER PROPHETIC MOMENT.

ANDY CAPP'S

NOT TWENTY-FOUR HOURS AFTER *PONG* GRACED THE PEANUT SHELL-COVERED FLOOR, AGENTS OF INDUSTRIAL ESPIONAGE--ENGINEERING FIRM *RAMTEK*--ARRIVED ON A SPY MISSION.

PONG

WITH THE SPEED OF *PEGASUS BOOTS* AND THE STING OF INSTANT KARMA, *PONG* IMITATIONS BEGAN POPPING UP *EVERY-WHERE* THE COIN-OP TRADE WAS PLIED...

...THEN PLACES IT NEVER HAD BEFORE, LIKE DENTAL OFFICES AND AIRPORTS.

THE *PONG* CLONES INCLUDED:

PADDLE BATTLE

TV PING PONG

VOLLY

A SPACEBALL *

ALLIED LEISURE'S *PADDLE BATTLE*

AMUTRONICS' *TV PING PONG*

RAMTEK'S *VOLLY*

EVEN BUSHNELL'S OLD PARTNER, NUTTING ASSOCIATES, THREW ITS HAT IN THE RING WITH *COMPUTER SPACEBALL*.

ATARI'S PARASITES WEREN'T LIMITED TO THE GOOD OL' U.S.A. EITHER.

OWN!!

ATARI

JACKALS!!

BY THE EARLY 1970S, THE PRIVATION JAPAN HAD FACED AFTER WORLD WAR II HAD UTTERLY EVAPORATED. THE ECONOMY HAD GROWN AT AN UNHEARD-OF 10 PERCENT PER YEAR.

SONY

ALL COULD ENJOY LUXURIES AND FREE TIME UNIMAGINABLE JUST DECADES AGO.

GINZA DISTRICT, TOKYO, 1970.

IN 1973, JAPAN'S *TAITO CORPORATION* RELEASED *ELEPONG*...

...DESIGNED BY *TOMOHIRO NISHIKADO*, A MAN ON TRACK TO MAKE VIDEO GAMES GO *SUPERNOVA* IN 1978.

THE MOMENTUM WAS POTENT ENOUGH TO PROJECT *PONG* CLONES DEEP INTO THE FUTURE.

DECADES LATER *GNOP!* WAS RELEASED FOR THE MAC BY *ALEX SEROPIAN*, WHO WOULD HELP ENSHRINE *ANOTHER JUGGERNAUT GAMING FRANCHISE*.

ATARI WISELY DID NOT EMBROIL ITSELF TOO DEEPLY IN CLONE WARS. IT HAD TO KEEP ON KEEPING ON--WITH *NEW GAMES*.

LET THOSE GUYS STAY BUSY COPYING *US* WHILE *WE* ACTUALLY *INNOVATE*. AND STAY THREE TO SIX MONTHS AHEAD OF THOSE IDIOTS.

THE ATARI LIBRARY'S FIRST EXPANSION INCLUDED MAZE CHASER *GOTCHA!*

A TRUE PRODUCT OF THE SMUT-ADJACENT "IF IT FEELS GOOD, DO IT" 1960S/1970S, ITS CONTROLLERS WERE SIMULACRA OF FEMALE ANATOMY.

ATARI DID FINALLY COUGH UP THE RACING GAME BUSHNELL WANTED, TOO...

...*GRAN TRAK 10*—LIKE *PONG*, ANOTHER EASY-TO-WRAP-YOUR-HEAD-AROUND SPORTS CONCEPT.

IT ACHIEVES ALL THE POINTS, FROM SKILL TO COMPETITION TO SPECTATOR APPEAL!

IT WAS ALSO THE FIRST VIDEO GAME WITH A STEERING WHEEL AND FOOT CONTROLS!

BUT AFTER AN INTERNAL ACCOUNTING BLUNDER, ATARI WOUND UP SELLING EACH *GRAN TRAK 10* AT A $100 LOSS.

THE COMPANY SLUMPED INTO THE RED.

TANK (RELEASED BY SECRET ATARI SUBSIDIARY *KEE GAMES*) BROUGHT *MUCHO* FIREPOWER AND STAVED OFF A RETREAT INTO BANKRUPTCY.

TANK

BUT QUARTERS WOULDN'T ADD UP TO THE CASH INFUSION ATARI NEEDED.

Approach Venture Capitalist

Menlo Park

LEGENDARY FOUNDER OF SEQUOIA CAPITAL *DON VALENTINE* SOBERED BUSHNELL, TELLING HIM:

Board limit on investment : None
Approach Don Valentine ?

Exit   Approach

THE COIN-OP BUSINESS... YOU THINK IT'S BIG? YOU AIN'T SEEN *NOTHING*!

THE FINANCIER WAS TALKING ABOUT THE *CONSUMER MARKET*. THE NUMBER OF ARCADES, PIZZA PARLORS, BOWLING ALLEYS, AND LAUNDROMATS WAS A *MOLEHILL* NEXT TO THE MOUNTAIN OF PRIVATE HOMES THERE WERE TO SELL TO.

AND ATARI HAD A PRODUCT IN DEVELOPMENT THAT ITS MANAGE-MENT THOUGHT JUST MIGHT MAKE BUYERS OUT OF MILLIONS OF THOSE POTENTIAL CUSTOMERS.

NOT LONG AFTER A SPATE OF TIME LIVING OUT OF A VAN, ATARI ELECTRICAL ENGINEER *HAROLD LEE* RETIRED TO THE CABIN OF A HILLTOP CHRISTMAS TREE FARM.

HIS MISSION?

BREAK DOWN ATARI'S FLAGSHIP TITLE TO A *SINGLE MICROCHIP*—ENABLING A DEVICE SMALL AND AFFORDABLE ENOUGH FOR EVERY AMERICAN LIVING ROOM.

IT WAS DONE. AND DONE WELL.

VALENTINE HELPED FIND A BUYER FOR THE RESULTING HOME VERSION OF *PONG:* RETAIL GIANT SEARS.

THE SAME OUTFIT THAT HAD INITIALLY JILTED RALPH BAER HELPED STAMP ATARI WITH THE IMPRIMATUR OF A VENERABLE TRUSTED HOUSEHOLD NAME.

SEARS EVEN HELPED MANUFACTURE AND MARKET *TELE-GAMES,* A RED-HOT SELLER FOR CHRISTMAS 1975. ATARI WAS SOON ALLOWED TO RELEASE THEIR OWN BRANDED CONSOLE.

IT OPERATES ON 4 "D" BATTERIES AND IS AVAILABLE FOR UNDER $100!

BY THE END OF THE GREEK MYTH, THE HERO OF *THE ODYSSEY* SLEW ALL THOSE WHO DEIGNED TO TAKE HIS PLACE.

THIS WOULD *NOT* BE THE FATE OF THE *ODYSSEY* FROM NEW HAMPSHIRE AND FORT WAYNE. HOME *PONG* OUTSOLD IT HANDILY.

HAROLD LEE, WHO MADE HOME *PONG* FEASIBLE, WAS GOOD. BUT OTHER *ENGINEERING DEMIGODS* WALKED AMONG MEN.

DR. STEPHEN FORTE, AKA "DR. PING-PONG."

SCOTLAND'S *GENERAL INSTRUMENTS* DESIGNED AND SHIPPED THE AY-3-8500 MICROCHIP TO PLAY *PONG*-LIKE GAMES.

AS A RELATIVELY CHEAP ALTERNATIVE TO FABRICATING CUSTOM CHIPS, THE AY-3-8500 ALLOWED MORE "JACKALS" INTO THE HOME VIDEO GAME MARKET.

KEEP IN MIND ALL THESE CONSOLES WERE "*DEDICATED.*" THEY COULD ONLY PLAY A FEW BUILT-IN GAMES.

OF NOTE AMONG THESE *PONG* DOPPELGANGERS IS A LITTLE MACHINE RELEASED IN 1977 JAPAN: THE "COLOR TV-GAME 6."*

?

TV-GAME 6

*NOT BECAUSE IT WAS SIXTH IN A SERIES, BUT BECAUSE IT PLAYED SIX SLIGHT VARIATIONS OF *PONG.*

AND TO PUT THE COLOR TV-GAME 6 IN PROPER PERSPECTIVE, WE MUST GO BACK ALMOST FIVE CENTURIES.

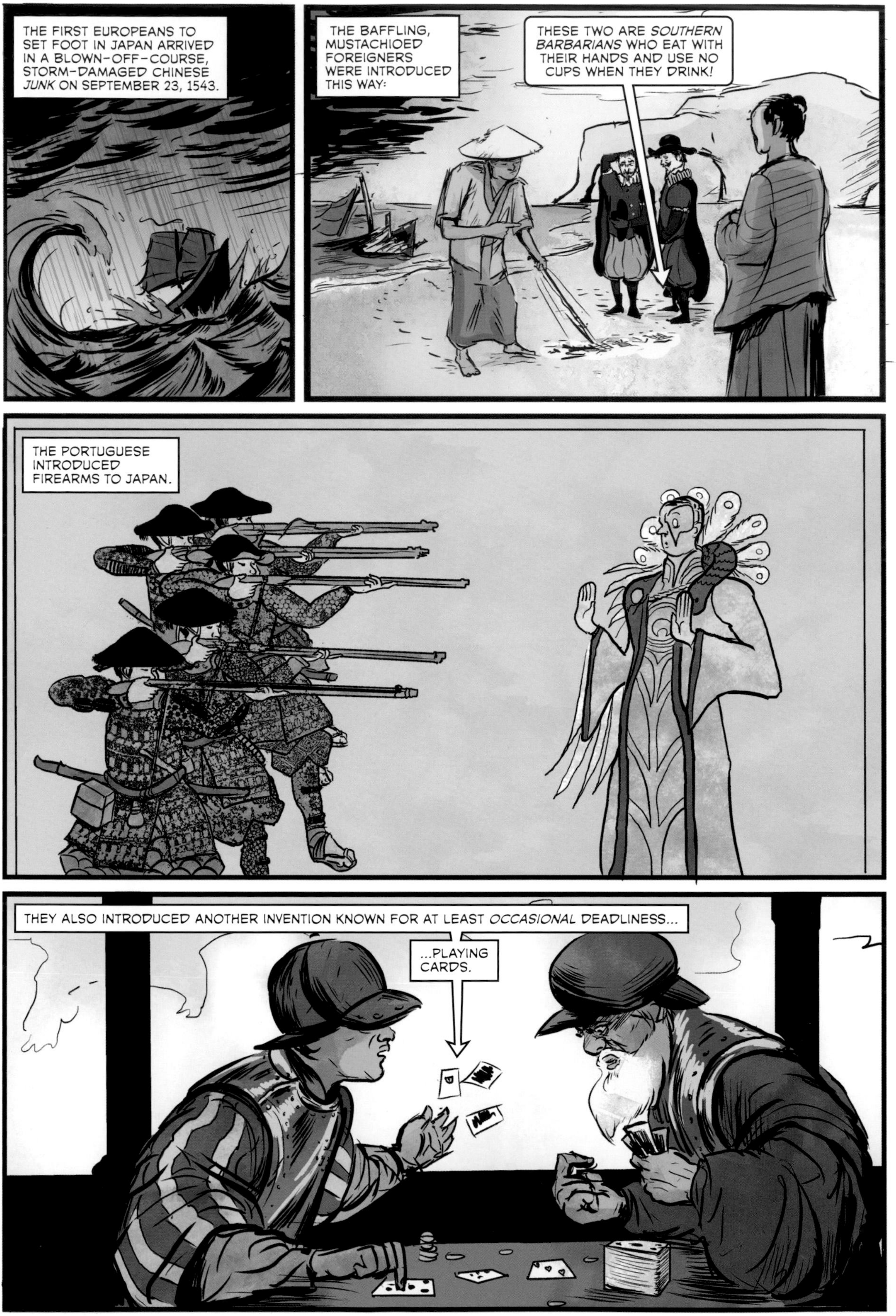
THE FIRST EUROPEANS TO SET FOOT IN JAPAN ARRIVED IN A BLOWN-OFF-COURSE, STORM-DAMAGED CHINESE *JUNK* ON SEPTEMBER 23, 1543.
THE BAFFLING, MUSTACHIOED FOREIGNERS WERE INTRODUCED THIS WAY:
THESE TWO ARE *SOUTHERN BARBARIANS* WHO EAT WITH THEIR HANDS AND USE NO CUPS WHEN THEY DRINK!
THE PORTUGUESE INTRODUCED FIREARMS TO JAPAN.
THEY ALSO INTRODUCED ANOTHER INVENTION KNOWN FOR AT LEAST *OCCASIONAL* DEADLINESS...
...PLAYING CARDS.

BY 1635, GUNS, CHRISTIANITY-- ALL THINGS FOREIGN-- WERE THOUGHT TO HAVE *WREAKED SO MUCH HAVOC* IN JAPAN THAT *SHOGUN TOKUGAWA IEMITSU* SHUT THE ISLANDS OFF FROM THE WORLD.

NO JAPANESE IS PERMITTED TO GO ABROAD. IF THERE IS ANYONE WHO ATTEMPTS TO DO SO SECRETLY, HE MUST BE EXECUTED!

THE DUTCH, MORE DEVOTED TO BUSINESS THAN RELIGIOUS CRUSADING, GOT AN EXCEPTION--AND CONTINUED TRADING WITH THEM.

UNDER SHOGUN RULE, CARDS ALSO BECAME ILLEGAL IN JAPAN.

BUT THE PEOPLE HAD FALLEN IN LOVE. ON THE SLY, THEY PLAYED ON.

EXERCISING THE SINGULAR JAPANESE GENIUS OF APPROPRIATING AND TRANSFORMING ALIEN INFLUENCES, OUT WENT THE HEARTS, CLUBS, SPADES, AND DIAMONDS...

...AND IN CAME MORE CULTURALLY APPROPRIATE SEASONAL ICONS--FLOWERS, TREES, AND ANIMALS.

HANAFUDA CARDS.

STARTING IN 1868 UNDER *EMPEROR MEIJI,* JAPAN MODERNIZED. ITS GOVERNMENT, BUSINESS, AND CULTURAL LEADERS ACTIVELY SOUGHT OUT EUROPEAN AND AMERICAN IDEAS.

IN 1889, A KYOTO MERCHANT NAMED *FUSAJIRO YAMAUCHI* BEGAN MAKING CARDS AVAILABLE IN A PLACE THEY HADN'T BEEN SOLD IN MORE THAN 250 YEARS: *OUT IN THE OPEN.*

IN 1959, YAMAUCHI'S GREAT-GRANDSON, AFTER HITTING IT BIG WITH A LINE OF DISNEY CHARACTER-THEMED CARDS, MOVED THE COMPANY INTO TOYS.

ATARI'S TRANSPACIFIC CRAZE SPURRED THAT COMPANY, *NINTENDO*...

PLAYING CARDS
THE NINTENDO PLAYING CARD CO.
SHOMEN-DORI OHASHI, KYOTO, JAPAN.

...INTO PRODUCING VIDEO GAMES...

...BEGINNING WITH THE COLOR TV-GAME 6.

NINTENDO WAS ONE REASON WHY, IN THE GAME OF HOME *PONG* COMPETITION, ATARI...

PONG CHAMPIONSHIPS: ATARIANS VS. THE WORLD

K-POP

...WAS FINDING ITS MARKET SHARE OVERWHELMED.

POP POP P-POP POP POP POP P-POP POP POP POP POP POP

THEN ATARI'S PLAN TO REMAIN THE MARKET LEADER BY BEING FIRST WITH MUST-HAVE, NEXT-GEN GAMING DEVICES...

...WAS HIT *DEAD CENTER* BY A TINY OUTFIT OF EX-BOWLING EQUIPMENT ENGINEERS FROM CONNECTICUT.

CLOBBER!

RECREATION GIANT AMF (NOW DEFUNCT) HAD TAKEN ITS RESEARCH AND DEVELOPMENT FROM NEW ENGLAND TO THE SUNNY SOUTH.

AMF XTREME BOWLING

BUT EMPLOYEE *NORMAN ALPERT* DIDN'T WANT TO GO.

SO HE STARTED HIS OWN COMPANY WITH COLLEAGUES *WALLACE KIRSCHNER* AND *LAWRENCE HASKEL*.

IT WASN'T LOST ON STRUGGLING NEWBIE **ALPEX COMPUTER** THAT GETTING IN ON THE GROUND FLOOR OF VIDEO GAMES WAS ONE PATH TO SUCCESS IN THE 1970S BUSINESS ENVIRONMENT.

GOLD RUSH!

AND THANKS TO MOORE'S LAW, MICROPROCESSORS WERE GETTING CHEAPER AND MORE POWERFUL WITH EVERY FLIP OF THE CALENDAR.

AFTER GINNING UP SOME SIMPLE GAMES TO SELL...

HEY, TURKEYS!

VIDEO GAME HOCKEY!

...ALPEX REACHED A "EUREKA" MOMENT:

WHY NOT INVENT A CONSOLE WITH *INTERCHANGEABLE, PROGRAMMABLE MEDIA?*

THAT WAY CONSUMERS WOULDN'T HAVE TO BUY NEW CONSOLES EVERY TIME THEY WANTED TO PLAY A NEW GAME.

THE ALPEX GUYS HACKED TOGETHER THE FIRST PROTOTYPE *VIDEO GAME CARTRIDGES* FROM *EPROM* MEMORY DEVICES AND 5X3" PLASTIC BOXES BOUGHT AT RADIO SHACK.

Fig.8

THEY SOLD THEIR SYSTEM TO *FAIRCHILD SEMICONDUCTOR*-- FOUNDED BY THE "TRAITOROUS 8" WHO HAD BURNED INVENTOR WILLIAM SHOCKLEY.

THE TRAITOROUS 8 [BIT]

FAIRCHILD ASSIGNED A NOTABLE EMPLOYEE TO THE ALPEX PROJECT...

SPOTLIGHT: JERRY LAWSON

BORN IN QUEENS, NEW YORK, *JERRY LAWSON* HAD ALWAYS BEEN A TECHNOLOGICAL WHIZ.

AS A KID, HE LEARNED TO REPAIR TVS. HE EVEN OPERATED HIS OWN RADIO STATION OUT OF HIS FAMILY'S APARTMENT.

A BELOVED TEACHER USED TO SAY OF THE PORTRAIT OF AFRICAN AMERICAN INVENTOR *GEORGE WASHINGTON CARVER* ON HIS CLASSROOM WALL:

THIS COULD BE YOU SOMEDAY.

LAWSON MADE HIS WAY TO SILICON VALLEY AND BEGAN WORKING IN TECH.

LAWSON BUILT--*FROM SCRATCH*--HIS VERY OWN ARCADE MACHINE IN HIS GARAGE, SO HE WAS DEEMED THE PERFECT MAN AT FAIRCHILD TO HELP COMPLETE ITS VIDEO GAME SYSTEM.

THE WHOLE REASON I DID GAMES WAS BECAUSE PEOPLE SAID, "YOU CAN'T DO IT."

I'M ONE OF [THOSE] GUYS, IF YOU TELL ME I CAN'T DO SOMETHING, I'LL TURN AROUND AND DO IT!

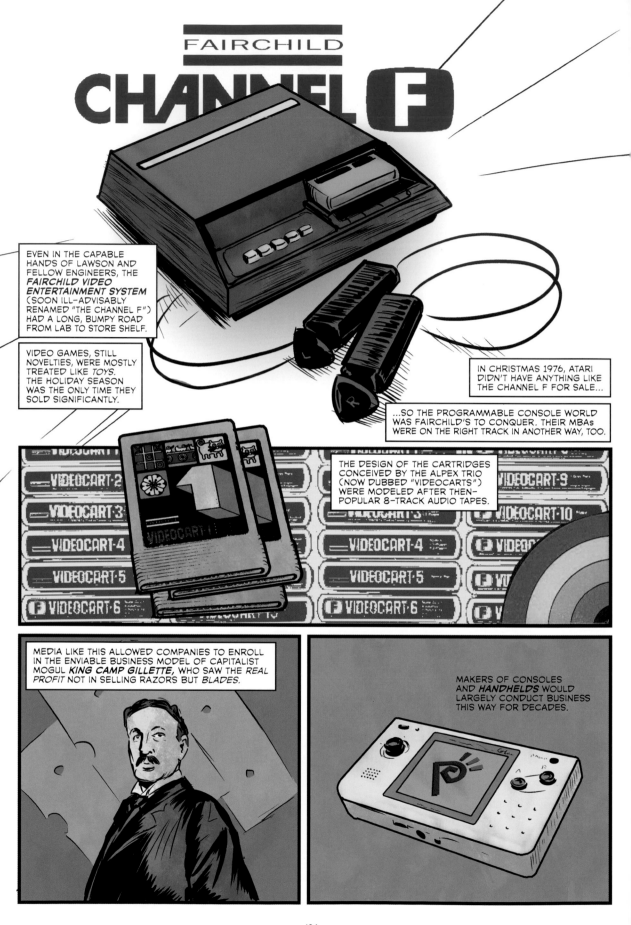

FAIRCHILD
CHANNEL F

EVEN IN THE CAPABLE HANDS OF LAWSON AND FELLOW ENGINEERS, THE *FAIRCHILD VIDEO ENTERTAINMENT SYSTEM* (SOON ILL-ADVISABLY RENAMED "THE CHANNEL F") HAD A LONG, BUMPY ROAD FROM LAB TO STORE SHELF.

VIDEO GAMES, STILL NOVELTIES, WERE MOSTLY TREATED LIKE *TOYS.* THE HOLIDAY SEASON WAS THE ONLY TIME THEY SOLD SIGNIFICANTLY.

IN CHRISTMAS 1976, ATARI DIDN'T HAVE ANYTHING LIKE THE CHANNEL F FOR SALE...

...SO THE PROGRAMMABLE CONSOLE WORLD WAS FAIRCHILD'S TO CONQUER. THEIR MBAs WERE ON THE RIGHT TRACK IN ANOTHER WAY, TOO.

THE DESIGN OF THE CARTRIDGES CONCEIVED BY THE ALPEX TRIO (NOW DUBBED "VIDEOCARTS") WERE MODELED AFTER THEN-POPULAR 8-TRACK AUDIO TAPES.

VIDEOCART-2
VIDEOCART-3
VIDEOCART-4
VIDEOCART-5
VIDEOCART-1
VIDEOCART-6
VIDEOCART-3
VIDEOCART-4
VIDEOCART-5
VIDEOCART-6
VIDEOCART-9
VIDEOCART-10

MEDIA LIKE THIS ALLOWED COMPANIES TO ENROLL IN THE ENVIABLE BUSINESS MODEL OF CAPITALIST MOGUL *KING CAMP GILLETTE,* WHO SAW THE *REAL PROFIT* NOT IN SELLING RAZORS BUT *BLADES.*

MAKERS OF CONSOLES AND *HANDHELDS* WOULD LARGELY CONDUCT BUSINESS THIS WAY FOR DECADES.

WHEN IT CAME TO GAMES, HOWEVER, THE CHANNEL F LIBRARY LACKED ÉLAN AND EXCITEMENT.

LIKE THEIR "MEH" *SPACEWAR!* PORT, THEY IGNITED LITTLE PASSION.

FAIRCHILD MIGHT HAVE WON THE 1976 PROGRAMMABLE CONSOLE RACE, BUT BY THE NEXT YEAR, ATARI WAS READYING A BOLD MOVE FROM BEHIND.

PC CD-ROM

Pro**Cycling**Manager

3+

ATARI ENGINEER *JOE DECUIR.*

28 00 00 73

NOLAN BUSHNELL WAS FED UP WITH A ROUGH ECONOMY. CASHFLOW ISSUES WERE HOLDING BACK ATARI'S POTENTIAL.

The New York Times.
Inflation Again?

IT WAS TIME TO TAKE A SHOT AT JOINING UP WITH A TEAM ALREADY IN THE CORPORATE BIG LEAGUES.

2K SPORTS COLLEGE HOOPS 2K8

EVERYONE
E
CONTENT RATED BY
ESRB

NCAA BASKETBALL

2K SPORTS

IN A SLAM DUNK, ATARI GOT ITSELF ACQUIRED BY MEDIA COLOSSUS *WARNER COMMUNICATIONS* FOR AROUND $28 MILLION...

...THE ROUGH EQUIVALENT OF $127 MILLION TODAY.

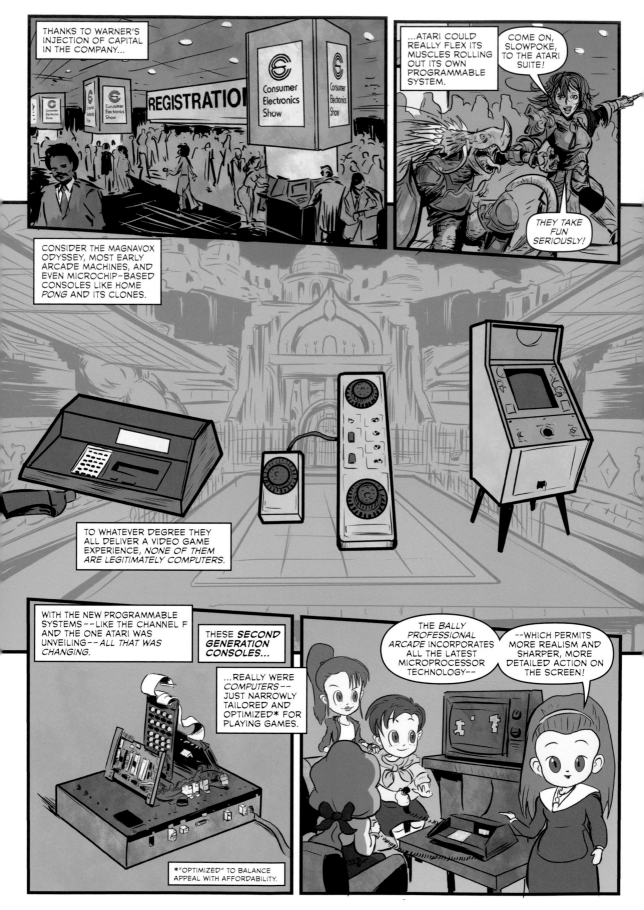

THANKS TO WARNER'S INJECTION OF CAPITAL IN THE COMPANY...

...ATARI COULD REALLY FLEX ITS MUSCLES ROLLING OUT ITS OWN PROGRAMMABLE SYSTEM.

COME ON, SLOWPOKE, TO THE ATARI SUITE!

THEY TAKE FUN SERIOUSLY!

CONSIDER THE MAGNAVOX ODYSSEY, MOST EARLY ARCADE MACHINES, AND EVEN MICROCHIP-BASED CONSOLES LIKE HOME *PONG* AND ITS CLONES.

TO WHATEVER DEGREE THEY ALL DELIVER A VIDEO GAME EXPERIENCE, *NONE OF THEM ARE LEGITIMATELY COMPUTERS.*

WITH THE NEW PROGRAMMABLE SYSTEMS--LIKE THE CHANNEL F AND THE ONE ATARI WAS UNVEILING--*ALL THAT WAS CHANGING.*

THESE *SECOND GENERATION CONSOLES...*

...REALLY WERE *COMPUTERS*-- JUST NARROWLY TAILORED AND OPTIMIZED* FOR PLAYING GAMES.

THE *BALLY PROFESSIONAL ARCADE* INCORPORATES ALL THE LATEST MICROPROCESSOR TECHNOLOGY--

--WHICH PERMITS MORE REALISM AND SHARPER, MORE DETAILED ACTION ON THE SCREEN!

*"OPTIMIZED" TO BALANCE APPEAL WITH AFFORDABILITY.

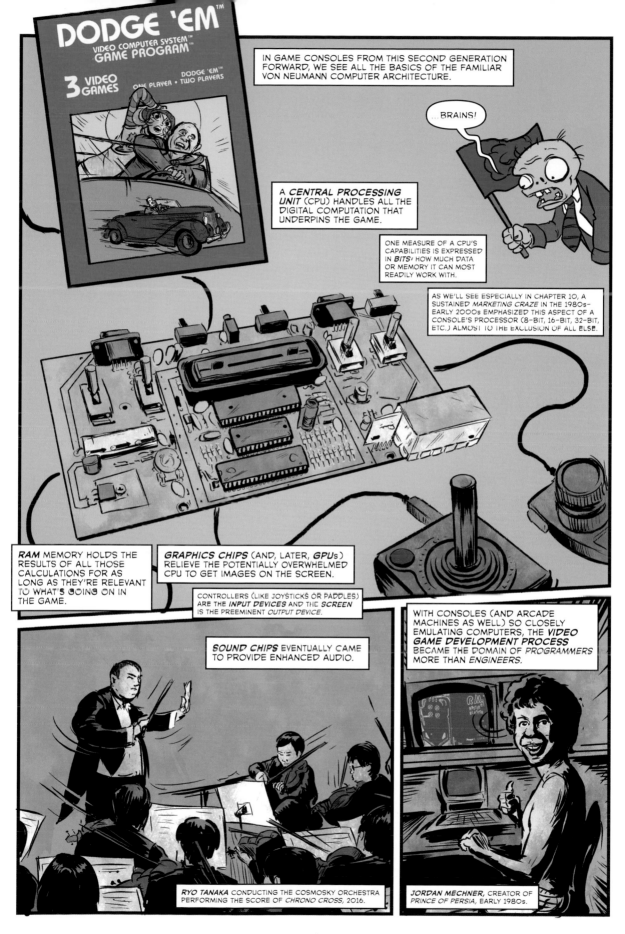

DODGE 'EM™
VIDEO COMPUTER SYSTEM™
·GAME PROGRAM™

3 VIDEO GAMES   ONE PLAYER · TWO PLAYERS   DODGE 'EM™

IN GAME CONSOLES FROM THIS SECOND GENERATION FORWARD, WE SEE ALL THE BASICS OF THE FAMILIAR VON NEUMANN COMPUTER ARCHITECTURE.

...BRAINS!

A *CENTRAL PROCESSING UNIT* (CPU) HANDLES ALL THE DIGITAL COMPUTATION THAT UNDERPINS THE GAME.

ONE MEASURE OF A CPU'S CAPABILITIES IS EXPRESSED IN *BITS:* HOW MUCH DATA OR MEMORY IT CAN MOST READILY WORK WITH.

AS WE'LL SEE ESPECIALLY IN CHAPTER 10, A SUSTAINED *MARKETING CRAZE* IN THE 1980s– EARLY 2000s EMPHASIZED THIS ASPECT OF A CONSOLE'S PROCESSOR (8-BIT, 16-BIT, 32-BIT, ETC.) ALMOST TO THE EXCLUSION OF ALL ELSE.

RAM MEMORY HOLDS THE RESULTS OF ALL THOSE CALCULATIONS FOR AS LONG AS THEY'RE RELEVANT TO WHAT'S GOING ON IN THE GAME.

GRAPHICS CHIPS (AND, LATER, *GPUs*) RELIEVE THE POTENTIALLY OVERWHELMED CPU TO GET IMAGES ON THE SCREEN.

CONTROLLERS (LIKE JOYSTICKS OR PADDLES) ARE THE *INPUT DEVICES* AND THE *SCREEN* IS THE PREEMINENT *OUTPUT DEVICE.*

SOUND CHIPS EVENTUALLY CAME TO PROVIDE ENHANCED AUDIO.

WITH CONSOLES (AND ARCADE MACHINES AS WELL) SO CLOSELY EMULATING COMPUTERS, THE *VIDEO GAME DEVELOPMENT PROCESS* BECAME THE DOMAIN OF *PROGRAMMERS* MORE THAN *ENGINEERS.*

RYO TANAKA CONDUCTING THE COSMOSKY ORCHESTRA PERFORMING THE SCORE OF *CHRONO CROSS*, 2016.

JORDAN MECHNER, CREATOR OF *PRINCE OF PERSIA*, EARLY 1980s.

**ATARI VCS
(AKA ATARI 2600)**

YEAR OF RELEASE: 1977

COUNTRY OF ORIGIN: UNITED STATES

CPU BITS: 8

RAM: 128 BYTES

CPU SPEED: 1.19 MHZ

MAX. DISPLAY RESOLUTION:
160X192 PIXELS

COLORS: 128

AUDIO: 2 CHANNELS/1 BIT MONO

MEDIA: ROM CARTRIDGES
(4 KB CAPACITY)

THE ATARI VCS (LATER REBRANDED THE 2600) HAD TO DELIVER ON THREE FRONTS.

IT HAD TO IMPRESS GAMERS. IT HAD TO OFFER ENOUGH POTENTIAL THAT PROGRAMMERS COULD KEEP CHURNING OUT NEW GAMES FOR IT.

AND, LIKE MOST CONSUMER PRODUCTS, IT HAD TO BE PROFITABLE TO THE MANUFACTURER AND THE RETAILERS--WHILE NOT TOO PRICEY FOR CONSUMERS.

WE'RE GUARANTEEING THAT YOU WON'T GET TIRED OF THE GAME FOR AT LEAST THE NEXT SEVEN YEARS!

THE SYSTEM SUCCEEDED BY THE SHEER SIMPLICITY OF ITS ENGINEERING: AN OUTSOURCED 8-BIT PROCESSOR AND A CRAFTY CRT TELEVISION-SPECIFIC GRAPHICS/SOUND CHIP DEVELOPED IN-HOUSE BY JOE DECUIR AND *JAY MINER.*

THE VCS *WAS* FLEXIBLE...BUT NOTORIOUSLY STINGY SYSTEM RESOURCES MEANT CODERS HAD TO BE *HYPERECONOMICAL* AND SUMMON FORTH *WIZARDLY TECHNO-TRICKS* LIKE *BANK SWITCHING* TO GIVE GAMES ALACRITY.

IT TAKES A REAL MAN TO PROGRAM THAT. NONE OF THIS HIGH-LEVEL LANGUAGE CRAP!

AND EVEN IF ATARI DIDN'T HAVE THE BEST TECHNOLOGY, IT HAD THE BEST *BRANDING.*

THEN, THE ATTRACTIVENESS OF CONSOLES LAY IN PLAYING *ARCADE TITLES* AT HOME-- NOT ORIGINALS. EARLY VCS GAMES HEWED FAITHFULLY TO THAT LOGIC.

AND FOR ITS TIME, THE VCS SERVED UP SERVICEABLE PORTS.

STANDARD ATARI VCS CARTRIDGES HELD ONLY 4K OF *ROM.* TO SHOW WHAT A *SKIMPY RATION OF HEXADECIMAL VALUES* THAT IS...

OUCH...

...THE NO-FRILLS, PACK-IN RINGTONE FOR AN IPHONE 6 IS A 427 KB DIGITAL FILE.

DONA BAILEY
501-555-1212

THAT MEANS AN ENTIRE VCS GAME HAD TO BE WRITTEN WITH LESS THAN 1/100TH OF THE DATA OF THAT RINGTONE...

...OR ABOUT A SINGLE PAGE OF TEXT.

THE VCS WAS UNLEASHED IN NORTH AMERICA FOR CHRISTMAS 1977. EVERY ONE TO ROLL OFF THE ASSEMBLY LINE--SOME 400,000-- WERE SNAPPED UP.

WITH NEW GAMES PRODUCED UNTIL *1990,* THE CONSOLE HAD EXTRAORDINARY LONGEVITY. IT PATRIATED *TENS OF MILLIONS* TO THE NATION OF GAMERS. THE VCS HELPED *HABITUATE THE WORLD* TO THE EVERYDAY FACT OF VIDEO GAMES' EXISTENCE.

IT WAS A *GATEWAY DRUG* FOR A LIFELONG OBSESSION WITH VIDEO GAMES.

HOLLYWOOD DIRECTOR *ZAK PENN,* 2015.

A FEW YEARS BEFORE THE VCS RELEASE, IN FEBRUARY 1974, A SHIFTLESS, UNSCRUBBED TEENAGER HAD AMBLED INTO THE ATARI OFFICES AND DECREED...

...I'M NOT LEAVING UNTIL THIS COMPANY HIRES ME.

AMUSED AND SEEING POTENTIAL IN THE ECCENTRIC, AL ALCORN HIRED **STEVE JOBS** AS A $5/HOUR TECHNICIAN.

AN OVERNIGHT SHIFT WAS INVENTED FOR JOBS BECAUSE FEW COULD TOLERATE HIS BODY ODOR AND JUDGMENTAL ATTITUDE.

NOLAN BUSHNELL HELPED JOBS APPRECIATE THE PURITY AND INTUITIVENESS OF ATARI GAMES...

...DESIGN APPROACHES THAT HAD LET BUSHNELL LEAP FROM SO-SO *COMPUTER SPACE* TO METEORIC *PONG*.

ATARI

JOBS PROBABLY ALSO LEARNED A THING OR TWO ABOUT *CONFIDENCE* AND *SHOWMANSHIP*.

(ALL THESE FACTORS WOULD BE CORPORATE SIGNATURES OF **APPLE COMPUTER,** WHICH JOBS COFOUNDED IN 1976.)

JOBS DRIFTED TO INDIA AND BACK TO ATARI.

HE INSISTED TO BE PUT ON A NEW COIN-OP DIVISION PROJECT FOR A JUICED-UP, SINGLE-PLAYER TAKE ON *PONG*.

JOBS DIDN'T MUCH RATE AS AN ENGINEER.

BUT HE HAD AN ACE UP HIS SLEEVE.

...HIS *WUNDERKIND* HARDWARE HACKER FRIEND *STEVE WOZNIAK.*

LATER WOZNIAK WOULD DESIGN AND BUILD THE APPLE II COMPUTER. BUT AT THE TIME HE STILL HAD A DAY JOB AT *HEWLETT-PACKARD.*

WOZNIAK WAS A *VIDEO GAMES FREAK.* HE USED TO RIDE HIS BIKE TO S.A.I.L. IN PALO ALTO TO PLAY *SPACEWAR!* ON THE PDP-11.

IN A NOW LEGENDARY FEAT OF FOUR DAYS STRAIGHT, SLEEPLESS PRODUCTIVITY, WOZ WHIPPED UP CIRCUIT BOARDS FOR THE *PONG* REMIX.

ONCE ATARI FIGURED OUT A WAY TO ADAPT WOZNIAK'S INGENIOUS YET *UNREPRODUCIBLE* DESIGN, THE GAME, *BREAKOUT,* BECAME A MASSIVE SUCCESS.

I WAS SO TIRED, IN AND OUT OF SLEEP...

...BUT YOU KNOW WHAT? THAT MAKES YOUR MIND CREATIVE.

BREAKOUT

111

THE GAME'S EARNINGS, HOWEVER, GOT A BIT *LOST IN TRANSLATION* IN ONE CRUCIAL OVERSEAS TERRITORY.

BREAKOUT TOOK TO JAPAN LIKE *KOI* TO A GARDEN POND.

IT BECAME SO POPULAR, IN FACT...

B—DEEP

B—D—DOOP

...THAT *JAPANESE ORGANIZED CRIME* MANUFACTURED ILLEGAL BOOTLEGS OF THE GAME. THIS UNDERMINED ATARI'S PROFITS SOMETHING FIERCE.

THE *YAKUZA* WERE NOT THE ONLY ONES ITCHING TO HITCH A RIDE ON THE *BREAKOUT* BANDWAGON.

AT TAITO, GAME DESIGNER *TOMOIHIRO NISHIKADO*'S BOSS CHALLENGED HIM...

⟨ MAKE THIS COMPANY A GAME THAT WILL OVERTAKE *BREAKOUT*. ⟩

TO SAY NISHIKADO *TOOK A SHOT* AND *SCORED A HIT*...

...

...IS AN UNDERSTATEMENT OF ALMOST *EXTRATERRESTRIAL* PROPORTIONS.

NISHIKADO CONFESSED TO BEING "ABSOLUTELY HOOKED" ON *BREAKOUT*.

CHAPTER SIX
THE GOLDEN AGE OF ARCADE GAMES
Video Games Give No Quarter

THE ARCADE HAD LONG BEEN SUBJECT TO THE VICISSITUDES OF THE LAW--AND THE WHIMS OF THE ENTERTAINMENT-SEEKING POPULACE.

PENNYLAND
ADMISSION FREE

BEFORE PORNOGRAPHY WAS AS CLOSE AS THE CONNECTED DEVICES IN OUR HANDBAGS, SOME "COINMEN" EARNED THEIR BREAD BY EXHIBITING X-RATED MATERIAL, THEN RARE AND TABOO.

PEEPORAMA
in COLOR MODELS

PEEP SHOW 25
8 MM ART FILM in COLOR
ON SALE THIS WEEK ½ 15¢

ARCADE SUPPLIERS BALLY, WILLIAMS, AND GOTTLIEB ALL HAILED FROM CHICAGO.

CHICAGO

THE WINDY CITY, GAMBLING, AND SMALL, CASH-ORIENTED BUSINESSES (ALL THE BETTER FOR TAX EVASION) WERE ALL DEEMED INSEPARABLE FROM THE MOB.

THE MAIN DISTRIBUTORS AND MANUFACTURERS [OF PINBALL] ARE SLIMY CREWS OF TINHORNS... LIVING IN LUXURY ON PETTY THIEVERY!

MAYOR *FIORELLO LA GUARDIA* CRUSADING AGAINST PINBALL IN 1940. IT WOULD BE BANNED IN NEW YORK CITY UNTIL 1976!

TAKE ALL THIS TOGETHER AND--FAIR OR NOT, ARCADES WERE WIDELY REPUTED TO BE PITS OF VICE AND INIQUITY.

ENTER VIDEO GAMES.

THOUGH HARDLY MISSIONARIES OF SUNDAY SCHOOL DECORUM, THEY DID CARRY AN APPEASING, APPEALING WHIFF OF HIGH TECH--OF *THE FUTURE*.

BRINGING AN EARLIER MANIA TO FRUITION, NOLAN BUSHNELL FOUNDED THE *CHUCK E. CHEESE'S PIZZA TIME THEATRE* CHAIN TO MAKE COIN-OP ARCADES MORE ACCEPTABLE TO PRICKLY SUBURBAN ZONING BOARDS.

AND FOLLOWING ON NISHIKADO'S INSIGHT TO REPLACE *BREAKOUT'S* PASSIVE BLOCKS WITH SOMETHING ACTIVELY HOSTILE AND CHILLINGLY DISCIPLINED...

...VIDEO GAMES, SOCIALLY DESIRABLE OR NOT, SUDDENLY SEEMED AS *UNSTOPPABLE* AS A *RUTHLESS ARMADA OF ALIENS*.

SPACE INVADERS

YEAR OF RELEASE: 1978

COUNTRY OF ORIGIN: JAPAN

GRAPHICS:
BLACK & WHITE CRT TELEVISION
(NTSC STANDARD)

PLATFORMS: ARCADE

DEVELOPER(S):
TOSHIHIRO NISHIKADO

PUBLISHER:
TAITO (JAPAN);
MIDWAY (NORTH AMERICA & EUROPE)

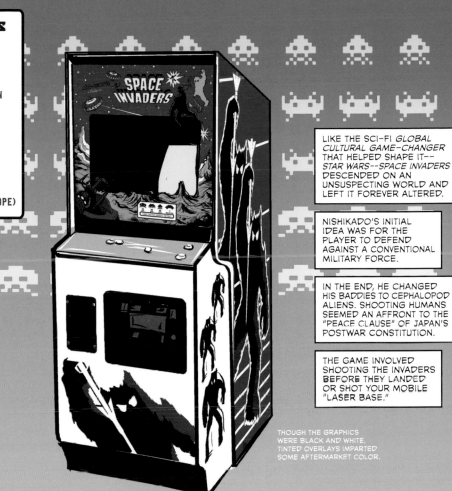

LIKE THE SCI-FI *GLOBAL CULTURAL GAME-CHANGER* THAT HELPED SHAPE IT-- *STAR WARS*--SPACE INVADERS DESCENDED ON AN UNSUSPECTING WORLD AND LEFT IT FOREVER ALTERED.

NISHIKADO'S INITIAL IDEA WAS FOR THE PLAYER TO DEFEND AGAINST A CONVENTIONAL MILITARY FORCE.

IN THE END, HE CHANGED HIS BADDIES TO CEPHALOPOD ALIENS. SHOOTING HUMANS SEEMED AN AFFRONT TO THE "PEACE CLAUSE" OF JAPAN'S POSTWAR CONSTITUTION.

THE GAME INVOLVED SHOOTING THE INVADERS BEFORE THEY LANDED OR SHOT YOUR MOBILE "LASER BASE."

THOUGH THE GRAPHICS WERE BLACK AND WHITE, TINTED OVERLAYS IMPARTED SOME AFTERMARKET COLOR.

SPACE INVADERS SWEPT JAPAN OFF ITS FEET. THE MACHINES SWELLED WITH SO MANY 100 YEN COINS THAT FOUR-TON TRUCKS WERE CALLED OUT TO COLLECT THEM. AND *STILL* THE SUSPENSIONS OF THE TRUCKS BUCKLED UNDER THE WEIGHT!

BEEEEP!!

ONE REASON *SPACE INVADERS* GETS *UNDER YOUR SKIN* SO EFFECTIVELY? ITS MUSIC *MATCHES A HUMAN HEARTBEAT*--PALPITATIONS QUICKENING AS DANGER BECOMES IMMINENT.

THE MAIN INNOVATION OF *SPACE INVADERS* WAS AS FOLLOWS: *IT GAVE YOU REAL DRAMA ON THE SCREEN.*

WHO CARES WHETHER YOU CAN ELIMINATE DOTS WITH AN ELECTRIC TENNIS BALL?

WRITER *MARTIN AMIS*, 1982.

SEVERAL NOTED GAME COMPANIES POUNCED ON THE CRAZE WITH *INVADERS* COPYCATS: *KENZO TSUJIMOTO* HOISTED UP HIS *CAPCOM* SHINGLE AFTER HIS FIRST COMPANY RELEASED *IPM INVADERS*.

NINTENDO WAS ADMITTED WITH *SPACE FEVER*, AN ARCADE MACHINE, IN 1979.

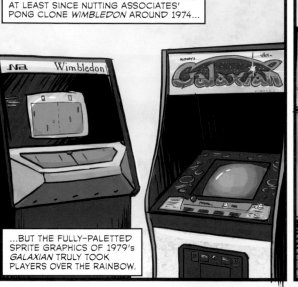

GAMES HAD FEATURED COLOR GRAPHICS AT LEAST SINCE NUTTING ASSOCIATES' PONG CLONE *WIMBLEDON* AROUND 1974...

...BUT THE FULLY-PALETTED SPRITE GRAPHICS OF 1979's *GALAXIAN* TRULY TOOK PLAYERS OVER THE RAINBOW.

EMERGING AS AN ALMOST LAUGHABLY EASY WAY TO MAKE A BUCK, THERE WAS NO STOPPING ARCADE MACHINES NOW.

I AM TOLD THAT EACH MACHINE CAN PRODUCE A WEEKLY INCOME OF $100 FOR THE STORE OWNER.

NOT BAD FOR A DOLLAR'S WORTH OF ELECTRICITY [AND] A FEW FEET OF SPACE!

SPOTLIGHT:
LARRY ROSENTHAL

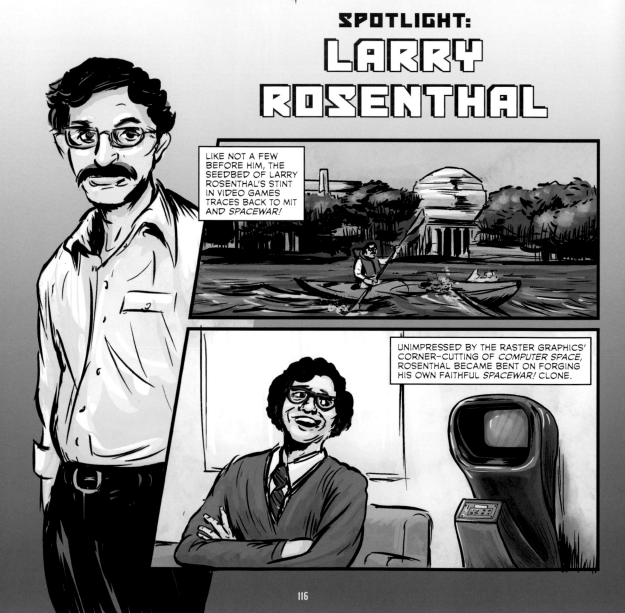

LIKE NOT A FEW BEFORE HIM, THE SEEDBED OF LARRY ROSENTHAL'S STINT IN VIDEO GAMES TRACES BACK TO MIT AND *SPACEWAR!*

UNIMPRESSED BY THE RASTER GRAPHICS' CORNER-CUTTING OF *COMPUTER SPACE*, ROSENTHAL BECAME BENT ON FORGING HIS OWN FAITHFUL *SPACEWAR!* CLONE.

ROSENTHAL, DAUNTED BUT UNDETERRED AFTER BUILDING HIS OWN CIRCUIT BOARDS FROM SCROUNGED PARTS...

...MODDED A CHEAP, STANDARD TV INTO AN AFFORDABLE *VECTOR DISPLAY.*

THE CRT'S ELECTRON GUN TOOK THE GAME FROM A DULL BITMAP TO A VIVID, GLOWING, *WIREFRAME* GEOMETRY.

AFTER POUNDING PAVEMENT, ROSENTHAL FOUND A STRUGGLING OUTFIT CONSTITUTED BY-- *WAIT FOR IT*--TWO EX-NFL PLAYERS AND A BEET FARMER.

IT SEEMED EVERYONE AND THEIR GRANDMA WANTED A PIECE OF THE VIDEO GAMES ACTION.

SPACE WARS

YEAR OF RELEASE: 1977

COUNTRY OF ORIGIN: U.S.

GRAPHICS: CUSTOM VECTOR MONITOR (1024 X 768 PIXELS)

PLATFORMS: ARCADE

DEVELOPER(S): LARRY ROSENTHAL

PUBLISHER: CINEMATRONICS

CINEMATRONICS DID NOT SEEM LIKE A FOOTNOTE IN VIDEO GAME HISTORY WHEN INDUSTRY TRADE MAGAZINES *REPLAY AND PLAY METER* RANKED SPACE WARS THE TOP GAME OF 1978.

SPACE WARS WAS, VERY MUCH, A FAITHFUL ARCADE PORT OF THE MIT HACKERS' UNCOPYRIGHTABLE 1961 OPUS.

ITS HI-RES GRAPHICS STARTED A FAD WITHIN A FAD. AND IT WOULDN'T BE CINEMATRONICS' LAST.

ASTEROIDS

YEAR OF RELEASE: 1979

COUNTRY OF ORIGIN: U.S.

GRAPHICS: WELLS-GARDNER B&W VECTOR MONITOR

PLATFORMS: ARCADE

DEVELOPER(S): ED LOGG, LYLE RAINS, ET AL.

PUBLISHER: ATARI

ATARI R&D TOOK NOTICE OF CINEMATRONICS' TRICK AND PROCEEDED TO HASH OUT A VECTOR SYSTEM OF THEIR OWN.

GAME DESIGNER ED LOGG MASTERFULLY SYNTHESIZED FUN AND TENSION IN THIS ROCK-SMASHING GAME THAT BECAME ATARI'S ALL-TIME TOP ARCADE EARNER.

THERE IS NO SUBSTITUTE FOR EXPERIENCING *ASTEROIDS* (OR ITS 1981 COUSIN *TEMPEST*) IN THEIR ORIGINAL VECTOR ARCADE FORMS.

THE COOLEST GAME PLANET EARTH HAS EVER SEEN!

JOHN ROMERO, COCREATOR OF *DOOM AND QUAKE,* AGE ELEVEN.

CREATING THE ILLUSION OF A 3-D WORLD IN A 2-D SPACE ESSENTIALLY COMES DOWN TO MAKING OBJECTS SMALLER AS THEY GET FARTHER AWAY.

SEEMS INTUITIVE, RIGHT?

BUT FOR MOST OF HISTORY, ARTISTS WEREN'T HIP TO THE TRICK.

DEPICTIONS OF DEPTH AND SPACE WERE UNDERDEVELOPED.

THE BATTLE OF SAN GILBOA IN THE SAN ISIDORO BIBLE, CIRCA 960 CE.

PERSPECTIVE SEEMS TO HAVE BEEN MASTERED FIRST BY FLORENTINE FILIPPO BRUNELLESCHI (1377-1446).

COMPUTERS CAN SUGGEST DEPTH BY SCALING GEOMETRIC SHAPES.

THE WIREFRAME VECTOR DISPLAYS OF *SPEED FREAK* (1978) AND *STAR WARS* (1983) HELPED VIDEO GAMES CONVERGE TOWARD WIDE ADOPTION OF *POLYGONAL 3-D GRAPHICS.*

BOTH CINEMATRONICS AND ATARI RECEIVED MILITARY CONTRACTS TO DEVELOP 3-D VIDEO GAME TRAINERS FOR THE U.S. MILITARY.

TOKYO-BORN NAMCO DESIGNER *TORU IWATANI* NOTICED THAT GAME CENTERS WERE JUST ABOUT *MONOPOLIZED* BY BOYS.

HE BEGAN SEARCHING FOR WAYS TO APPEAL TO THE FEMALE PERSUASION.

THE ACT OF EATING CUT ACROSS BOTH GENDERS. IWATANI STARTED THERE...

...AND ENDED WITH A MONEYMAKER THAT RACKED UP OVER $10 BILLION.

パクパク食べる!!

PAC-MAN

YEAR OF RELEASE: 1980

COUNTRY OF ORIGIN: JAPAN

GRAPHICS: COLOR CRT TELEVISION (NTSC STANDARD)

PLATFORMS: ARCADE

DEVELOPER(S): TORU IWATANI, ET AL.

PUBLISHER: NAMCO (JAPAN); MIDWAY (NORTH AMERICA)

RUNNING A MAZE, CLEARING AWAY DOTS, RUSHING TO KEEP AHEAD OF ENEMIES--THERE WAS ALREADY A PRECEDENT FOR SUCH GAMEPLAY IN SEGA'S *HEAD ON*, A 1979 CAR RACER.

YET ONE OF MANY STROKES OF GENIUS IN *PAC-MAN* IS MAKING THOSE DOTS MEANINGFUL-- THAT IS, THEY ARE *FOOD TO EAT*, NOT ARBITRARY MARKERS OF PROGRESS.

IWATANI ADDED TENSION TO THE RECIPE WITH FOUR CUTE BUT DEADLY GHOSTS. AT INTERVALS, PIECES OF FRUIT POP UP FOR BONUS POINTS. THESE ELEMENTS HELPED ENDEAR THE GAME TO THE FEMALE DEMOGRAPHIC.

THE GHOSTS' MECHANICS ARE A DIRECT REACTION TO THE REPETITIVE, PREDICTABLE MOTION OF *SPACE INVADERS* ALIENS. HERE EACH BRIGHTLY COLOR-COORDINATED GHOST HAS ITS OWN SIGNATURE FORM OF AI MOVEMENT.

PAC-MAN IS CREDITED FOR INTRODUCING THE "POWER-UP" TROPE IN GAMING. BUT WHAT MAKES *PAC-MAN* SO EXCITING IS THAT IN ONE MOMENT *THE ACTION COMPLETELY FLIPS*. THE GAME BECOMES ONE ABOUT *CHASING* RATHER THAN *BEING CHASED*!

JAPAN'S VIRTUOSITY IN THIS MEDIUM IS EVIDENT IN *PAC-MAN'S* SEQUELS, ADAPTATIONS, AND ENDLESS ECHOES IN POP CULTURE. BUT THIS TITLE'S MOST BELOVED SPINOFF CAME STRAIGHT OUT OF THE AMERICAN CRADLE OF VIDEO GAMING.

PAC-MAN, ASTEROIDS, AND MORE HAD *DESIGN FLAWS* VETERAN GAMERS COULD *EXPLOIT*...

...RESULTING IN LONG PLAY TIME PER COIN DROP AND SHORTING OPERATORS' CASH FLOW.

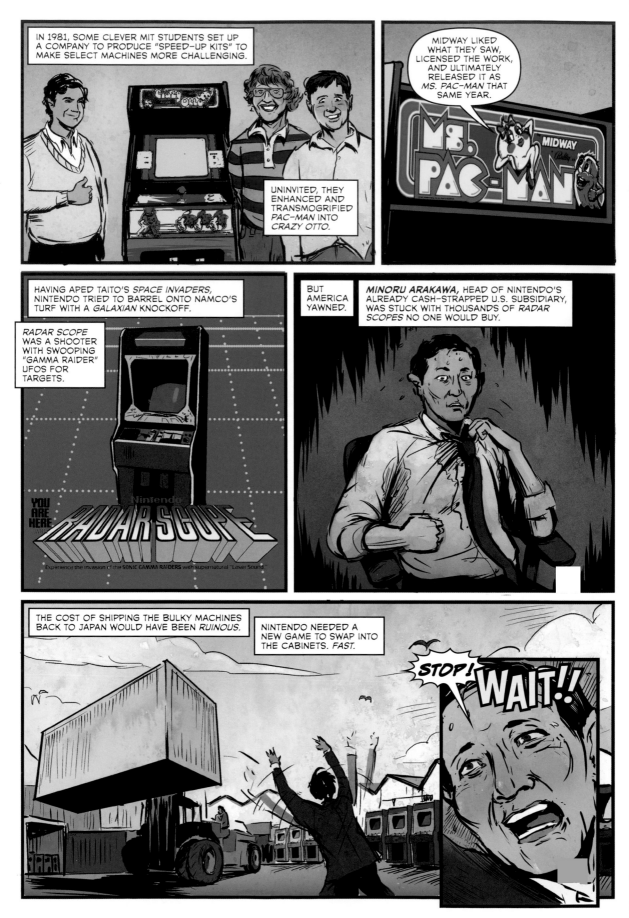

IN 1981, SOME CLEVER MIT STUDENTS SET UP A COMPANY TO PRODUCE "SPEED-UP KITS" TO MAKE SELECT MACHINES MORE CHALLENGING.

UNINVITED, THEY ENHANCED AND TRANSMOGRIFIED *PAC-MAN* INTO *CRAZY OTTO*.

MIDWAY LIKED WHAT THEY SAW, LICENSED THE WORK, AND ULTIMATELY RELEASED IT AS *MS. PAC-MAN* THAT SAME YEAR.

HAVING APED TAITO'S *SPACE INVADERS*, NINTENDO TRIED TO BARREL ONTO NAMCO'S TURF WITH A *GALAXIAN* KNOCKOFF.

RADAR SCOPE WAS A SHOOTER WITH SWOOPING "GAMMA RAIDER" UFOS FOR TARGETS.

BUT AMERICA YAWNED.

MINORU ARAKAWA, HEAD OF NINTENDO'S ALREADY CASH-STRAPPED U.S. SUBSIDIARY, WAS STUCK WITH THOUSANDS OF *RADAR SCOPES* NO ONE WOULD BUY.

THE COST OF SHIPPING THE BULKY MACHINES BACK TO JAPAN WOULD HAVE BEEN *RUINOUS.* NINTENDO NEEDED A NEW GAME TO SWAP INTO THE CABINETS. *FAST.*

STOP! WAIT!!

SPOTLIGHT: SHIGERU MIYAMOTO

THE BOY SCOUTS, ASSUMED BY MANY AMERICANS TO BE A HOMEGROWN INSTITUTION, BEGAN IN GREAT BRITAIN AS A WAY TO READY THE YOUTH OF THE NEW 20th CENTURY FOR WAR.

SCOUTING SPREAD TO JAPAN...

...DRAWING IN A DREAMY, MULTITALENTED, BORN EXPLORER FROM THE RURAL VILLAGE OF *SONOBE* (NOW *NANTAN*).

MIYAMOTO TRAMPED THROUGH THE LUSH LOCAL TERRAIN, DISCOVERING CAVES AND BREATHTAKING MOUNTAIN LAKES,

I WISH THAT CHILDREN NOWADAYS COULD HAVE SIMILAR EXPERIENCES, BUT IT'S NOT ALWAYS EASY.

A BANJO-PLAYING ART STUDENT MIGHT SHRIVEL UNDER THE HEAT LAMPS OF THE *ALL-WORK-ALL-THE-TIME* JAPANESE BUSINESS WORLD.

THE HIGH STAKES TASK OF REPURPOSING THOSE ORPHANED, WORTHLESS *RADAR SCOPE* CABINETS FELL TO HIM.

POPEYE SPINACH

BUT CONNECTIONS AND SAMPLE TOYS GOT MIYAMOTO HIRED AT NINTENDO.

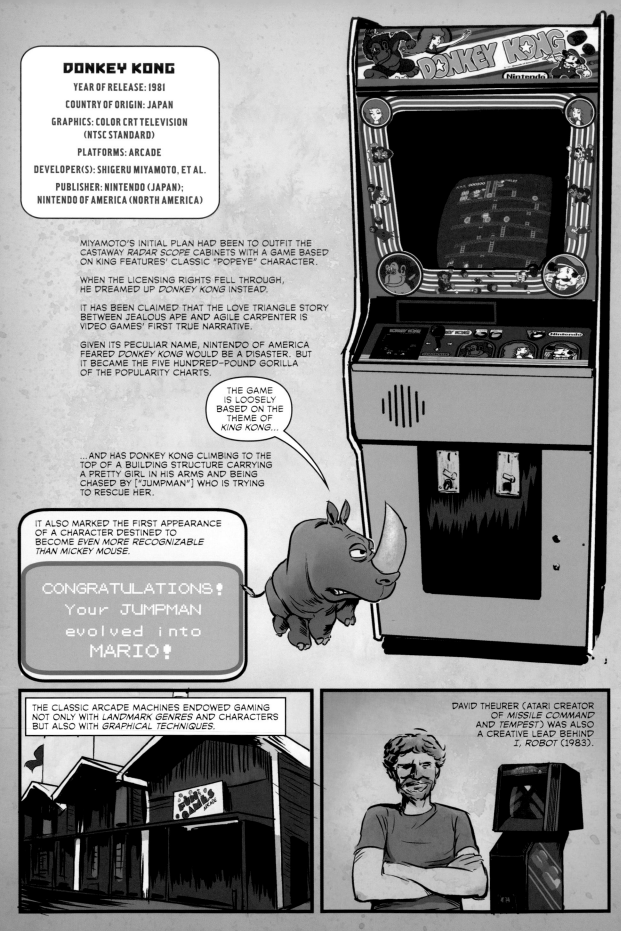

DONKEY KONG

YEAR OF RELEASE: 1981

COUNTRY OF ORIGIN: JAPAN

GRAPHICS: COLOR CRT TELEVISION (NTSC STANDARD)

PLATFORMS: ARCADE

DEVELOPER(S): SHIGERU MIYAMOTO, ET AL.

PUBLISHER: NINTENDO (JAPAN); NINTENDO OF AMERICA (NORTH AMERICA)

MIYAMOTO'S INITIAL PLAN HAD BEEN TO OUTFIT THE CASTAWAY *RADAR SCOPE* CABINETS WITH A GAME BASED ON KING FEATURES' CLASSIC "POPEYE" CHARACTER.

WHEN THE LICENSING RIGHTS FELL THROUGH, HE DREAMED UP *DONKEY KONG* INSTEAD.

IT HAS BEEN CLAIMED THAT THE LOVE TRIANGLE STORY BETWEEN JEALOUS APE AND AGILE CARPENTER IS VIDEO GAMES' FIRST TRUE NARRATIVE.

GIVEN ITS PECULIAR NAME, NINTENDO OF AMERICA FEARED *DONKEY KONG* WOULD BE A DISASTER. BUT IT BECAME THE FIVE HUNDRED-POUND GORILLA OF THE POPULARITY CHARTS.

THE GAME IS LOOSELY BASED ON THE THEME OF *KING KONG*...

...AND HAS DONKEY KONG CLIMBING TO THE TOP OF A BUILDING STRUCTURE CARRYING A PRETTY GIRL IN HIS ARMS AND BEING CHASED BY ["JUMPMAN"] WHO IS TRYING TO RESCUE HER.

IT ALSO MARKED THE FIRST APPEARANCE OF A CHARACTER DESTINED TO BECOME *EVEN MORE RECOGNIZABLE THAN MICKEY MOUSE.*

CONGRATULATIONS! Your JUMPMAN evolved into MARIO!

THE CLASSIC ARCADE MACHINES ENDOWED GAMING NOT ONLY WITH *LANDMARK GENRES* AND CHARACTERS BUT ALSO WITH *GRAPHICAL TECHNIQUES.*

DAVID THEURER (ATARI CREATOR OF *MISSILE COMMAND* AND *TEMPEST*) WAS ALSO A CREATIVE LEAD BEHIND *I, ROBOT* (1983).

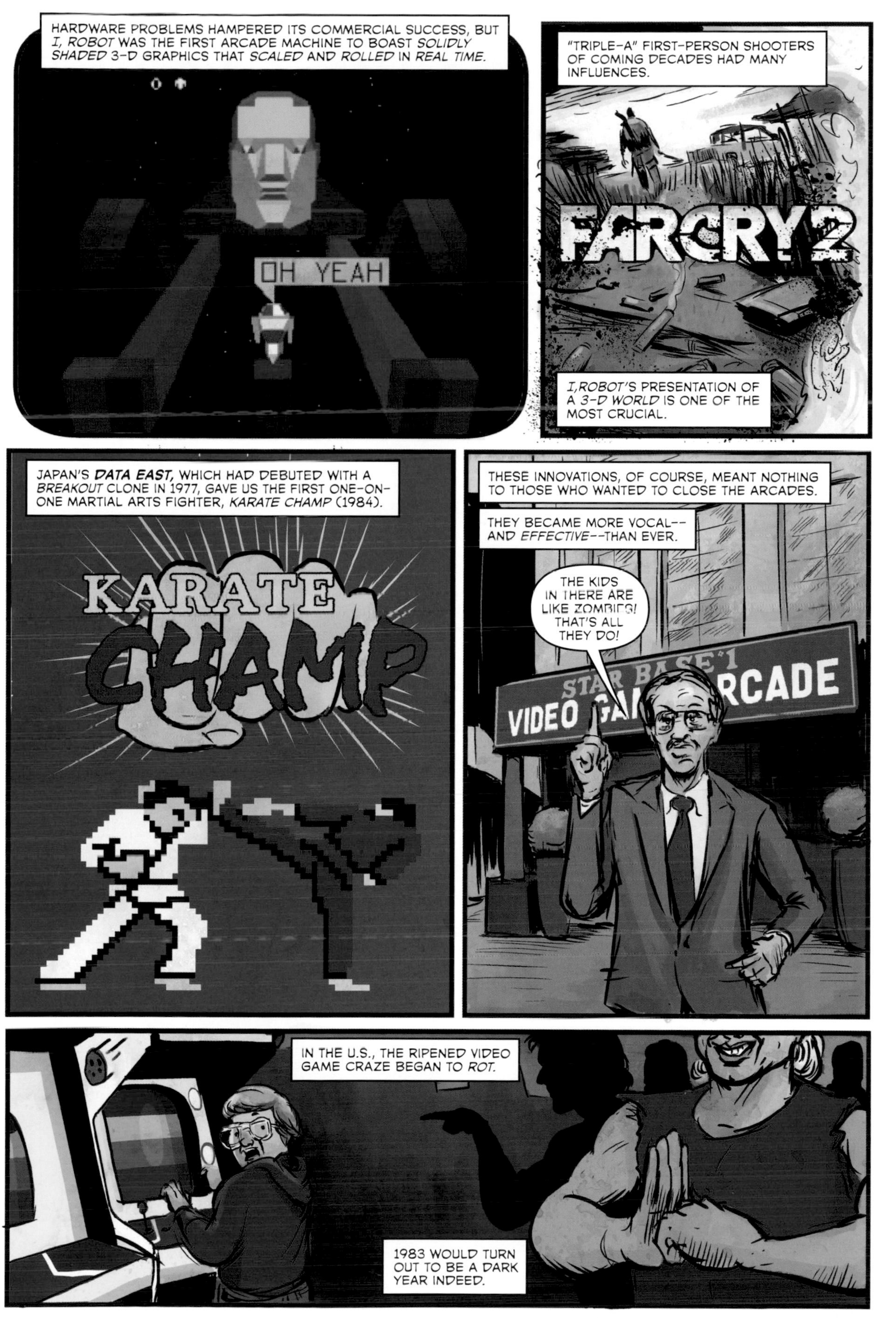

HARDWARE PROBLEMS HAMPERED ITS COMMERCIAL SUCCESS, BUT *I, ROBOT* WAS THE FIRST ARCADE MACHINE TO BOAST *SOLIDLY SHADED* 3-D GRAPHICS THAT *SCALED* AND *ROLLED* IN *REAL TIME.*
OH YEAH
"TRIPLE-A" FIRST-PERSON SHOOTERS OF COMING DECADES HAD MANY INFLUENCES.
FARCRY 2
I,ROBOT'S PRESENTATION OF A *3-D WORLD* IS ONE OF THE MOST CRUCIAL.
JAPAN'S ***DATA EAST,*** WHICH HAD DEBUTED WITH A *BREAKOUT* CLONE IN 1977, GAVE US THE FIRST ONE-ON-ONE MARTIAL ARTS FIGHTER, *KARATE CHAMP* (1984).
KARATE CHAMP
THESE INNOVATIONS, OF COURSE, MEANT NOTHING TO THOSE WHO WANTED TO CLOSE THE ARCADES.
THEY BECAME MORE VOCAL--AND *EFFECTIVE*--THAN EVER.
THE KIDS IN THERE ARE LIKE ZOMBIES! THAT'S ALL THEY DO!
STAR BASE 1
VIDEO
RCADE
IN THE U.S., THE RIPENED VIDEO GAME CRAZE BEGAN TO *ROT.*
1983 WOULD TURN OUT TO BE A DARK YEAR INDEED.

CHAPTER SEVEN
CRASH 'N' DON'T SCORE
The Disaster That Almost Spelled "Games Over"

VIDEO GAMING AT THIS TIME WAS WHAT ECONOMISTS WOULD CALL AN "IMMATURE INDUSTRY."

IN THE UNITED STATES, FOLKS WERE IN AN *INFATUATED STATE* WITH GAMES. THEY COULDN'T GET ENOUGH OF THEM--*OR SPEND ENOUGH ON* THEM.

EVEN HOME EDITIONS THAT FELL WAY SHORT OF ARCADE "GAME-FEEL," LIKE THE ATARI VCS *PAC-MAN* PORT, WERE, FOR A TIME, RELIABLE CASH COWS.

THE VIDEO GAME INDUSTRY (ARCADE AND HOME COMBINED) HAD HAD REVENUES OF $400 MILLION IN 1977.

BUT BY 1982, THOSE REVENUES HAD *SKYROCKETED 3,900 PERCENT* TO AN ESTIMATED *$15.6 BILLION*-- MAKING GAMES BIGGER THAN SPORTS, MOVIES, AND MUSIC!

"GET RICH QUICK" FANTASIES SENT TOY, ELECTRONICS, AND MEDIA COMPANIES ELBOWING IN.

FIRE FLY video game cartridge
For Atari® 2600™ VCS™ and compatible systems
$9.95

ATARI HAD NO POWER TO STOP THEM FROM RUSHING *HALF-BAKED* VCS GAMES INTO CIRCULATION.

BY 1983, THERE WERE TOO MANY GAMES ON THE MARKET. AND TOO MANY ARCADE MACHINES IN TOO MANY LOCATIONS. THE BUSINESS SECTOR HAD LARGELY FAILED TO REALIZE...

ACT 4: THE HONEYMOON IS OVER

...INFATUATION DOESN'T LAST FOREVER.

AS GAMERS GREW MORE SOPHISTICATED, MEDIOCRE GAMES NO LONGER SATISFIED.

LEGENDARY ATARI FIZZLER *E.T.* WAS *NOT*, HOWEVER, THE UNILATERAL CAUSE OF THE 1983 GAMING "CRASH."

ATARI 260

E.T. THE EXTRA-TERRESTRIAL

Games 'n' Gadgets

FACED WITH A GLUT OF UNWANTED STOCK, RETAILERS *SLASHED PRICES*-- AND LOST FAITH IN BUYING NEW GAMES.

THE NOSE DIVE AFFECTED THE HARDWARE SIDE, TOO.

RIP CORD

PLAYERS WITH *TECHNOLOGICAL SUPERIORITY* TO ATARI HAD BOWED...

...SUCH AS *MATTEL* WITH ITS "INTELLIVISION" AND *COLECO* WITH ITS "COLECOVISION."

Intellivision

COLECO, A PORTMANTEAU OF *CO*NNECTICUT *LE*ATHER *CO*MPANY, HAD SEEN AN OPPORTUNITY WITH THE 1950s DAVY CROCKETT CRAZE TO ENTER THE TOY MARKET.

Coleco's AUTHENTIC INDIAN FIGHTER DAVY CROCKETT

MOCCASIN KIT

GENUINE LEATHER

FROM TOYS, IT WAS NOT AN ILLOGICAL LEAP TO VIDEO GAMES.

COLECO'S *DONKEY KONG,* [IN JANUARY 1983] THE SECOND BIGGEST SELLER ACCORDING TO *BILLBOARD'S* BIWEEKLY POLL, [HAD] ALREADY EARNED OVER $5 MILLION IN ROYALTIES FOR ITS ARCADE MANUFACTURER, NINTENDO!

BUT IN LIGHT OF THE HEAVY-DUTY LIQUIDATION GOING ON IN STORES, QUALITY COULD NOT KEEP THE NEWCOMERS AFLOAT.

$50.00 INTELLIVISION CASH REBATE
BUY ANY INTELLIVISION® AND ANY TWO MATTEL ELECTRONICS® INTELLIVISION CARTRIDGES

$99.99
-50.00
$49.99

INTELLIVISION WAS DISCONTINUED IN 1984...

...AND COLECOVISION IN 1985.

THE DEVASTATION WROUGHT BY *THE BURST OF THE VIDEO GAMES BUBBLE* NEARLY BANKRUPTED MATTEL, MAKER OF THE ICONIC BARBIE DOLL.

EPYX PRESENTS Barbie™
©1984 MATTEL INC.
©1984 EPYX INC.
GAME DEVELOPED BY A. EDDY GOLDFARB & ASSOC.

FOR SUCH COMPANIES, THE IDEA OF BEATING ATARI AT ITS OWN GAME HAD LOST ITS GIRLISH CHARM.

MEANWHILE, ATARI'S MANAGEMENT WAS ALL BUT *HELPING* ITS RIVALS *BURY IT ALIVE.*

BREAKOUT
BREAKOUT
BREAKOUT

ATARI'S CORPORATE CULTURE HAD *OUTRAGED* THE BUTTONED-UP EAST COAST EXECUTIVE WARNER HAD SENT TO OVERSEE BUSHNELL'S CREW.

≈GASP≈
(INHALE)
≈COUGH≈

YOU PARTAKING, BUD?

WHAT KIND OF COMPANY ARE YOU PEOPLE RUNNING HERE?!

RAY KASSAR, 1978.

126

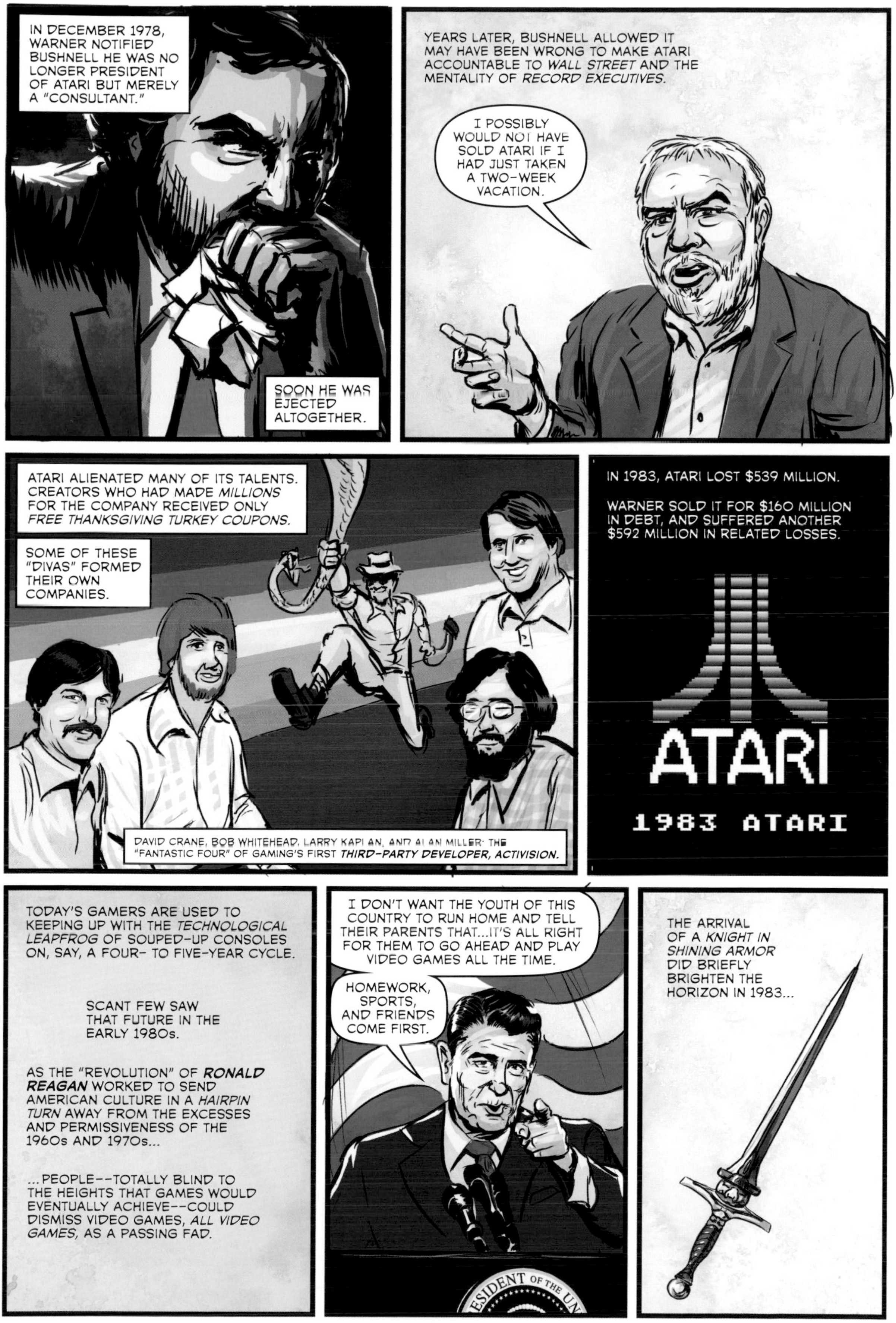
IN DECEMBER 1978, WARNER NOTIFIED BUSHNELL HE WAS NO LONGER PRESIDENT OF ATARI BUT MERELY A "CONSULTANT."
SOON HE WAS EJECTED ALTOGETHER.
YEARS LATER, BUSHNELL ALLOWED IT MAY HAVE BEEN WRONG TO MAKE ATARI ACCOUNTABLE TO *WALL STREET* AND THE MENTALITY OF *RECORD EXECUTIVES.*
I POSSIBLY WOULD NOT HAVE SOLD ATARI IF I HAD JUST TAKEN A TWO-WEEK VACATION.
ATARI ALIENATED MANY OF ITS TALENTS. CREATORS WHO HAD MADE *MILLIONS* FOR THE COMPANY RECEIVED ONLY *FREE THANKSGIVING TURKEY COUPONS.*
SOME OF THESE "DIVAS" FORMED THEIR OWN COMPANIES.
DAVID CRANE, BOB WHITEHEAD, LARRY KAPLAN, AND ALAN MILLER: THE "FANTASTIC FOUR" OF GAMING'S FIRST *THIRD-PARTY DEVELOPER, ACTIVISION.*
IN 1983, ATARI LOST $539 MILLION.
WARNER SOLD IT FOR $160 MILLION IN DEBT, AND SUFFERED ANOTHER $592 MILLION IN RELATED LOSSES.
ATARI
1983 ATARI
TODAY'S GAMERS ARE USED TO KEEPING UP WITH THE *TECHNOLOGICAL LEAPFROG* OF SOUPED-UP CONSOLES ON, SAY, A FOUR- TO FIVE-YEAR CYCLE.
SCANT FEW SAW THAT FUTURE IN THE EARLY 1980s.
AS THE "REVOLUTION" OF ***RONALD REAGAN*** WORKED TO SEND AMERICAN CULTURE IN A *HAIRPIN TURN* AWAY FROM THE EXCESSES AND PERMISSIVENESS OF THE 1960s AND 1970s...
...PEOPLE--TOTALLY BLIND TO THE HEIGHTS THAT GAMES WOULD EVENTUALLY ACHIEVE--COULD DISMISS VIDEO GAMES, *ALL VIDEO GAMES,* AS A PASSING FAD.
I DON'T WANT THE YOUTH OF THIS COUNTRY TO RUN HOME AND TELL THEIR PARENTS THAT...IT'S ALL RIGHT FOR THEM TO GO AHEAD AND PLAY VIDEO GAMES ALL THE TIME.
HOMEWORK, SPORTS, AND FRIENDS COME FIRST.
THE ARRIVAL OF A *KNIGHT IN SHINING ARMOR* DID BRIEFLY BRIGHTEN THE HORIZON IN 1983...

RICK DYER WAS A SELF-TAUGHT BOY INVENTOR WHO HAD LANDED A JOB ON MATTEL'S INTELLIVISION PROJECT...

...BUT HE DREAMED OF CROSS-BREEDING VIDEO GAMES AND ANIMATION INTO A SINGLE INTERACTIVE EXPERIENCE.

THE INVENTION OF THE LASERDISC MADE THIS FEASIBLE.

DYER LOOPED IN DISSIDENT EX-DISNEY ANIMATOR DON BLUTH. THEY WON A GAMING ALLY IN CINEMATRONICS.

THE RESULT WAS A PILE OF LOOT AFTER A LONG AND PERILOUS JOURNEY.

DRAGON'S LAIR

YEAR OF RELEASE: 1983

COUNTRY OF ORIGIN: U.S.

GRAPHICS: COLOR CRT TELEVISION (NTSC STANDARD)

PLATFORMS: ARCADE

DEVELOPER(S):
RICK DYER, DON BLUTH, ET AL.
PUBLISHER: CINEMATRONICS

DRAGON'S LAIR WAS THE CULMINATION OF A LONG, EVOLUTIONARY PROCESS UNDERTAKEN BY RICK DYER-- BEGINNING WITH AN "ELECTRONIC BOOK" ON CASH REGISTER PAPER.

EVEN AS ARCADES WERE BEGINNING TO CLOSE IN LARGE NUMBERS, BLUTH'S JAUNTY ANIMATIONS WERE A BLOCKBUSTER HIT.

PLAYERS THRILLED TO CONTROL "DIRK THE DARING" THROUGH SIMPLE, DECISION-MAKING JOYSTICK AND BUTTON MOVES.

ALTHOUGH TO A FIRST-TIMER, *DRAGON'S LAIR* SEEMED CONVINCING...

...GAMERS SOON SAW THAT THE GAME WAS JUST A MEMORY CHALLENGE WITH A CLOSED ENDING.

SLASH!

BUT THERE WOULD BE NO CLOSED ENDING FOR VIDEO GAMES IN JAPAN.

THE ISLAND NATION PROVED ITSELF A FAITHFUL SUITOR TO ITS FOREIGN-BORN BRIDE.

FOR MANY AMERICAN FANS, VIDEO GAMES HAD BEEN *JUST A FLING.*

I'M TERMINATING MY LEASE.

I HAVE A LOT OF BILLS TO PAY. I'M MOVING TO FLORIDA TO GET A JOB.

WALTER DAY CLOSING THE TWIN GALAXIES ARCADE IN OTTUMWA, IOWA, MARCH 1984.

HARDCORE DEVOTEES STILL PLAYED IN THEIR LIVING ROOMS AND IN DIMLY-LIT PUBLIC PLACES WHERE ARCADE MACHINES HUNG ON.

BUT IF GAMES WERE GOING TO SAVE THEMSELVES FROM EXTINCTION, IT SEEMED THE WAY FORWARD WAS NOT GOING TO COME WITH *DISCONTINUED CONSOLES* OR *DISCREDITED COIN-OP.*

INDUSTRY PROGNOSTICATORS FIGURED THE FUTURE WOULD BE ALL ABOUT *COMPUTERS.*

IN SOME WAYS, *THEY WERE RIGHT.*

CHAPTER EIGHT
BACK TO COMPUTERS
And This Time It's Personal

FROM THE SPARTAN FEATURES OF THE MAGNAVOX ODYSSEY TO THE ALMOST ARCADE-QUALITY COLECOVISION, FROM THE SIMPLISTIC SYMBOLISM OF *PONG* TO THE SHADED 3-D POLYGONS OF *I, ROBOT*, A DOZEN YEARS HAD BORNE WITNESS TO A *FULL-SCALE INVASION* OF CONSOLES AND ARCADE GAMES.

TODAY IT MAY BE HARD TO GRASP. BUT DURING THOSE SAME TWELVE YEARS IT WAS STILL *UNCONVENTIONAL* TO HAVE A *COMPUTER IN THE HOME.*

EVEN AS LATE AS 1984, LESS THAN ONE IN TEN AMERICAN HOUSEHOLDS OWNED A COMPUTER. THE WIDE-OPEN INTERNET WAS YEARS OFF. AND JUST 1.4 PERCENT OF U.S. FAMILIES HAD ANY WAY TO SEND OR RECEIVE TINY BITS OF INFORMATION VIA COMPUTER.

THE MEMORABLE EARLY CONSOLE AND ARCADE GAMES RETAIN A WILD AMOUNT OF *CULTURAL RELEVANCE.*

THE SAME PERIOD'S *COMPUTER GAMES,* THOUGH, NEVER HAD THE *USERS* OR *EXPOSURE* TO LOCK IN EQUAL STAYING POWER.

WHY? FRANKLY, IT'S BECAUSE-- BEFORE THE 1990s OR THEREABOUTS-- COMPUTERS STILL *INTIMIDATED THE HELL OUT* OF ALMOST EVERYONE.

STARTING MS-DOS...

HIMEM IS TESTING EXTENDED MEMORY... DONE.

C:\>C:\DOS\SMARTDRV.EXE /X

C:\>

DROP IN A QUARTER, POP IN A CARTRIDGE... THAT KIND OF USER EXPERIENCE WAS *IDIOT-PROOF.* BUT WRANGLE RESULTS FROM THE "COMMAND LINE ENVIRONMENT" OF A BLINKING CURSOR ON A BLACK SCREEN? FOR THE MASSES, THAT WAS *SOMETHING ELSE ENTIRELY.*

BACK IN THE DAY, COMPUTERS HAD *ANOTHER* PROBLEM BESIDES BEING *IMPENETRABLE* TO AVERAGE JOES.

c:\>!

c:\>!!

MOMMY!!

IN THE ABSENCE OF A FAST, OPEN INTERNET, COMPUTERS--TO BE BLUNT--OFFERED *ALMOST NOTHING* ANYONE REALLY WANTED.

SO GUYS, *I* KNOW... HOW ABOUT WE BALANCE MY MOM'S CHECKBOOK?

♪ I'VE GOT VISICALC...! ♪

ALMOST NOTHING, THAT IS, EXCEPT *GAMES*.

King's Quest

1

Quest for the Crown

AND SINCE THERE WAS THIS *UNSHAKEABLE ANXIETY* THAT MEMBERS OF THE UPCOMING GENERATION SHOULD HAVE COMPUTERS--AND KNOW HOW TO USE THEM...

Why Every Kid Should Have An Apple After School.

THE APPLE II WAS FIRST RELEASED IN JUNE 1977.

...THE FIX WAS IN.

[THE APPLE II] WAS BUILT WITH GAMING IN MIND.

...AND SO SUDDENLY YOU HAVE THIS MACHINE THAT'S *A PERFECT TROJAN HORSE* FOR GETTING GAMES INTO YOUR HOUSE.

UNDER THE RULE OF MOORE'S LAW, CHEAPER, MORE *MUSCULAR* PERSONAL COMPUTERS WERE SOON STAGING AN INVASION OF THEIR OWN.

BUSINESS IS WAR.

AUSCHWITZ SURVIVOR AND *COMMODORE* FOUNDER *JACK TRAMIEL* BROUGHT LOW-COST PCs TO MASS MERCHANDISERS IN THE EARLY 1980s. THE COMMODORE 64 IS THE *ALL-TIME HIGHEST-SELLING SINGLE MODEL OF PC.*

AND SO WERE IRRIGATED THE FIELDS OF *PC GAMES.* GAMES WRITTEN ON COMPUTERS, *FOR* COMPUTERS...

...AND TO BE PLAYED BY THE IMAGINATIVE *SMARTY-PANTS* CAPABLE OF ACTUALLY *DEALING WITH* COMPUTERS.

WHEN I WAS REALLY, REALLY YOUNG, LIKE EIGHT YEARS OLD, MY DAD GOT US A COMMODORE 128.

AND WE STARTED SUBSCRIBING TO A MAGAZINE THAT HAD, LIKE, CODE LISTINGS FOR GAMES. AND I STARTED ENTERING THEM AND STARTED TOYING WITH THEM.

MARKUS "NOTCH" PERSSON, CREATOR OF *MINECRAFT.*

THE NATURE OF PC GAMES WAS ELEMENTALLY DISTINCT FROM ARCADE GAMES.

TO JUSTIFY THEIR EXPENSE, ARCADE GAMES HAD TO EAT UP MANY QUARTERS PER HOUR.

LETHAL ENFORCERS MYST

SO ARCADE GAMEPLAY WAS DESIGNED TO BE AS *SHORT* AND AS *DIFFICULT* AS THE AVERAGE COIN-DROPPER COULD TOLERATE.

IN THE HIT-DRIVEN BUSINESS, *EASILY CATEGORIZED* AND *WIDELY RELATABLE* PRODUCTS WERE OPTIMAL: SPORTS GAMES, SHOOTERS, FIGHTERS, PLATFORMERS, AND SO ON.

OH, COME ON!!!

(GRUMBLE GRUMBLE) I GUESS I'LL TRY AGAIN...

PC GAMES WEREN'T DEPENDENT ON QUARTERS.

NOR, IN THE POST-1983 *CRASH* ATMOSPHERE WHEN BIG RETAIL CHAINS CONSIDERED VIDEO GAMES *TOXIC*, WERE HUGE SALES REQUIRED TO MAKE A GAME "SUCCESSFUL."

YOUR FIRST GAME ON THE TRS-80... DID IT EVER GET PUBLISHED?

YEP! THERE WAS ONE TRS-80 PUBLISHER IN THE COUNTRY...

...I THINK THEY MUST HAVE SOLD ABOUT FIFTY COPIES IN TOTAL, WHICH WAS PRETTY GOOD!

BRITISH DESIGNER *MATTHEW SMITH*, CREATOR OF 1983s *MANIC MINER*.

SO PC GAMES COULD BE *LONG* IN DURATION; *NUANCED* IN BOTH CONCEPT AND EXECUTION.

SURE, ARCADE- AND CONSOLE-TYPE PURSUITS *ARE* ENJOYABLE ON PCS. BUT CERTAIN GENRES UNQUESTIONABLY PLAY TO THEIR STRENGTHS.

JAPANESE GAME DESIGNER *YUJI HORII* DISCOVERING *WIZARDRY* AT SAN FRANCISCO APPLEFEST, 1983.

AND WHAT COULD BE MORE DISTANT FROM THE *WHAM, BAM, THANK YOU, MA'AM* ARCADE PARADIGM THAN *SIMULATIONS* OR *SANDBOX GAMES*...

ACQUIRE

COMPUTER ACQUIRE
The object of the game is to become the wealthiest person in this "business" game about hotel acquisitions and mergers. For 2 to 6 players it is a subtle game of interplayer strategy. As a SOLITAIRE game you play against the computer. One can even pit the computer against itself in this faithful recreation of the classic board game.

16K cass. TRS-80 II, Apple II, Pet 2001 $20
32K disk: TRS-80 II, Apple II $25

OFTEN DEVOID OF PLOTS, GOALS, ENDINGS, AND EVEN ANTAGONISTS?

BRUCE ARTWICK ALL BUT BROKE AN *AIR SPEED RECORD* BY ZOOMING THROUGH COLLEGE AND GRADUATE SCHOOL IN FOUR YEARS.

HE COMBINED A LOVE OF SPEED, ELECTRONICS, PLANES, AND 3-D COMPUTER GRAPHICS INTO *A2FS1 FLIGHT SIMULATOR*.

THRT

FUEL   020
TACH   240
SCORE 000
BOMBS 004
AMMO   080

CLIMB
-999
HEADING
353
TURN RT
-454

ELEV

ROLL

2 4 6 8 10 12 14 16 18 20   0 1 2 3 4 5 6 7 8 9
AIRSPEED   ALTITUDE

WE HAD TO KEEP IT SIMPLE... EVEN A FEW LINES WERE ENOUGH TO GIVE YOU A SENSE OF MOVEMENT.

IT BECAME A LONG-RUNNING AND HUGELY PROFITABLE FRANCHISE.

BUT NOT EVEN *FLIGHT SIMULATOR* COULD RIVAL THE BRAINCHILD OF ANOTHER *SPEED ADDICT.*

WILL WRIGHT USED A CAR TRICKED OUT WITH GADGETS AND COMPUTERS TO WIN AN ILLEGAL CROSS-COUNTRY RACE IN 1980.

RAAAAAARRRR!!!

← Tucumcari
Amarillo →

GAMERS TOOK NOTICE OF THE IMPRESSIVE AI AND MODELING DYNAMICS IN HIS ACTION PC GAME *RAID ON BUNGELING BAY* (1984).

I FOUND THAT I WAS HAVING MUCH MORE FUN BUILDING THESE LITTLE WORLDS THAN FLYING AROUND AND BLOWING THEM UP.

WORLD BUILDING WAS SO GRATIFYING THAT, WITH HIS NEXT RELEASE, HE MADE IT EASY FOR OTHERS TO SHARE THE EXPERIENCE.

SimCity The City Simulator · SIMCITY CREATOR · SIMCITY 4 · SIMCITY 3000 · SIMCITY BOX · SIMCITY · SIMCITY DS · SIM CITY · SIM CITY 2000

SIMCITY (1989) WAS THE FOUNDATION FOR ONE OF THE BEST-SELLING SERIES OF ALL TIME.

THE BIGGEST SELLING COMMODORE MAG IN BRITAIN! ZZAP! 64 · MONTHLY REVIEW FOR C · COMMODORE SOFTWARE · ANOTHER CHANCE TO WIN A COMPUTER · MOVIE MAKER · STEVE EVANS

ANOTHER PC GENRE REALLY ALLOWED GAMERS TO *LET THEIR FREAK FLAGS FLY.*

ONCE A WILD, UNDISCOVERED, AND SCANTILY-VISITED CONTINENT, THE DOMAIN OF NERD CULTURE...

...WAS PERHAPS MOST EXTENSIVELY *OPENED FOR HOMESTEADING* BY A *TWEEDY, ALE-QUAFFING, PIPE-PUFFING* SCHOLAR...

...A MAN MOST AT HOME IN A LEATHER-CUSHIONED ARMCHAIR IN OXFORD, ENGLAND.

J. R. R. TOLKIEN IS MOST REMEMBERED FOR THE *LORD OF THE RINGS* TRILOGY (PUBLISHED BETWEEN 1954 AND 1955), A *HIGH FANTASY* ABOUT A QUEST TO RID A MIGHTY EVIL FROM A WORLD OF HOBBITS, DWARVES, AND ELVES.

I WANTED TO TRY MY HAND AT WRITING A REALLY, STUPENDOUSLY LONG NARRATIVE...

...AND TO SEE WHETHER I HAD THE SUFFICIENT ART, CUNNING, OR MATERIAL TO HOLD THE AVERAGE READER RIGHT THROUGH.

THE BOOKS EMERGED AS A MONOLITHIC INFLUENCE ON COLLEGE STUDENTS OF THE 1960s AND 1970s...

...SINCE TOLKIEN'S PROTAGONISTS EMBRACED IDEALISTIC CAUSES AND SAW THEM THROUGH WITH PERSEVERANCE AND DETERMINATION.

TRULY A MYTH FOR THE TIMES.

THEN, COLLEGE STUDENTS WERE SOME OF THE ONLY PEOPLE WITH *ACTUAL ACCESS TO COMPUTERS,* SO TOLKIEN ALSO INSPIRED A GENERATION OF PC GAMERS.

[TOLKIEN] SHOWED IT COULD BE DONE. HE SHOWED YOU COULD CREATE A CONSISTENT, BELIEVABLE, ENTHRALLING WORLD THAT DIDN'T--*COULDN'T*--POSSIBLY EXIST.

RICHARD BARTLE, COCREATOR IN 1978 OF THE UNIVERSITY OF ESSEX [U.K.]-BASED *MUD1,* THE FIRST *MULTIUSER DUNGEON (MUD).*

TABLETOP GAMES THAT REPLICATED WAR OR SPORTS HAD BEEN BELOVED OF HOBBYISTS FOR CENTURIES.

ONE LOVER--AND INITIALLY SMALL-FRY MAKER-- OF SUCH GAMES WAS A HIGH SCHOOL DROPOUT AND JEHOVAH'S WITNESS LIVING IN LAKE GENEVA, WISCONSIN.

GARY GYGAX AND MATE DAVE ARNESON CREATED DUNGEONS & DRAGONS...

...WHICH WAS AT ITS HEART AN ATTEMPT TO TURN A TOLKIEN- OR CONAN THE BARBARIAN-STYLE WORLD INTO AN OPEN-ENDED ROLE-PLAYING GAME (RPG).

DUNGEONS & DRAGONS

Rules for Fantastic Medieval Wargames Campaigns Playable with Paper and Pencil and Miniature Figures

GYGAX & ARNESON

MEN & MAGIC
VOLUME 1 OF THREE BOOKLETS

PUBLISHED BY
TACTICAL STUDIES RULES
Price $3.50

IN TABLETOP RPGS, PLAYERS ASSUME THE PART OF ALTER EGOS WHOSE TRAITS AND SKILLS ARE REPRESENTED NUMERICALLY.

THE GAME ACTION RELIES ON MATH, STATISTICS, AND RANDOM NUMBERS GENERATED BY ROLLING SPECIAL MULTISIDED DICE.

RPGS RELIED ON CONSTANT CALCULATION.

THE PEOPLE WHO ENJOYED THEM OFTEN HAPPENED ALSO TO BE COMPUTER LITERATE...

...SO IT WAS NOT LONG BEFORE RPG PROGRAMS BEGAN POPPING UP ON MAINFRAMES.

Level 4
Death

fight, evade, magic
or cleric (f,e,m,c) >

GARY WHISENHUNT AND RAY WOOD'S 1975 DND ON THE SOUTHERN ILLINOIS UNIVERSITY'S "PLATO" SYSTEM.

THE WORLD OF VIDEO GAME RPGS OWES IT ALL TO THIS FAN-BASED URGE TO DELIVER A DIGITAL D&D.

Official **Advanced Dungeons & Dragons**
PLAYERS HANDBOOK
by E. Gary Gygax

AS I WAS LEARNING THE [VIDEO GAMES JOURNALISM] BEAT AND MEETING PEOPLE WHO MAKE VIDEO GAMES...

...I ALWAYS LIKED TO ASK PEOPLE, "WHAT MADE YOU WANT TO DO THIS FOR A LIVING?"

OVER AND OVER AGAIN THEY GAVE ME THE SAME ANSWER.

THEY ALL SAID, "OH, I PLAYED A LOT OF *DUNGEONS & DRAGONS* WHEN I WAS A KID."

JOURNALIST DAVID EWALT

SPOTLIGHT:
RICHARD "LORD BRITISH" GARRIOTT

HOUSTON HAD NO PROBLEM HELPING THE IMAGINATION OF RICHARD GARRIOTT ACHIEVE ESCAPE VELOCITY.

A NASA PILOT, GARRIOTT'S FATHER FLEW BOTH ON A SATURN IB ROCKET MISSION IN 1973 AND ON THE SPACE SHUTTLE COLUMBIA IN 1983.

HI, DAD. GO TO THE MOON TODAY?

NO, SON, NOT TODAY.

LITERALLY BEING ABLE TO PATCH DAD IN ON THE TELEPHONE FROM ORBIT TO HELP WITH MATH HOMEWORK *IS* A BIT EXTRAORDINARY.

YET GARRIOTT'S PATH TO VIDEO GAME CREATOR WAS MORE TYPICAL. HE TRIED TO ADAPT *D&D* FOR COMPUTER PLAY.

DUNGEONS & DRAGONS

SOON AFTER, I WAS INTRODUCED TO *DUNGEONS & DRAGONS*...

...I QUICKLY BUILT ONE OF THE EARLIEST AND LARGEST PLAYING GROUPS, WHICH BROUGHT TOGETHER 30-100 PEOPLE FOR ALL-NIGHT GAMING SESSIONS.

GARRIOTT CAME UNDER THE GRAVITATIONAL INFLUENCE OF TWO OTHER MUSES: SILAS WARNER'S GROUNDBREAKING 3-D MAZE GAME *ESCAPE* AND THE APPLE II.

GAME DESIGNER *SILAS WARNER*

COMPACT CASSETTES WERE COMMONLY USED FOR DATA STORAGE IN THE 1970s AND 1980s. A NINETY-MINUTE AUDIO TAPE COULD HOLD ABOUT 1.2MB OF DATA.

ENCOURAGED BY THE RECEPTION OF A PREVIOUS GAME, *AKALABETH*, GARRIOTT NEXT PRODUCED *ULTIMA* (1981).

Ultima II

ULTIMA WOULD BECOME A SPRAWLING RPG SERIES AND, LATER, A *MASSIVELY MULTIPLAYER ONLINE RPG* (MMORPG).

NOW AVAILABLE FOR THE APPLE

GARRIOTT WOULD SEE THE DARK SIDE OF GAMER URGES. THERE WAS RAMPANT *PLAYER-KILLING* IN THE ROLLOUT OF *ULTIMA ONLINE*. IN 1996, A DELUSIONAL FAN ALSO STALKED HIM IN HIS HOME.

GARRIOTT TWEAKED HIS GAMES TO STEER PLAYERS IN A MORE MORALLY CONSCIOUS DIRECTION.

911? IF THIS GUY COMES UPSTAIRS, WHAT SHOULD I DO?!

SUCCESS ALSO ENABLED GARRIOTT TO FULFILL A LIFETIME DREAM: SPACE TRAVEL. IN 2007, HE SELF-FINANCED A TRIP TO THE INTERNATIONAL SPACE STATION IN A RUSSIAN *SOYUZ* ROCKET.

BELOW, UNTOLD THOUSANDS PLAYED THE RPGS HE HELPED BRING INTO THE GAMING MAINSTREAM...

...BUT, UNFORTUNATELY, GARRIOTT WAS NOT ALLOWED TO JOIN IN FROM SPACE.

IT TURNS OUT THAT EVEN THOUGH THERE IS AN IP PATHWAY, THEY WERE WORRIED ABOUT [HACKERS] TUNNELING BACKWARDS TO THE ISS AND WREAKING HAVOC...

ANOTHER DIFFERENCE BETWEEN ARCADE AND CONSOLE OFFERINGS AND EARLY PC GAMES?

THE FORMER WERE TO *GRAPHICS* WHAT OLYMPIANS ARE TO *ATHLETIC PROWESS.* EVEN THE VAUNTED APPLE II WAS *UNDERCRANKED* BY COMPARISON.

INITIALLY, THE PC TRADITION CONDONED THE *CRUDEST* OF GRAPHICS...

...OR NO GRAPHICS AT ALL!

```
59  REM ***INSTRUCTIONS***
60  PRINT "THIS PROGRAM SIMULATES A TRIP OVER THE OREGON TRAIL FROM"
65  PRINT "INDEPENDENCE, MISSOURI TO OREGON CITY, OREGON IN 1847."
70  PRINT "YOUR FAMILY OF FIVE WILL COVER THE 2000 MILE OREGON TRAIL"
75  PRINT "IN 5 MONTHS --- IF YOU MAKE IT ALIVE."
```

YOU ARE IN A DEBRIS ROOM, FILLED WITH STUFF WASHED IN FROM THE SURFACE.

A NOTE ON THE WALL SAID, "MAGIC WORD XYZZY."

>XYZZY

ADVENTURE WAS A PUZZLE GAME WITH NO VISUAL INTERFACE AT ALL. *JUST TEXT.*

ADVENTURE BEGAN IN THE EARLY 1970s WITH *WILL CROWTHER:* PROGRAMMER, *D&D* PLAYER, ROCK CLIMBER, AND CAVER.

THIS WAS RELATED TO [MY] DIVORCE...

...AND I WAS FEELING KIND OF LONELY AND I WANTED TO WRITE A GAME FOR MY KIDS.

NATURAL ENTRANCE MAMMOTH CAVE

IT *PARSED* SIMPLE TWO-WORD COMMANDS (LIKE "GO NORTH") TYPED IN BY THE PLAYER.

THEN, USING JUST TYPE, *ADVENTURE* WOULD DESCRIBE THE OUTCOME OF THE PLAYER'S CHOSEN ACTIONS.

HMMM. WHY DO I THINK I'M IN THE WRONG PLACE AT THE WRONG TIME...?

>Go North

YOU ARE IN the hall of the Mountain king, with passages off in several directions. A fierce green snake bars your way.

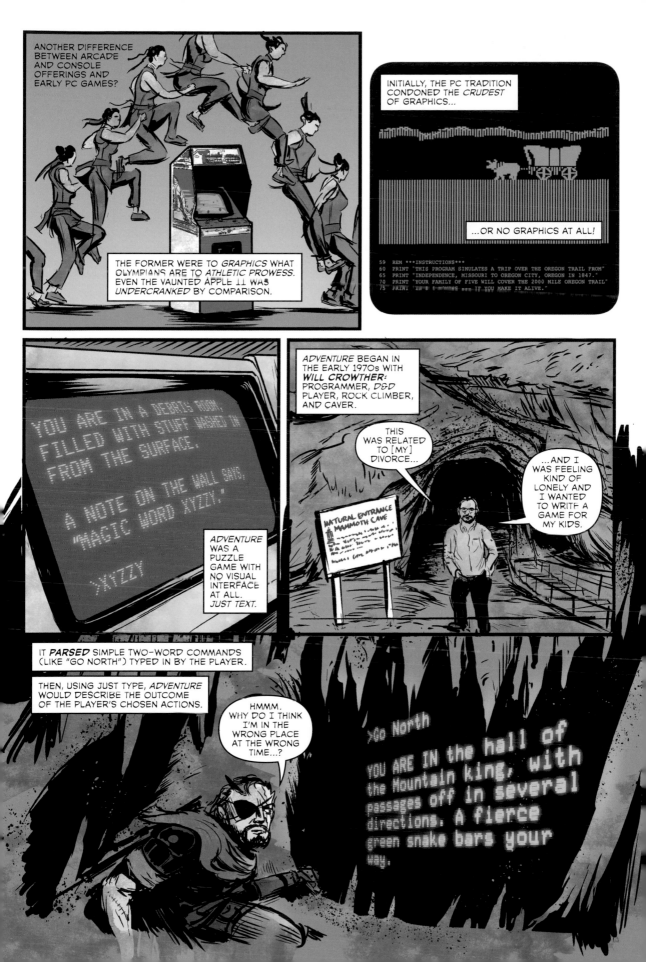

ADVENTURE WAS ONLY ON MAINFRAMES-- AND ALMOST EXCLUSIVELY ACCESSIBLE TO THOSE WITH UNIVERSITY COMPUTER LAB ACCESS...

...LIKE **DON WOODS** AT STANFORD'S S.A.I.L.

THE VERSION [OF ADVENTURE] I FOUND CONSISTED MOSTLY OF EXPLORATION, WITH ALMOST NO PUZZLES.

BUT I THOUGHT IT WAS AN INTERESTING IDEA FOR A GAME, AND WANTED TO TINKER WITH IT.

BEFORE MODERN DIGITAL COMMUNICATIONS, COMPUTERS HAD BEEN ABLE TO SLOWLY TRANSFER DATA OVER DEDICATED TELEPHONE CIRCUITS.

BUT ADVENTURE HAD REACHED PALO ALTO FROM BOSTON VIA FAR MORE RESILIENT **PACKET-SWITCHING** PROTOCOLS...

...THANKS IN PART TO CROWTHER'S WORK AT MIT-BASED TECH CONSULTANCY **BOLT BERANEK & NEWMAN**.

IN 1969, BBN HAD BEEN SELECTED TO ENGINEER THE ROUTERS ON WHICH A *NATIONWIDE COMPUTER NETWORK* WOULD BE CONSTRUCTED.

CROWTHER.

WM. CROWTHER.

THE ARPANET--THE MILITARY-INDUSTRIAL-ACADEMIC FORERUNNER OF THE *WORLD WIDE WEB*...

...PROGRESSIVELY SCALED UP AND EVOLVED TO (AMONG MANY OTHER THINGS) SUPPLY PC GAMES WITH ANOTHER INHERENT SUPERPOWER...

THE FIRST NODE OF THE ARPANET CAME ONLINE IN 1969 IN BOELTER HALL, ROOM 3420, UNIVERSITY OF CALIFORNIA, LOS ANGELES.

...THE ABILITY TO PLAY IN A *MULTIPLAYER ENVIRONMENT.*

NORTH AMERICA'S CONSOLES WOULD ONLY START TAKING *BABY STEPS* IN THE MID-1990s TO EMBRACE GAMING OVER A NETWORK.

OVER THE EXPANDING "INFORMATION SUPERHIGHWAY," DON WOODS'S MORE IMMERSIVE AND TOLKIEN-ESQUE *ADVENTURE* PINGED BACK TO MIT...

...WHERE AN UPDATED SLATE OF HACKERS LIKE *MARC BLANK, TIM ANDERSON,* AND *DAVE LEBLING* ENCOUNTERED IT.

ENGINEERS' INSTINCTS KICKED IN: SOON THEY WANTED TO IMPROVE ON THE TINY WORLD AND SIMPLISTIC LANGUAGE PARSING OF CROWTHER AND WOODS.

ZORK

GENRE: ADVENTURE

YEAR OF RELEASE: 1977

COUNTRY OF ORIGIN: U.S.

PLATFORMS: ORIGINALLY PDP-10; PORTED ACROSS PC LANDSCAPE

DEVELOPER(S): TIM ANDERSON, MARC BLANK, DAVE LEBLING, BRUCE DANIELS

PUBLISHER: PERSONAL SOFTWARE (INFOCOM & OTHERS FOLLOWED)

Your greatest challenge lies ahead–and downwards.

ZORK

ZORK, YET ANOTHER LANDMARK VIDEO GAME REPLETE WITH MIT DNA, WAS A *TEXT ADVENTURE* ORDERS OF MAGNITUDE RICHER THAN *ADVENTURE.*

ZORK PAVED THE WAY FOR ITS DEVELOPERS TO FOUND A COMPANY--*INFOCOM.* IT LIVED UP TO THEIR HIGH HOPES OF RUNNING A SOFTWARE POWERHOUSE... BUT ONLY BRIEFLY.

...CTIVE FICTION

FANTASY

STANDARD LEVEL

INFOCOM
SOFTWARE FOR YOUR
APPLE II
(48K 16-SECTOR DISK)
(Z1-AP1)

INFOCOM'S WRITERS ACHIEVED SUCH HEIGHTS OF LITERARY DESCRIPTION THAT THE COMPANY *TRUMPETED* ITS LACK OF GRAPHICS--BOASTING THAT THEIR INTERFACE WITH *HUMAN IMAGINATION* WAS SUPERIOR TO ANY GRAPHICS.

WE UNLEASH THE WORLD'S MOST POWERFUL GRAPHICS TECHNOLOGY

infocom

ZORK SEQUELS AND AMBITIOUS ORIGINAL RELEASES FOLLOWED. BUT WHEN INFOCOM TRIED TO PIVOT TO BUSINESS SOFTWARE, NO MAGIC OR ALIEN TECHNOLOGY COULD SAVE IT.

IF PC GAMES IN THEIR CHILDHOOD WEREN'T ALL ABOUT GRAPHICS...

MYSTERY HOUSE

YOU ARE IN THE FENCED BACK YARD. THE FENCE FOLLOWS THE SIDE OF THE HOUSE TO THE NORTH. THERE IS A DEAD BODY HERE
--------------- ENTER COMMAND?※

ROBERTA AND *KEN WILLIAMS*'S *MYSTERY HOUSE* (1980)

...THINGS WOULD MIGHTILY CHANGE BY THE TIME THEY HIT ADOLESCENCE.

GRAPHICS EVOLUTION ASIDE, THE DEMAND FOR VIDEO GAMES-- AND THE DRIVE TO MAKE THEM EVER MORE POTENT..

第3回ゲームホビー プログラムコンテスト

THIS 1984 CALL FOR ENTRIES BY JAPANESE COMPANY *ENIX* (LATER *SQUARE ENIX*) PROMISED BIG MONEY FOR GAME PROGRAMMERS AS TALENTED AS *KOICHI NAKAMURA,* CREATOR OF THE *DRAGON QUEST* RPG FRANCHISE.

...TRANSFORMED THE ENTIRE PERSONAL COMPUTER INDUSTRY.

FAST PROCESSORS?
VAST STORES OF MEMORY?
VIDEO RENDERING?
3-D GRAPHICS?
HIGH-FIDELITY SOUND?

THE FACT THAT THESE FEATURES HAVE BECOME *STANDARD* IN EVERYDAY COMPUTERS OWES MUCH TO VIDEO GAMES.

EVEN THE *UNIX OPERATING SYSTEM* (ON WHICH *LINUX* IS BASED) STEMS FROM PROGRAMMER KEN THOMPSON'S EFFORTS TO WRITE HIS GAME *SPACE TRAVEL* AT BELL LABS IN 1969.

Think different.

Honk, if you love digital.

CREDIT FOR A LOT OF THESE ADVANCES GOES TO THE AFOREMENTIONED, EVERGREEN PC GAME GENRE OF THE *FIRST-PERSON SHOOTER* (FPS).

The COLONY

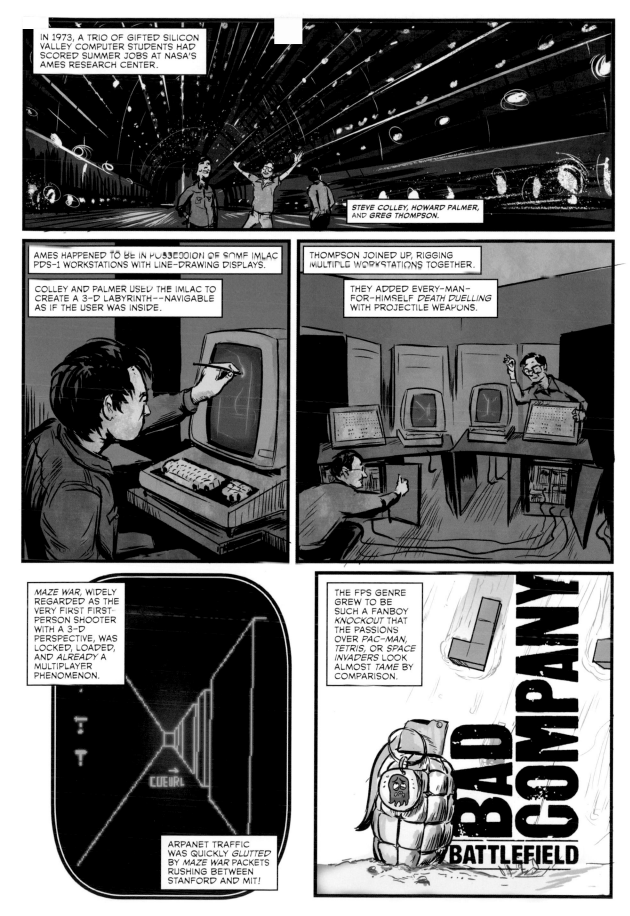

IN 1973, A TRIO OF GIFTED SILICON VALLEY COMPUTER STUDENTS HAD SCORED SUMMER JOBS AT NASA'S AMES RESEARCH CENTER.

STEVE COLLEY, HOWARD PALMER, AND GREG THOMPSON.

AMES HAPPENED TO BE IN POSSESSION OF SOME IMLAC PDS-1 WORKSTATIONS WITH LINE-DRAWING DISPLAYS.

COLLEY AND PALMER USED THE IMLAC TO CREATE A 3-D LABYRINTH--NAVIGABLE AS IF THE USER WAS INSIDE.

THOMPSON JOINED UP, RIGGING MULTIPLE WORKSTATIONS TOGETHER.

THEY ADDED EVERY-MAN-FOR-HIMSELF *DEATH DUELLING* WITH PROJECTILE WEAPONS.

MAZE WAR, WIDELY REGARDED AS THE VERY FIRST FIRST-PERSON SHOOTER WITH A 3-D PERSPECTIVE, WAS LOCKED, LOADED, AND *ALREADY* A MULTIPLAYER PHENOMENON.

ARPANET TRAFFIC WAS QUICKLY *GLUTTED* BY *MAZE WAR* PACKETS RUSHING BETWEEN STANFORD AND MIT!

THE FPS GENRE GREW TO BE SUCH A FANBOY *KNOCKOUT* THAT THE PASSIONS OVER *PAC-MAN, TETRIS,* OR *SPACE INVADERS* LOOK ALMOST *TAME* BY COMPARISON.

BAD COMPANY

BATTLEFIELD

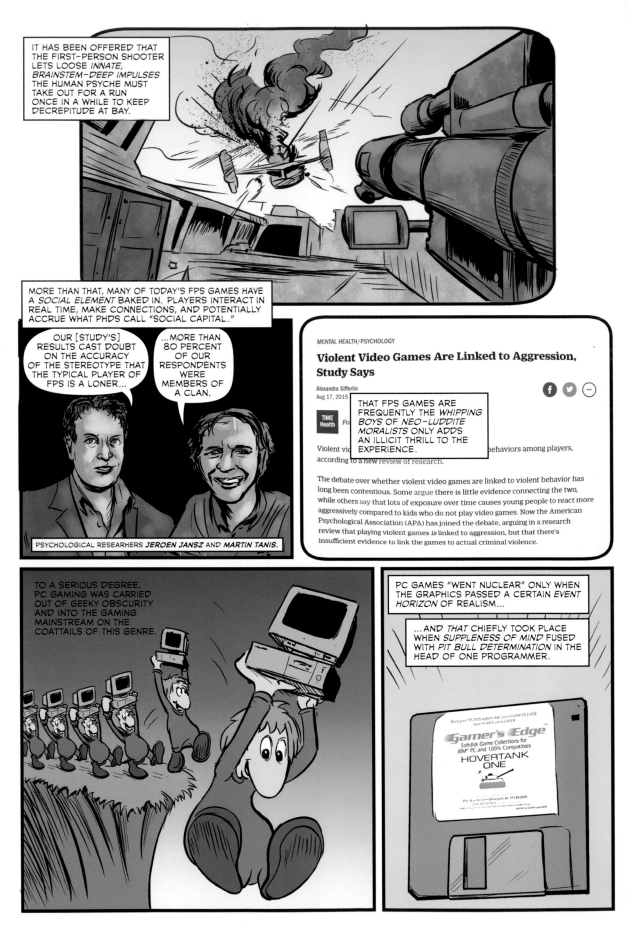

IT HAS BEEN OFFERED THAT THE FIRST-PERSON SHOOTER LETS LOOSE *INNATE, BRAINSTEM-DEEP IMPULSES* THE HUMAN PSYCHE MUST TAKE OUT FOR A RUN ONCE IN A WHILE TO KEEP DECREPITUDE AT BAY.

MORE THAN THAT, MANY OF TODAY'S FPS GAMES HAVE A *SOCIAL ELEMENT* BAKED IN. PLAYERS INTERACT IN REAL TIME, MAKE CONNECTIONS, AND POTENTIALLY ACCRUE WHAT PHDS CALL "SOCIAL CAPITAL."

OUR [STUDY'S] RESULTS CAST DOUBT ON THE ACCURACY OF THE STEREOTYPE THAT THE TYPICAL PLAYER OF FPS IS A LONER...

...MORE THAN 80 PERCENT OF OUR RESPONDENTS WERE MEMBERS OF A CLAN.

PSYCHOLOGICAL RESEARHERS *JEROEN JANSZ* AND *MARTIN TANIS*.

MENTAL HEALTH/PSYCHOLOGY

Violent Video Games Are Linked to Aggression, Study Says

Alexandra Sifferlin
Aug 17, 2015

TIME Health

THAT FPS GAMES ARE FREQUENTLY THE *WHIPPING BOYS* OF *NEO-LUDDITE MORALISTS* ONLY ADDS AN ILLICIT THRILL TO THE EXPERIENCE.

Violent vi... ...behaviors among players, according to a new review of research.

The debate over whether violent video games are linked to violent behavior has long been contentious. Some argue there is little evidence connecting the two, while others say that lots of exposure over time causes young people to react more aggressively compared to kids who do not play video games. Now the American Psychological Association (APA) has joined the debate, arguing in a research review that playing violent games *is* linked to aggression, but that there's insufficient evidence to link the games to actual criminal violence.

TO A SERIOUS DEGREE, PC GAMING WAS CARRIED OUT OF GEEKY OBSCURITY AND INTO THE GAMING MAINSTREAM ON THE COATTAILS OF THIS GENRE.

PC GAMES "WENT NUCLEAR" ONLY WHEN THE GRAPHICS PASSED A CERTAIN *EVENT HORIZON* OF REALISM...

...AND *THAT* CHIEFLY TOOK PLACE WHEN *SUPPLENESS OF MIND* FUSED WITH *PIT BULL DETERMINATION* IN THE HEAD OF ONE PROGRAMMER.

Gamer's Edge
Softdisk Game Collections for IBM® PC and 100% Compatibles
HOVERTANK ONE

SPOTLIGHT:
JOHN CARMACK

AS A YOUTH IN KANSAS CITY, GRAPHICS MASTER "CARMACK THE MAGNIFICENT" SO DESIRED AN APPLE II THAT HE TRIED TO LIBERATE ONE FROM A SCHOOL USING A HOMEBREW CHEMICAL GEL TO MELT THE WINDOW GLASS.

K-SCHWOOF!!!

HIGH SCHOOL

A SPAN IN JUVY HALL FOLLOWED, COURTESY OF A FELLOW HEISTER WHO CARELESSLY TRIGGERED THE ALARM.

DRIVEN, INTELLIGENT, DERISIVE OF AUTHORITY, *JOHN CARMACK* SEEMED MOST LIKELY TO BECOME A SUPERVILLAIN. OR A TECH MULTIMILLIONAIRE.

"BUCKLE OF THE BIBLE BELT" SHREVEPORT, LOUISIANA, ISN'T THE SORT OF TOWN KNOWN FOR ENGENDERING EITHER.

606 COMMON

BUT IT IS WHERE CARMACK--BY THEN A BEDROOM PROGRAMMER CHURNING OUT GAMES FOR SMALL TIME PUBLISHERS--MET *JOHN ROMERO.*

WITH TWO OTHER COHORTS, THEY COFOUNDED *ID SOFTWARE* IN 1991.

HARD KNOCKS AND HEAVY METAL HAD GIVEN ROMERO A TASTE FOR MAYHEM AND MORBIDITY.

DEATH METAL AND HEAD-BANGS

CARMACK WAS A SAVANT WITH CREATING *VIDEO GAME ENGINES:* CUSTOM SOFTWARE USED TO GENERATE A GAME'S VISUAL ENVIRONMENT.

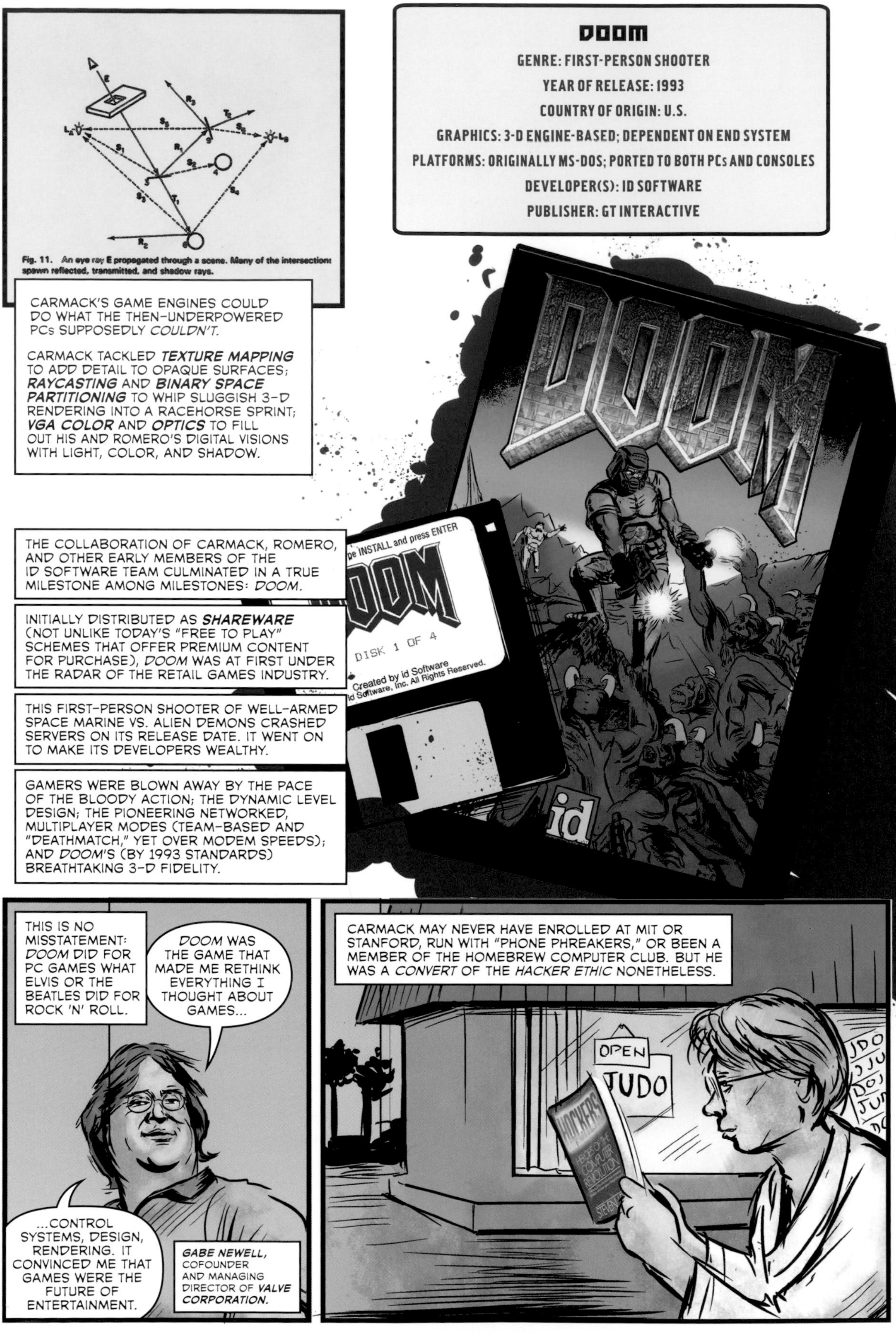
Fig. 11. An eye ray E propagated through a scene. Many of the intersections spawn reflected, transmitted, and shadow rays.
DOOM
GENRE: FIRST-PERSON SHOOTER
YEAR OF RELEASE: 1993
COUNTRY OF ORIGIN: U.S.
GRAPHICS: 3-D ENGINE-BASED; DEPENDENT ON END SYSTEM
PLATFORMS: ORIGINALLY MS-DOS; PORTED TO BOTH PCs AND CONSOLES
DEVELOPER(S): ID SOFTWARE
PUBLISHER: GT INTERACTIVE
CARMACK'S GAME ENGINES COULD DO WHAT THE THEN-UNDERPOWERED PCs SUPPOSEDLY *COULDN'T.*
CARMACK TACKLED ***TEXTURE MAPPING*** TO ADD DETAIL TO OPAQUE SURFACES; ***RAYCASTING*** AND ***BINARY SPACE PARTITIONING*** TO WHIP SLUGGISH 3-D RENDERING INTO A RACEHORSE SPRINT; ***VGA COLOR*** AND ***OPTICS*** TO FILL OUT HIS AND ROMERO'S DIGITAL VISIONS WITH LIGHT, COLOR, AND SHADOW.
DOOM
THE COLLABORATION OF CARMACK, ROMERO, AND OTHER EARLY MEMBERS OF THE ID SOFTWARE TEAM CULMINATED IN A TRUE MILESTONE AMONG MILESTONES: *DOOM.*
INITIALLY DISTRIBUTED AS ***SHAREWARE*** (NOT UNLIKE TODAY'S "FREE TO PLAY" SCHEMES THAT OFFER PREMIUM CONTENT FOR PURCHASE), *DOOM* WAS AT FIRST UNDER THE RADAR OF THE RETAIL GAMES INDUSTRY.
THIS FIRST-PERSON SHOOTER OF WELL-ARMED SPACE MARINE VS. ALIEN DEMONS CRASHED SERVERS ON ITS RELEASE DATE. IT WENT ON TO MAKE ITS DEVELOPERS WEALTHY.
GAMERS WERE BLOWN AWAY BY THE PACE OF THE BLOODY ACTION; THE DYNAMIC LEVEL DESIGN; THE PIONEERING NETWORKED, MULTIPLAYER MODES (TEAM-BASED AND "DEATHMATCH," YET OVER MODEM SPEEDS); AND *DOOM*'S (BY 1993 STANDARDS) BREATHTAKING 3-D FIDELITY.
pe INSTALL and press ENTER
DOOM
DISK 1 OF 4
Created by id Software
id Software, Inc. All Rights Reserved.
id
THIS IS NO MISSTATEMENT: *DOOM* DID FOR PC GAMES WHAT ELVIS OR THE BEATLES DID FOR ROCK 'N' ROLL.
DOOM WAS THE GAME THAT MADE ME RETHINK EVERYTHING I THOUGHT ABOUT GAMES...
...CONTROL SYSTEMS, DESIGN, RENDERING. IT CONVINCED ME THAT GAMES WERE THE FUTURE OF ENTERTAINMENT.
GABE NEWELL, COFOUNDER AND MANAGING DIRECTOR OF ***VALVE CORPORATION.***
CARMACK MAY NEVER HAVE ENROLLED AT MIT OR STANFORD, RUN WITH "PHONE PHREAKERS," OR BEEN A MEMBER OF THE HOMEBREW COMPUTER CLUB. BUT HE WAS A *CONVERT* OF THE *HACKER ETHIC* NONETHELESS.
OPEN
JUDO
HACKERS
HEROES OF THE COMPUTER REVOLUTION

SO ID SOFTWARE ACTIVELY WELCOMED THE MODDING OF *DOOM* AS PLAYERS SAW FIT. THIS AMOUNTED TO A *JARRING U-TURN* FROM MOST OTHER COMPANIES TRYING TO LOCK DOWN THEIR *INTELLECTUAL PROPERTY* BY ANY MEANS NECESSARY.

DOOM MODDERS THOMAS AND DENIS MÖLLER, HAMBURG, GERMANY, 1994.

SOFTWARE HACKING WAS RIGHT IN LINE WITH THE *MODULAR NATURE* OF PC HARDWARE.

UNLIKE CONSOLES, PCS CAN BE BUILT AND REBUILT AS FAST AS SKILLED USERS CAN GET THEIR HANDS ON NEW COMPONENTS.

THE RUNAWAY SUCCESS OF *DOOM* AMPLIFIED WHAT *WILLIAM M. "TRIP" HAWKINS,* FOUNDER OF *ELECTRONIC ARTS,* SAID HE HAD SEEN COMING (AND BEEN PREPARING FOR) SINCE THE EARLY 1970S...

...THAT THERE WAS A BIG AUDIENCE FOR VIDEO GAMES AND TALENTED AUTEURS WAITING TO SERVE THEM...

WE SEE FARTHER

...AND THAT *COMPUTERS* WOULD BE THE ULTIMATE PLATFORM TO PLAY THOSE GAMES ON.

BUT EVEN HAWKINS WOULD COME TO EAT HIS WORDS.

BACK IN THE LAND OF THE RISING SUN, THERE WERE *POWERFUL* AND *INFLUENTIAL FIGURES* PLANNING TO BRING CONSOLES BACK.

CHAPTER NINE NINTENDO
"The Name of the Game is the Games"

AFTER THE 1983 CRASH, THE NORTH AMERICAN RETAIL ESTABLISHMENT HAD WRITTEN OFF VIDEO GAMES.

BUT THERE WAS SOMETHING NINTENDO OF AMERICA'S MINORU ARAKAWA COULDN'T HELP BUT NOTICE...

WHOA! OIL SLICK!

GET BACK ON! GET BACK ON!

I'M TRYIN'!

...AMERICAN KIDS WERE STILL PLAYING VIDEO GAMES.

GOT 'IM!

COULD IT BE THAT *SHODDY BUSINESS PRACTICES* WERE TO BLAME FOR THE CRASH...

...NOT LACK OF INTEREST IN GAMES?

IF SO, WERE THE RIGHT CORPORATE PLAYER TO REINTRODUCE CONSOLES TO THE VAST U.S. MARKET, AND THIS TIME, DO IT *RIGHT*...

...THE SKY WOULD BE THE LIMIT.

THANKS TO HIS FATHER-IN-LAW BACK IN KYOTO, ARAKAWA COULD TAKE A SHOT WITHOUT EVEN HAVING TO START AT THE FIRST LEVEL.

THE COLOR TV GAME LINE HAD DONE *WELL ENOUGH* FOR NINTENDO. BUT THE ADVANTAGES OF A PROGRAMMABLE SYSTEM WERE CLEAR...

...ESPECIALLY IF THE COMPANY FOLLOWED ITS SUCCESS FORMULA: COMBINING LOW-COST TECHNOLOGY FROM OTHER INDUSTRIES WITH PLAYFUL IDEAS FOR TOYS.

NINTENDO'S POPULAR GAME & WATCH SERIES WAS BUILT ON DIGITAL CALCULATOR CHIPS FROM *SHARP.*

NINTENDO'S YAMAUCHI REALIZED THAT KEEPING COSTS LOW WOULDN'T BE ENOUGH. QUALITY GAMES WERE PARAMOUNT.

SO HIS MOST TRUSTED CREATIVES, HE DECIDED, MUST HAVE TOP PRIORITY--AND NOT BE BEHOLDEN TO THE MARKETING DEPARTMENT.

YAMAUCHI ORGANIZED NINTENDO'S ENGINEER-ARTISTS INTO FOUR SEPARATE DIVISIONS.

AN ORDINARY MAN CANNOT DEVELOP GOOD GAMES NO MATTER HOW HARD HE TRIES. [ONLY] A HANDFUL OF PEOPLE IN THIS WORLD CAN DEVELOP GAMES THAT EVERYBODY WANTS.

THOSE ARE THE PEOPLE WE WANT AT NINTENDO.

R&D 1

LED BY:
GUNPEI YOKOI

PREVIOUS CREDENTIALS: PRE-VIDEO GAME TOYS LIKE ULTRA HAND; GAME & WATCH; SUPERVISED MIYAMOTO ON *DONKEY KONG* ARCADE GAME

WOULD BE RESPONSIBLE FOR: SOFTWARE FOR HOME GAMES; ARCADE GAMES; GAME & WATCH SERIES; *GAME BOY* HANDHELD PROJECT

R&D 2

LED BY:
MASAYUKI UEMURA

PREVIOUS CREDENTIALS: OPTICAL LIGHT GUN ARCADE ATTRACTIONS, "BEAM GUN"

WOULD BE RESPONSIBLE FOR: GAME SOFTWARE AND SYSTEM PERIPHERALS

R&D 3

LED BY:
GENYO TAKEDA

PREVIOUS CREDENTIALS: ALSO WORKED ON OPTICAL LIGHT GUN ATTRACTIONS

WOULD BE RESPONSIBLE FOR: GAME SOFTWARE AND HARDWARE-PUSHING TECHNICAL INNOVATIONS LIKE ROM CHIPS INSIDE CARTRIDGES

R&D 4

LED BY:
SHIGERU MIYAMOTO

PREVIOUS CREDENTIALS: *DONKEY KONG, POPEYE*

WOULD BE RESPONSIBLE FOR: GAME SOFTWARE; OVERSIGHT OF COMPANY'S EVENTUAL FRANCHISES

IN 1983, THE COMPANY RELEASED ITS HIT 8-BIT, CARTRIDGE-BASED SYSTEM IN JAPAN: THE "FAMILY COMPUTER" OR FAMICOM.

NINTENDO NEGOTIATED WITH ATARI TO MAKE AN AMERICAN VERSION OF THE FAMICOM THE SUCCESSOR TO THE VCS.

BUT ATARI FLOUNDERED. AND THE DEAL FIZZLED.

ADVENTURE™

WITH TREPIDATION, ARAKAWA UNDERTOOK LAUNCHING THE FAMICOM IN THE WEST.

BUT HE NEEDED TO MAKE CHANGES. STARTING WITH THAT NAME...

FAO Schwarz

LOOK! NO MORE STICK FIGURE GRAPHICS AND UNCHALLENGING PLAY!

NINTENDO ENTERTAINMENT SYSTEM

YEAR OF RELEASE (U.S.): 1985

COUNTRY OF ORIGIN: JAPAN

CPU BITS: 8

RAM: 2 KB

CPU SPEED: 1.79 MHZ

MAX. DISPLAY RESOLUTION: 256X240 PIXELS (NTSC)

COLORS: 48

AUDIO: 5 CHANNELS/1 BIT MONO

MEDIA: ROM CARTRIDGES (4 MB STANDARD CAPACITY; EXPANDABLE)

THE *NES* (A SECOND GENERATION CONSOLE WITH A MUCH HIGHER PERFORMING *CHIPSET* THAN THE ATARI VCS) WAS STYLED TO LOOK LIKE A VCR OR COMPUTER--*NOT* A TOY!

MEDIA WERE TERMED "GAME PAKS" INSTEAD OF "CARTRIDGES." UNLIKE THE TOP-LOADING FAMICOM DESIGN, THEY WERE HIDDEN AWAY UNDER A FLAP.

WITH THE NES, NINTENDO *FIXATED* ON PREVENTING A REPEAT OF THE TOO-MANY-GAMES-ON-THE-MARKET DYNAMIC THAT HAD BROUGHT OTHERS TO RUIN.

EVEN ESTABLISHED THIRD-PARTY PUBLISHERS LIKE CAPCOM, BANDAI, TAITO, AND KONAMI COULD PUBLISH NO MORE THAN FIVE NES GAMES A YEAR. AND THEY HAD TO BUY CARTRIDGES FROM NINTENDO, CASH UP FRONT!

Nintendo ENTERTAINMENT SYSTEM

A "LOCKOUT" CHIP INSURED THAT *ONLY* TITLES SANCTIONED BY NINTENDO WOULD PLAY ON THE NES.

THE SUCCESS OF THESE SEMIMONOPOLISTIC PRACTICES *ELEVATED* JAPAN TO TOTAL CONTROL OF CONSOLES FOR THE NEXT TWENTY YEARS.

THE ALLURE OF UNIQUE, BEWITCHING GAMES DIDN'T HURT EITHER.

THE EVOLUTION OF VIDEO GAMES IN THE U.S. CANNOT BE EXTRICATED FROM WARFARE. THAT WAS *NOT* THE CASE, HOWEVER, IN JAPAN--WHERE THEY WENT HAND-IN-HAND WITH TOYS AND ENTERTAINMENT.

PERHAPS THE WHIMSICAL, PSYCHEDELIC SETTING AND PLAY OF *SUPER MARIO BROTHERS* ARISES NOT JUST FROM SHIGERU MIYAMOTO'S ACCLAIMED IMAGINATION BUT ALSO THE LESS BELLICOSE NATURE OF POSTWAR JAPAN.

SUPER MARIO BROTHERS SOLD A TOWERING 6.8 MILLION UNITS IN JAPAN. IN THE U.S., IT OFTEN SHIPPED IN-BOX WITH THE CONSOLE ITSELF.

DISTINCT FROM THE OTHER NES LAUNCH TITLES, *SUPER MARIO BROTHERS* ENDOWED NINTENDO WITH AN ENDURING, ENDEARING BRAND.

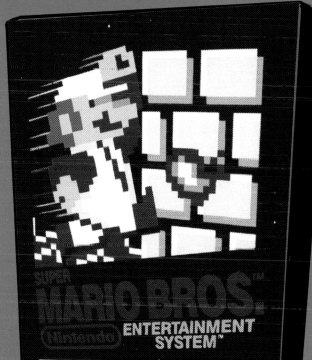

SUPER MARIO BROTHERS

GENRE: PLATFORMER

YEAR OF RELEASE (U.S.): 1985

COUNTRY OF ORIGIN: JAPAN

PLATFORMS: ORIGINALLY NES; PORTED TO ARCADE, GAME BOY SYSTEMS, AND MORE

DEVELOPER(S): SHIGERU MIYAMOTO, ET AL.

PUBLISHER: NINTENDO

BY 1990, A JAW-DROPPING ONE IN THREE AMERICAN HOMES SPORTED AN NES.

A STRING OF *MULTIPLATINUM HITS* CONTINUED NINTENDO'S SHEER MARKET DOMINANCE.

THE LEGEND OF ZELDA

GENRE: ADVENTURE

YEAR OF RELEASE (U.S.): 1987

COUNTRY OF ORIGIN: JAPAN

PLATFORMS: ORIGINALLY FAMICOM DISK SYSTEM; PORTED TO NES, GAME BOY SYSTEMS, AND MORE

DEVELOPER(S): NINTENDO R&D 4

PUBLISHER: NINTENDO

EVEN MORE VISCERALLY INSPIRED BY MIYAMOTO'S CHILDHOOD EXPLORATIONS, *THE LEGEND OF ZELDA* (DISTRIBUTED IN A GOLD CARTRIDGE THAT FANS WENT NUTS FOR) WAS ONLY THE BEGINNING OF A STORIED LINE OF TITLES SET IN THE KINGDOM OF HYRULE AND ITS MULTIVERSE.

METROID

GENRE: ACTION-ADVENTURE

YEAR OF RELEASE (U.S.): 1987

COUNTRY OF ORIGIN: JAPAN

PLATFORMS: ORIGINALLY FAMICOM DISK SYSTEM; PORTED TO NES, GAME BOY SYSTEMS, AND MORE

DEVELOPER(S): NINTENDO R&D 1

PUBLISHER: NINTENDO

DARK, EDGY, ATMOSPHERIC, SOMETIMES *REPULSIVE,* THIS RELEASE FROM GUNPEI YOKOI'S R&D 1 DEMONSTRATED NINTENDO HAD MORE THAN JUVENILIA AND WHIMSY ON TAP. *METROID* ALSO MARKED A NEW LEVEL OF SOPHISTICATION WITH DEEP MYTHOLOGY AND NONLINEAR EXPLORATION.

"NINTENDO'S COMPETITORS ARE FURIOUS," ASSERTED A 1990 ARTICLE IN BUSINESS JOURNAL *FORBES.*

AND THOSE RIVALS WERE GEARING UP TO TRY TO PROVE THE OLD MAXIM...

..."THE BIGGER THEY COME, THE HARDER THEY FALL."

CHAPTER TEN
TIMES THAT TRY CONSOLES
From Genesis to "Revelations"

JAPAN HAS ALMOST NO FOREIGN-BORN PEOPLE NOR MINORITY ETHNIC GROUPS OF ANY REAL SIZE.

A SINGLE SCHOOL CURRICULUM IS TAUGHT NATIONWIDE.

WHEN A PRODUCT BECOMES A HIT THERE, IT IS ADOPTED QUICKLY AND WIDELY-- WITHOUT GIVING RIVALS MUCH ROOM FOR PROFIT.

SO, ALTHOUGH JAPANESE CULTURE IS FAMOUS FOR EVERYONE ACTING LIKE THEY'RE *ALL IN IT TOGETHER*...

...COMPETITION CAN BE FIERCE.

I DON'T LIKE THE IDEA OF ONE COMPANY MONOPOLIZING AN INDUSTRY.

SEGA IS NOTHING.

IN JAPAN IN 1988, SEGA HAD OUTPLAYED NINTENDO BY RELEASING ITS "MEGA DRIVE." THIS NEXT-GENERATION CONSOLE WITH A *16-BIT PROCESSOR* PREEMPTED THE 16-BIT "SUPER NES" BY TWO YEARS.

HAYAO NAKAYAMA, PRESIDENT OF *SEGA OF JAPAN,* IN 1991.

HIROSHI YAMAUCHI, PRESIDENT OF *NINTENDO,* IN 1991.

SEGA

時代か求めた16ヒット
MEGA DRIVE

時代は・
すでに16ヒット

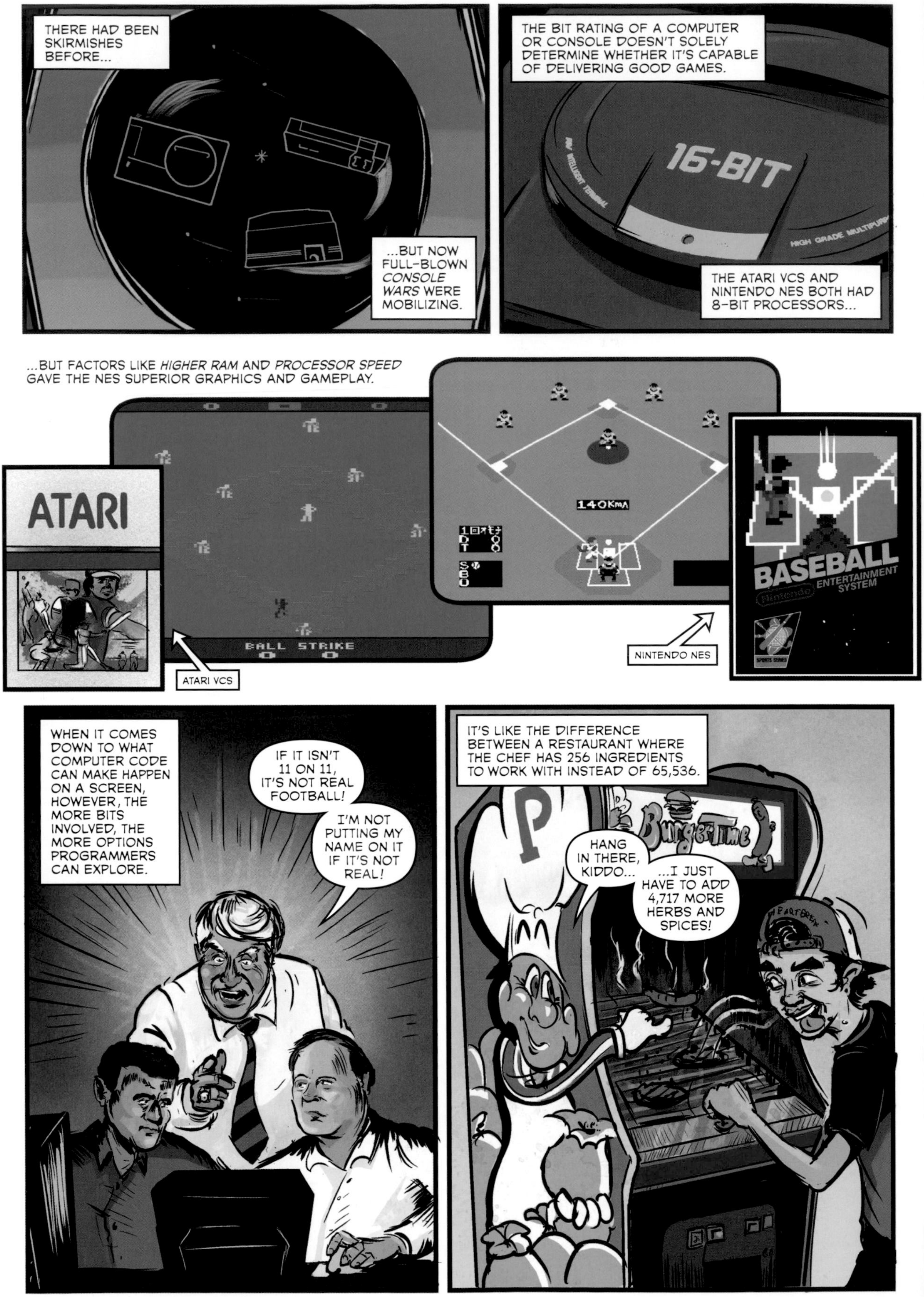
THERE HAD BEEN SKIRMISHES BEFORE...
...BUT NOW FULL-BLOWN *CONSOLE WARS* WERE MOBILIZING.
THE BIT RATING OF A COMPUTER OR CONSOLE DOESN'T SOLELY DETERMINE WHETHER IT'S CAPABLE OF DELIVERING GOOD GAMES.
16-BIT
INTELLIGENT TERMINAL
HIGH GRADE MULTIPURPOSE
THE ATARI VCS AND NINTENDO NES BOTH HAD 8-BIT PROCESSORS...
...BUT FACTORS LIKE *HIGHER RAM* AND *PROCESSOR SPEED* GAVE THE NES SUPERIOR GRAPHICS AND GAMEPLAY.
ATARI
BALL STRIKE
0 0
140Kmh
BASEBALL
ENTERTAINMENT SYSTEM
Nintendo
SPORTS SERIES
ATARI VCS
NINTENDO NES
WHEN IT COMES DOWN TO WHAT COMPUTER CODE CAN MAKE HAPPEN ON A SCREEN, HOWEVER, THE MORE BITS INVOLVED, THE MORE OPTIONS PROGRAMMERS CAN EXPLORE.
IF IT ISN'T 11 ON 11, IT'S NOT REAL FOOTBALL!
I'M NOT PUTTING MY NAME ON IT IF IT'S NOT REAL!
IT'S LIKE THE DIFFERENCE BETWEEN A RESTAURANT WHERE THE CHEF HAS 256 INGREDIENTS TO WORK WITH INSTEAD OF 65,536.
BurgerTime
HANG IN THERE, KIDDO...
...I JUST HAVE TO ADD 4,717 MORE HERBS AND SPICES!

BUT THE LIKES OF *QUAKE* OR *GOD OF WAR* JUST *WOULDN'T* BE POSSIBLE WITHIN 8-BIT ARCHITECTURE.

THE NEWLY RECRUITED *SEGA OF AMERICA* PRESIDENT BELIEVED CONSOLE GAMERS WOULD GO *ALL-IN* FOR A 16-BIT SYSTEM...

...IF HE COULD BREW UP A PERFECT STORM OF GAMES AND PR BUZZ.

TOM KALINSKE.

IT WASN'T EASY GETTING PERMISSION FROM THE JAPANESE HOME OFFICE FOR THESE PLANS. BUT HE DID.

...EVEN THOUGH WE THINK YOU'RE CRAZY AND DON'T AGREE WITH IT, GO AHEAD AND DO IT.

SEGA GENESIS

YEAR OF RELEASE (U.S.): 1989

COUNTRY OF ORIGIN: JAPAN

CPU BITS: 16/32

RAM: 72 KB, 64 KB VIDEO RAM

CPU SPEED: 7.6 MHZ

MAX. DISPLAY RESOLUTION: 320 X 224 PIXELS (NTSC)

COLORS: 512

MEDIA: ROM CARTRIDGES

(16 MB STANDARD CAPACITY; EXPANDABLE)

SEGA OF AMERICA FACED A STEEP UPHILL BATTLE JUST GETTING THE GENESIS STOCKED IN ENOUGH STORES TO GIVE THE NES A RUN FOR ITS MONEY. TOYS'R'US, WAL-MART...FEW WERE EAGER TO MAKE ANY MOVES THAT MIGHT BE PERCEIVED AS DISLOYALTY TO NINTENDO.

YET SEGA WROTE ITS OWN ROLE AS THE BRASH, TEEN-FRIENDLY ALTERNATIVE TO NINTENDO'S "KID STUFF"--THE CHEMICAL-SPIKED BUZZ OF AN ENERGY DRINK INSTEAD OF APPLE JUICE.

GENESIS DOES WHAT NINTENDON'T.

THE UPSTART PROBABLY WOULD NEVER HAVE HAD A SHOT WITHOUT SEVERAL GAMES THAT WOULD BECOME ALL BUT *SYNONYMOUS* WITH "SEGA GENESIS"...

SONIC THE HEDGEHOG

GENRE: PLATFORMER

YEAR OF RELEASE: 1991

COUNTRY OF ORIGIN: JAPAN

PLATFORMS: ORIGINALLY SEGA GENESIS; PORTED TO GAME BOY ADVANCE, IOS, ADROID, MORE

DEVELOPER(S): SONIC TEAM

PUBLISHER: SEGA

A "MASCOT WITH ATTITUDE," *SONIC THE HEDGEHOG* WAS MORE THAN JUST AN ANTIDOTE TO THE WHOLE-SOMENESS OF MARIO AND LINK.

THE GAME WAS *EXHILARATINGLY FAST* FOR ITS DAY--LIKE QUICKSILVER COMPARED TO THE MORE AMBLING NES.

SONIC HIMSELF, WHO WAS COOKED UP BY AN IN-HOUSE DESIGN CONTEST OF SEGA EMPLOYEES, BECAME AN ICON.

IN THE 1990s, A STRING OF HOT FIGHTING GAMES BRIEFLY RETURNED ARCADES TO RELEVANCY.

ONLY ONE COMPANY WAS AUDACIOUS ENOUGH TO FAITHFULLY PORT THE MOST CONTROVERSIAL ONE OF THESE.

MOOOR-TAL KOMMM-BAT!!

MORTAL KOMBAT

YEAR OF RELEASE (U.S.): 1992

COUNTRY OF ORIGIN: U.S.

GRAPHICS: COLOR CRT RASTER TELEVISION

PLATFORMS: ARCADE

DEVELOPER(S): ED BOON, JOHN TOBIAS

PUBLISHER: MIDWAY (NORTH AMERICA AND EUROPE)

MORTAL KOMBAT WAS A CABINET OF SECRETS. EACH OF ITS SURPRISINGLY EFFECTIVE PLAYABLE CHARACTERS WERE CAPABLE OF ATTACKS THAT ONLY TIME AND EXPERTISE WITH THE MACHINE WOULD YIELD.

IT WAS AND REMAINS NOTORIOUS FOR ITS BLOODY, ORGAN- AND VISCERA-SHREDDING EXECUTION SCENES.

THE SEGA GENESIS PORT PRESERVED THE ARCADE GAME'S GORE. NINTENDO HAS SIGNIFICANTLY TONED IT DOWN--FROM SPRAYING RED BLOOD TO FLYING GRAY "SWEAT."

MORTAL KOMBAT, LETHAL ENFORCERS, AND "B" HORROR-MOVIE-STYLE NIGHT TRAP SENT THE U.S. GOVERNMENT INTO SPASMS OF APPREHENSION.

INSTEAD OF ENRICHING A CHILD'S MIND, THESE GAMES TEACH A CHILD TO ENJOY INFLICTING TORTURE.

SENATOR "JOE" LIEBERMAN (D-CT), 1993.

SEN. JOSEPH LIEBERMAN (D)

C-SPAN TODAY

IN RESPONSE, THE VIDEO GAMES INDUSTRY CONSTITUTED THE ENTERTAINMENT SOFTWARE RATING BOARD (ESRB) TO KEEP EXPLICIT MATERIAL FROM YOUNG CHILDREN.

EVERYONE
TM
E
CONTENT RATED BY
ESRB

SEGA IN 1994 BROKE NINTENDO'S NORTH AMERICAN DOMINANCE-- EVEN CRIMPING THE ROLLOUT OF ITS NEXT-GEN SYSTEM.

Babbage's

NINTENDO JUST ISN'T COOL ANYMORE. THIS ONE IS 16 BITS, SO IT'S BETTER THAN THE ORIGINAL NINTENDO.

SNES

BUT THE COMPANY ONLY MADE IT TO COMPETE WITH SEGA. THAT'S JUST IDIOTIC.

SUPER NINTENDO

GAMER JACOB HAJDU, AGE TEN, 1993.

SUPER NES.

GAMERS WHO HAD TEST-DRIVEN SUPER MARIO KART (1992) WOULD HAVE PUT ON THE BRAKES BEFORE DISMISSING NINTENDO.

1 00' 06"49

THE GAME RAN IN THE SUPER NES'S "MODE 7": A SNAPPY 3-D EFFECT ACHIEVED THROUGH SCALING AND ROTATING BACKGROUND LAYERS.

1

2 00' 06"47

2

AND NINTENDO HAD EVEN MORE WONDERS TO REVEAL IN THE 1990s...

GASP!

⟨I FOUND ONE!⟩

GROWING UP ON THE STILL-RUSTIC OUTSKIRTS OF TOKYO, *SATOSHI TAJIRI* WAS AN AVID COLLECTOR OF *INSECTS*.

NEIGHBORHOOD KIDS CALLED HIM "DR. BUG."

LARVAL STAGE OF MONEMA FLARESCENS MOTH, KNOWN IN JAPAN AS THE *DENKIMUSHI* OR "ELECTRIC BUG."

AS IF THIS ALONE WASN'T ENOUGH TO ESTABLISH SOME SERIOUS *NERD CREDIBILITY,* TAJIRI STARTED A VIDEO GAME FANZINE ENTITLED *GAME FREAK.*

HE AND HIS CREATIONS WOULD NOT BE ON THE FRINGE FOR VERY LONG...

GAME FREAK

SPECIAL MAGAZINE OF VIDEO GAMES

17

THOUSANDS OF MILES AWAY, IN 1984, A PUZZLE-LOVING MOSCOW COMPUTER SCIENTIST-- *ALEXEY PAJITNOV*--CREATED A SIMPLE VIDEO GAME ON A SOVIET CLONE OF THE PDP-11.

PAJITNOV'S *TETRIS* EVENTUALLY SNUCK OUT OF *COMMUNIST LOCKDOWN*...

...AND BEGAN *MESMERIZING* SMALL POCKETS OF GAMERS AROUND THE WORLD.

Next:

Play TETRIS ?

ONE WAS *HENK ROGERS,* AN EXPATRIATE DUTCH GAMER WHO HAD BONDED WITH NINTENDO'S HIROSHI YAMAUCHI OVER THE GAME *GO.*

...I FINALLY FELL IN LOVE WITH A JAPANESE GIRL. I CHASED HER TO JAPAN.

ROGERS PERSUADED YAMAUCHI TO INCLUDE *TETRIS* ON THE GAME BOY HANDHELD SYSTEM, RELEASED IN 1989.

TETRIS AND GAME BOY WERE BOTH UNQUALIFIED SUCCESSES.

GAME BOY

TETRIS

Nintendo GAME BOY™

B A

SELECT START

AND PAJITNOV'S GAME HELPED COMPLETE THE PICTURE FOR ANOTHER IMMENSE VIDEO GAME HIT.

ONE DAY SATOSHI TAJIRI SAW SOME BOYS COMPETING AT *TETRIS.* THEY WERE PLAYING ON GAME BOYS CONNECTED VIA LINK CABLE.

Nintendo GAME BOY™

...do GAME BOY

FOR TAJIRI, SOMETHING JUST WENT *"CLICK."*

SELECT START

SELECT START

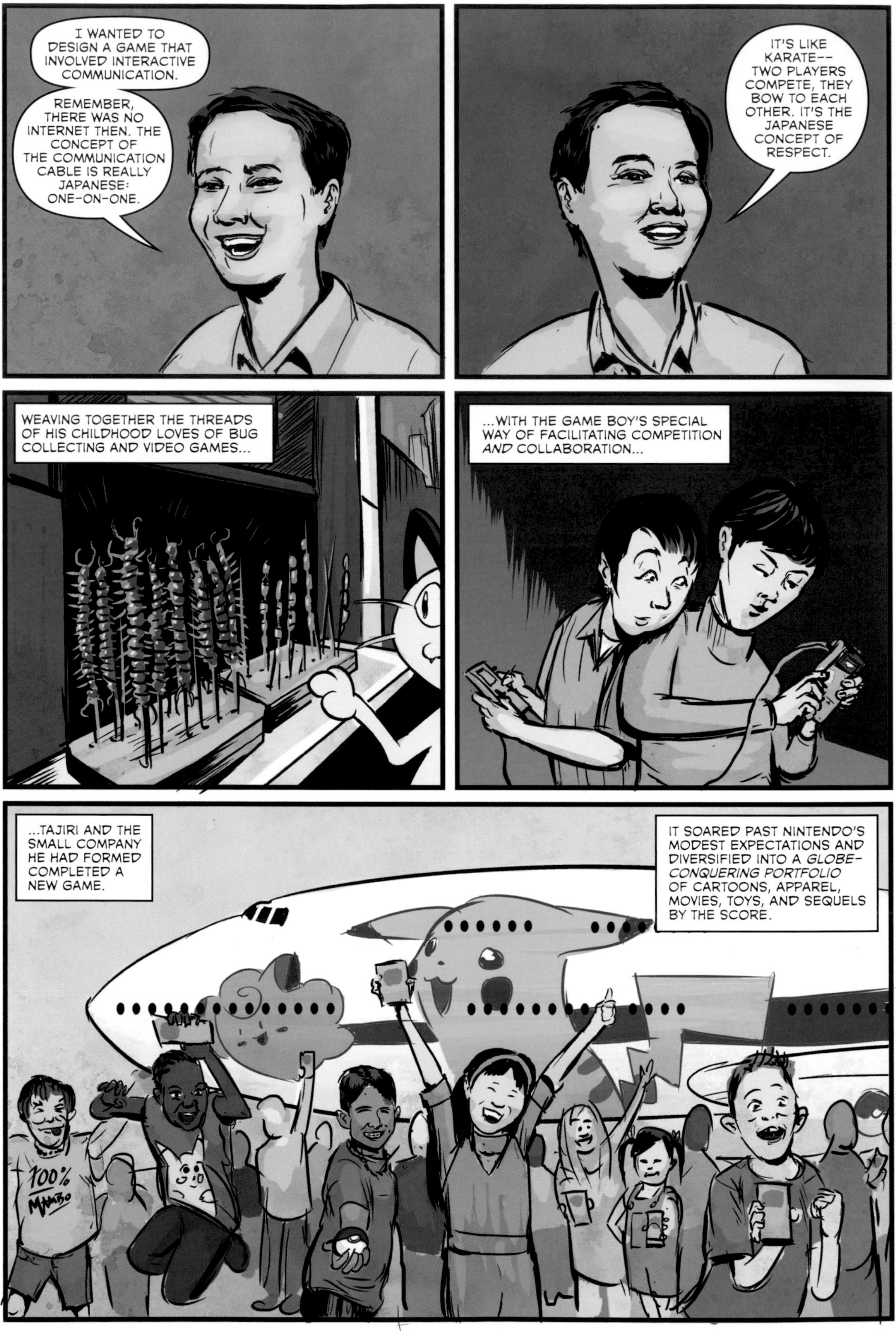
I WANTED TO DESIGN A GAME THAT INVOLVED INTERACTIVE COMMUNICATION.
REMEMBER, THERE WAS NO INTERNET THEN. THE CONCEPT OF THE COMMUNICATION CABLE IS REALLY JAPANESE: ONE-ON-ONE.
IT'S LIKE KARATE-- TWO PLAYERS COMPETE, THEY BOW TO EACH OTHER. IT'S THE JAPANESE CONCEPT OF RESPECT.
WEAVING TOGETHER THE THREADS OF HIS CHILDHOOD LOVES OF BUG COLLECTING AND VIDEO GAMES...
...WITH THE GAME BOY'S SPECIAL WAY OF FACILITATING COMPETITION *AND* COLLABORATION...
...TAJIRI AND THE SMALL COMPANY HE HAD FORMED COMPLETED A NEW GAME.
IT SOARED PAST NINTENDO'S MODEST EXPECTATIONS AND DIVERSIFIED INTO A *GLOBE-CONQUERING PORTFOLIO* OF CARTOONS, APPAREL, MOVIES, TOYS, AND SEQUELS BY THE SCORE.
100%

POKÉMON RED VERSION AND POKÉMON BLUE VERSION

GENRE: RPG

YEAR OF RELEASE (U.S.): 1998

COUNTRY OF ORIGIN: JAPAN

PLATFORMS: GAME BOY

DEVELOPER(S): GAME FREAK

PUBLISHER: NINTENDO

THESE SIMULTANEOUSLY RELEASED HANDHELD SYSTEM TITLES STARTED IT ALL. THEY BECAME THE MANIA OF AN ENTIRE GENERATION OF TRANSPACIFIC YOUTH.

IN *POKÉMON* PLAYERS ASSUME THE ROLE OF A COLLECTOR AND TRAINER OF "POCKET MONSTERS"--EACH WITH ITS OWN STRENGTHS AND WEAKNESSES. THEY THEN DO BATTLE.

ONE OF THE MOST INSPIRED ASPECTS OF THE GAME WAS THAT PLAYERS, TO ACQUIRE ALL 150 OF THE FIGHTING CRITTERS, MUST PLUG IN AND TRADE WITH EACH OTHER. IT WAS AT ITS CORE A CHARMINGLY SOCIAL GAME.

IN 2016, THE BECALMED *POKÉMON* CAUGHT A FAST-MOVING TRADEWIND AND SAILED BACK TO DOMINATE THE CROWDED SHIPPING LANES OF INTERNATIONAL CULTURE.

POKÉMON GO, AN ***AUGMENTED REALITY*** GAME FOR ***MOBILE PLATFORMS,*** MARSHALED MILLIONS OF PLAYERS OUTSIDE TO HUNT FOR POCKET MONSTERS ALONG ROADSIDES, IN PARKS, CEMETERIES, AND PUBLIC BUILDINGS.

GAME BOYS WERE A BREEZE TO USE.

YET THAT WAS STILL NOT THE CASE FOR PC GAMING. FOR DECENT PERFORMANCE, WEAKLING SYSTEMS STILL NEEDED TO BE GOOSED. BUT CONFIGURING ALL THE NEEDED GIZMOS WAS WAY TOO MUCH FOR MOST PEOPLE TO HANDLE.

AUTOEXEC.BAT!

CONFIG.SYS!

Start

THE SPREAD OF **MICROSOFT'S WINDOWS OPERATING SYSTEM** (OS) BEGAN TO MITIGATE THESE WOES-- ESPECIALLY FOLLOWING THE RELEASE OF WINDOWS 95.

FOR YEARS, ELECTRONIC ARTS' TRIP HAWKINS HAD REPUDIATED CONSOLES.

THEN HE CHANGED HIS TUNE.

WE HAD TO LET GO OF OUR ATTACHMENT TO MACHINES THAT THE PUBLIC *DID NOT WANT TO BUY...*

...AND SUPPORT THE HARDWARE THE PUBLIC *WOULD* EMBRACE.

SEGA

GENESIS

HAWKINS WANTED TO MAKE AND SELL GAMES FOR THE GENESIS, BUT THE TERMS OF SEGA'S EARLY LICENSING AGREEMENTS WERE STRICT.

SO TO GET IN A BETTER BARGAINING POSITION...

C'MON!

NOW! NOW! NOW!

...HAWKINS HAD A TEAM SECRETLY *REVERSE-ENGINEER* THE CONSOLE AND BREAK ITS SECURITY.

THE GAMBIT PAID OFF. ELECTRONIC ARTS BROUGHT ITS STABLE OF RESPECTED SPORTS GAMES TO THE CONSOLE WORLD.

JOHN MADDEN FOOTBALL
GENRE: SPORTS
YEAR OF RELEASE: 1990
COUNTRY OF ORIGIN: U.S.
PLATFORMS: SEGA GENESIS; SEQUELS RELEASED ACROSS POPULAR PLATFORMS
DEVELOPER(S): (ORIGINAL) PARK PLACE PRODUCTIONS
PUBLISHER: ELECTRONIC ARTS

NOT JUST A FRANCHISE, AN INDUSTRY-ALTERING *DYNASTY*, THE GAME THAT WOULD BECOME SIMPLY *MADDEN NFL* BEGAN WHEN TRIP HAWKINS STALKED THE AIRPLANE-PHOBIC COACH AND COMMENTATOR WHILE EN ROUTE VIA TRAIN FROM DENVER TO OAKLAND, CALIFORNIA.

FOOTBALL SIMS FROM GAMING'S EARLIER DAYS WERE HAMSTRUNG BY THE PALTRY NUMBER OF MOVING SPRITES SYSTEMS COULD HANDLE. AFTER A COMPROMISED APPLE II ITERATION IN 1988 (AND PROGRAMMING CHALLENGES THAT REPORTEDLY ALMOST KILLED PRODUCER JOE YBARRA), PERFORMANCE PICKED UP APPRECIABLY WITH THE ONSET OF 16-BIT CONSOLES.

SEGA EVEN SCORED AN OFFICIAL NFL LICENSE IN 1992, RENDERING THIS FOOTBALL SIM THE CYBER WORLD'S MOST BONA FIDE. ALTHOUGH SEGA WOULD ABANDON HARDWARE, *MADDEN* FULFILLED AN INCREDIBLE DESTINY.

THE TITLE HAS BEEN LAVISHED WITH CONSTANT UPDATES OVER THE YEARS, AND HAS RACKED UP OVER *$4 BILLION* IN REVENUE FOR ELECTRONIC ARTS.

IT WAS THE FIRST GAME THAT REALLY GAVE YOU AN INSIDE LOOK INTO THE PROFESSIONAL GAME.

BARRY SANDERS, DETROIT LIONS HALL OF FAME RUNNING BACK.

IN 1989, HAWKINS OFFERED MADDEN "AS MUCH [ELECTRONIC ARTS] STOCK AS HE WANTED" FOR $7.50 A SHARE.

MADDEN TURNED HAWKINS DOWN. IN 2016, THOSE SHARES WERE WORTH ALMOST $85.

THAT WAS THE DUMBEST THING I EVER DID IN MY LIFE.

TRIP HAWKINS KEPT CANDOR LIKE MADDEN'S IN RESERVE. HE LEFT EA TO LAUNCH A HIGHLY ADVANCED BUT PRICEY CONSOLE IN 1993: THE *3DO*.

THE 3DO WAS NO TOUCHDOWN. THE NEW COMPANY WENT BANKRUPT IN 2003.

PUBLISHING FOR SEGA--OR NINTENDO'S SYSTEMS FOR THAT MATTER--HAD DRAWBACKS, THOUGH...

...LIKE COSTLY-TO-MANUFACTURE CARTRIDGES.

SINCE DEBUTING WITH THE FAIRCHILD CHANNEL F, CONSOLE HARDWARE MAKERS HAD PREFERRED CARTRIDGES FOR SEVERAL REASONS.

THEY WITHSTOOD ABUSE IN HOMES WITH SMALL CHILDREN. THEY ACCOMMODATED EXTRA CHIPS OR BATTERIES TO PUNCH UP GAMEPLAY. AND THEIR DATA WAS CHALLENGING TO COPY. THIS HELPED KEEP A LID ON SOFTWARE PIRACY.

NINTENDO HAD A HUGE FINANCIAL STAKE IN CARTRIDGES.

JAPAN AND THE NETHERLANDS HAVE HAD ECONOMIC TIES FOR MANY CENTURIES.

NO GREAT SURPRISE, THEN, THAT DUTCH ELECTRONICS COMPANY *PHILIPS* AND SONY COOPERATED IN 1988 TO STANDARDIZE CD-ROMS FOR COMPUTER DATA.

GERARD PHILIPS, CO-FOUNDER OF *PHILIPS.*

DEJIMA ISLAND, A DUTCH TRADING PORT IN NAGASAKI BAY, 1641-1853.

MASARU IBUKA AND AKIO MORITA, CO-FOUNDERS OF SONY.

CD-ROMS, ALREADY ADOPTED BY PC GAMERS, POSED SERIOUS ADVANTAGES IN TERMS OF PRICE--PLUS THEIR HIGH DATA CAPACITIES WOULD ALLOW FOR *MUCH* ENHANCED GAMES.

164

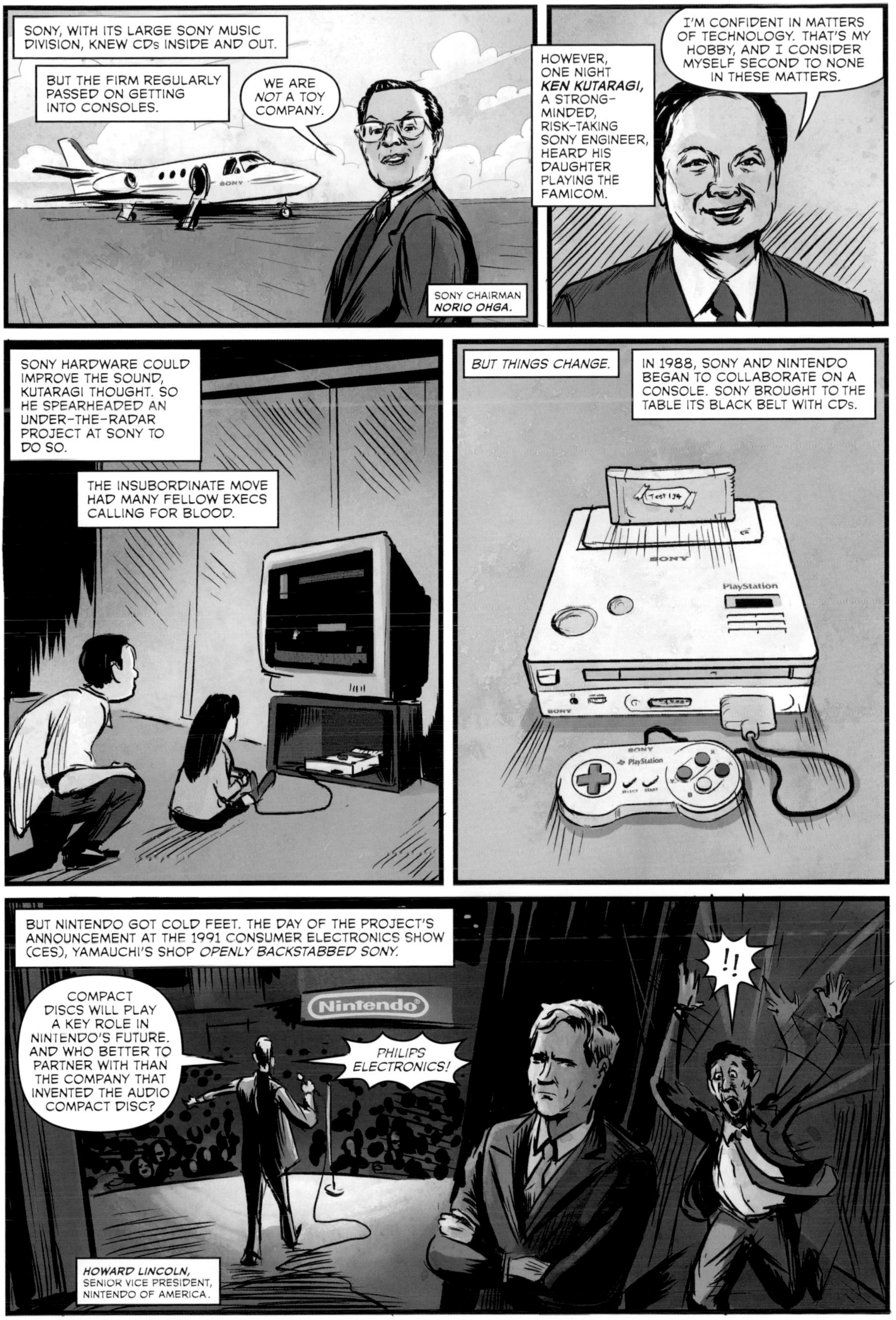
SONY, WITH ITS LARGE SONY MUSIC DIVISION, KNEW CDs INSIDE AND OUT.
BUT THE FIRM REGULARLY PASSED ON GETTING INTO CONSOLES.
WE ARE *NOT* A TOY COMPANY.
SONY
SONY CHAIRMAN ***NORIO OHGA.***
HOWEVER, ONE NIGHT ***KEN KUTARAGI,*** A STRONG-MINDED, RISK-TAKING SONY ENGINEER, HEARD HIS DAUGHTER PLAYING THE FAMICOM.
I'M CONFIDENT IN MATTERS OF TECHNOLOGY. THAT'S MY HOBBY, AND I CONSIDER MYSELF SECOND TO NONE IN THESE MATTERS.
SONY HARDWARE COULD IMPROVE THE SOUND, KUTARAGI THOUGHT. SO HE SPEARHEADED AN UNDER-THE-RADAR PROJECT AT SONY TO DO SO.
THE INSUBORDINATE MOVE HAD MANY FELLOW EXECS CALLING FOR BLOOD.
BUT THINGS CHANGE.
IN 1988, SONY AND NINTENDO BEGAN TO COLLABORATE ON A CONSOLE. SONY BROUGHT TO THE TABLE ITS BLACK BELT WITH CDs.
Test 134
SONY
PlayStation
SONY
SONY
PlayStation
BUT NINTENDO GOT COLD FEET. THE DAY OF THE PROJECT'S ANNOUNCEMENT AT THE 1991 CONSUMER ELECTRONICS SHOW (CES), YAMAUCHI'S SHOP *OPENLY BACKSTABBED SONY.*
Nintendo
COMPACT DISCS WILL PLAY A KEY ROLE IN NINTENDO'S FUTURE. AND WHO BETTER TO PARTNER WITH THAN THE COMPANY THAT INVENTED THE AUDIO COMPACT DISC?
PHILIPS ELECTRONICS!
!!
HOWARD LINCOLN, SENIOR VICE PRESIDENT, NINTENDO OF AMERICA.

THE PUBLIC SHAMING MAY WELL HAVE INSTILLED A *LUST FOR REVENGE* AT SONY.

OHGA TOLD KUTARAGI TO DEVELOP THE CD-BASED CONSOLE ANYWAY, NINTENDO BE DAMNED.

DO IT!

THUMP!!

THE ADVENT OF CD-ROMS AND 32-BIT SYSTEMS MEANT THAT TRUE 3-D POLYGONAL GRAPHICS-- RENDERED IN REAL TIME--WERE BECOMING A REALITY FOR CONSOLE GAMERS.

TIE FIGHTER

RIDGE RACER

namco

THE QUESTION WAS, WHOSE SYSTEM WOULD HAVE THE BIGGEST "WOW FACTOR?"

SONY PLAYSTATION

YEAR OF RELEASE (U.S.): 1995

COUNTRY OF ORIGIN: JAPAN

CPU BITS: 32

RAM: 2 MB, 1 MB VIDEO RAM

CPU SPEED: 33.87 MHZ

MAX. DISPLAY RESOLUTION: UP TO 640X480 PIXELS (NTSC)

COLORS: 16.7 MILLION

MEDIA: 660MB CD-ROM

THE SONY PLAYSTATION, THE FLAGSHIP OF THE FIFTH GENERATION OF VIDEO GAME CONSOLES, ASTONISHED MANY GAMERS WHEN THEY SAW IT FOR THE FIRST TIME.

IN TERMS OF HARDWARE, THE PLAYSTATION WAS *CONCEIVED* AS A 3-D GRAPHICS MACHINE. IT WAS ENGINEERED THAT WAY FROM THE GROUND UP--UNLIKE SEGA'S SATURN, FOR WHICH 3-D SUPPORT WAS AN ELEVENTH-HOUR ADDITION TACKED ON TO AN ESSENTIALLY 2-D SPRITE GRAPHICS SYSTEM.

THE PLAYSTATION ALSO FEATURED EXCELLENT CD-QUALITY SOUND CAPABILITIES.

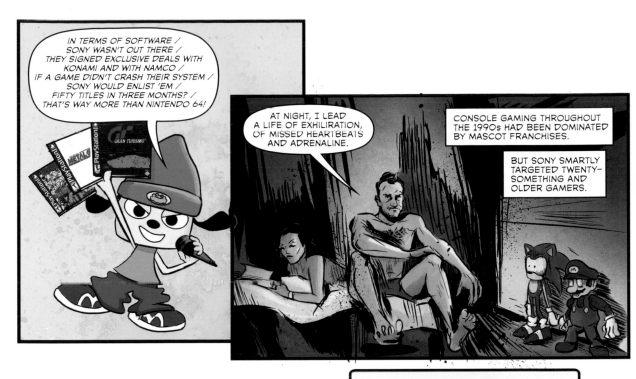

FINAL FANTASY VII

GENRE: RPG (OR "JRPG")

YEAR OF RELEASE (U.S.): 1997

COUNTRY OF ORIGIN: JAPAN

PLATFORMS: PLAYSTATION; PORTED TO MICROSOFT WINDOWS, IOS, STEAM

DEVELOPER(S): SQUARE

PUBLISHER (U.S.): SONY COMPUTER ENTERTAINMENT

IN 1997, THE PLAYSTATION'S HIGH-OCTANE 3-D GRAPHICS WERE A CLARION CALL TO THE WORLD'S MOST POPULAR RPG FRANCHISE: SQUARE'S *FINAL FANTASY.*

A DECADE EARLIER, JAPANESE PUBLISHER SQUARE HAD BEEN AT BANKRUPTCY'S DOOR. SQUARE HAD RELEASED *FINAL FANTASY* AS NOTHING MORE THAN A PARTING SHOT. (THUS THE "FINAL" IN THE TITLE: IT WAS MEANT TO BE THEIR LAST GAME.)

FINAL FANTASY VII'S GRAPHICS WERE LAUDED AS "INCREDIBLE." THE RECEPTION OF ITS NARRATIVE WENT ABOVE AND BEYOND--DUBBED "SO COMPLEX AND INTRIGUING THAT IT'S ALMOST IMPOSSIBLE TO SHUT OFF THE GAME."

FINAL FANTASY VII COULD NOT HAVE EXISTED ON CONSOLES WITHOUT THE HIGH DATA CAPACITIES OF PLAYSTATION'S CD-ROM.

THE MASTERPIECE OF CINEMATIC, OPEN-ENDED, INTERACTIVE STORYTELLING HELPED ELEVATE CONSOLES. IT PROVED THAT THEY, TOO, WERE CAPABLE OF ARTISTIC, HIGH-MINDED GAME EXPERIENCES.

THE WRITING ON THE WALL WAS NO BLURRY TEXTURE MAPPING: A *NEW FRONTIER* WAS OPENING UP. GAMES ONCE ALMOST *UNTHINKABLE* OUTSIDE OF THE PC TRADITION COULD NOW FIND LUCRATIVE EXPOSURE ELSEWHERE.

IT WAS TIME FOR THE BOLD AND THE BRAZEN TO TAKE THINGS IN THEIR OWN HANDS...OR RISK MISSING THE BOAT.

THE PLAYSTATION RECALIBRATED THE ASSUMPTIONS OF ANOTHER FORMER PC HARDLINER: SCOTLAND-BASED **DMA DESIGN.**

WITH SOME EARLY 1990s HITS UNDER THEIR BELT, **BMG INTERACTIVE** CONTRACTED WITH DMA FOR SEVERAL NEW GAMES.

SAM HOUSER, A WELL-CONNECTED YOUNG MAN FROM A SMART LONDON FAMILY, HAD BEEN BROUGHT INTO BMG IN HOPES HE COULD FERTILIZE GROWTH IN THE TECH-SAVVY YOUTH MARKET.

A FORTUITOUS *CROSS-POLLINATION* THUS ENSUED. DAVID JONES'S AMBITION TO CREATE *LIVING, BREATHING DIGITAL WORLDS*...

...TRANSFUSED WITH HOUSER'S *GANGSTER MOVIE/HIP-HOP SENSIBILITIES* OF *VIOLENCE* AND *SWAGGER*.

DMA DELIVERED UP A GAME CONCEPT CALLED *RACE 'N' CHASE*...

...A "COPS & ROBBERS" VEHICULAR PURSUIT WITH THE TOP-DOWN PERSPECTIVE OF A POLICE HELICOPTER.

JONES HAD RICHLY OUTFITTED HIS DIGITAL ENVIRONMENT WITH LOADS OF AUTONOMOUS PEDESTRIANS, CARS, AND LAW ENFORCEMENT.

JONES AFFIXED A FURTHER CREATIVE STAMP BY SETTING THE ACTION IN VAST, DISTINCT CITIES.

LibertyCity

SanAndreas

IMPRESSIVE? SURE! AND YET...

Vice city

THIS IS A F*CKING SIMULATION!

...NOT A FEW TESTERS FOUND *RACE 'N' CHASE... UNDERWHELMING.*

GARY PENN, THEN A PRODUCER AT BMG INTERACTIVE.

IN THE GAME, CARS COULD SOMETIMES RUN OVER JONES'S AI PEDESTRIANS. THIS COST THE PLAYER POINTS.

BUT THEN SOMEONE SUGGESTED, WHY NOT *REWARD* THESE GNARLY HIT-AND-RUNS INSTEAD?

HIRING NOW

FROM THAT POINT, THE DESIGNERS TRULY *FLIPPED THE SCRIPT* OF *RACE 'N' CHASE.*

IT SEIZED UPON A STYLE OF PLAY THAT *COMPUTER GAMES MAGAZINE* WOULD DESCRIBE AS "A GLEEFUL EMBRACE OF ANARCHY." THE PLAYER COULD FOLLOW A PLOT *OR* FREELY COMMIT ALL MANNER OF VIOLENT MAYHEM IN JONES'S OPEN-ENDED "SANDBOX" WORLD.

BY THE TIME OF ITS RELEASE, THE TITLE APPLIED TO THE GAME'S EARLY ITERATIONS LOOKED STALER THAN EVER.

RACE 'N' CHASE WAS RENAMED, TAKING ON A MONIKER THAT WOULD BECOME ONE OF THE BIGGEST NAMES EVER IN THE ENTIRE GAMING UNIVERSE...

ONCE WE MADE YOU ABLE TO KILL POLICEMEN, WE KNEW WE HAD SOMETHING THAT WOULD TURN HEADS!

GRAND THEFT AUTO

GENRE: ACTION-ADVENTURE

YEAR OF RELEASE: 1997

COUNTRY OF ORIGIN: U.S.

PLATFORMS: MS-DOS, MICROSOFT WINDOWS, PLAYSTATION, GAME BOY COLOR

DEVELOPER: DMA DESIGN

PUBLISHER: BMG INTERACTIVE ET AL.

IN SPITE OF THIS, *GRAND THEFT AUTO* RUMBLED OVER A SPIKE STRIP OF NEGATIVE REVIEWS...

GRAPHICS ARE TERRIBLE.

THE WORD "ORDINARY" COMES TO MIND

...NOT FOR ITS ANTISOCIAL BEARING BUT FOR ITS PERCEIVED *PASSÉ GRAPHICS.*

A CRITICAL MASS OF GAMERS WOULD ACCEPT NOTHING LESS THAN THE REALISM, FLUID ANIMATION, AND OPENNESS OF "KILLER 3-D" ENVIRONMENTS...

...MADE POSSIBLE BY FIFTH GENERATION CONSOLES AND PCS WHOSE 3-D RENDERING CHOPS WERE INTENSIVELY TOOLED UP WITH HARDWARE ACCELERATORS: GPUS FROM CHIPMAKERS LIKE *3DFX, ATI,* AND *NVIDIA.*

YOU DIDN'T HAVE TO BE SONY TO TAKE TRADITIONAL PC GENRES AND COAX THEM INTO FULL FLOWER ON CONSOLES.

1997'S *GOLDENEYE 007* FOR THE NINTENDO 64 WAS A CREDITABLE ENOUGH FPS TO BECOME A GAMING CLASSIC.

SAM HOUSER, WHO HAD GONE ON TO FORM THE LABEL *ROCKSTAR GAMES,* VOWED TO BRING THE GTA SERIES UP TO SPEC.

THE PLATFORM OF RELEASE FOR THIS NEW VISION OF THE GAME? THE *PLAYSTATION 2.*

&#@*#!!

THE ICONIC *LARA CROFT* FROM *EIDOS INTERACTIVE'S TOMB RAIDER* (1996).

RELEASED IN 2000, THE PLAYSTATION 2 (A SIXTH-GENERATION CONSOLE) TURNED HEADS WITH A *128-BIT* CPU, 16X THE PS1'S RAM, AND OVER 9X ITS PROCESSOR SPEED. WITH *DVD*S AS STORAGE MEDIA, GAME CONTENT COULD SOAR INTO MULTIPLE GIGABYTES IN SIZE.

IT WAS SO *POWERFUL* THAT IRAQI STRONGMAN *SADDAM HUSSEIN* WAS REPORTED TO BE STOCKPILING THEM FOR USE IN A DEADLY MISSILE SYSTEM.

TO DATE, IT REMAINS *THE HIGHEST-SELLING CONSOLE OF ALL TIME.*

HITTING SHELVES IN 2001, *GRAND THEFT AUTO III* HIT THE RICHTER SCALE SO HARD EVEN THOSE WHO HADN'T PLAYED A GAME SINCE *PONG* FELT THE EARTH MOVE.

ITS DIGITAL PLAYGROUND SETTING-- "LIBERTY CITY"-- HAD A STIRRINGLY APT NAME: IT LEFT MILLIONS OF GAMERS REELING WITH THE SENSE THEY COULD DO *ANYTHING* WITHIN IT.

INTERCONNECTED COMPUTERS WERE PROMULGATING EVERYWHERE PHONE LINES AND COAXIAL CABLE COULD REACH. AND NETWORKED MULTIPLAYER GAMING HADN'T BEEN NEW SINCE THE DAWN OF THE ARPANET.

STILL, PRECIOUS FEW SAW THE SHAPE THE INTERNET WAS GRADUALLY TAKING.

ONE SYSTEM ARRIVED TAKING ONLINE GAMING *FOR GRANTED:* SEGA'S DREAMCAST IN 1999.

THIS FIRST-TO-MARKET OF THE 128-BIT SIXTH-GENERATION CONSOLES CAME STANDARD WITH AN ON-BOARD MODEM.

IT ALSO RAN WINDOWS CE AND HAD AN OPTIONAL KEYBOARD FOR ONLINE BROWSING.

BUILDING ON PREVIOUS ONLINE EFFORTS, SEGA'S STRONG LEAD IN CYBER-SPACE ALSO OFFERED DIGITAL DISTRIBUTION AND DOWNLOADABLE CONTENT.

BUT WITH SEGA'S LACK OF MARKET SHARE--JUST 12 PERCENT PRIOR TO THE DREAMCAST--THE COMPANY LOST ALTITUDE FAST.

THIRTY-SIX YEARS AFTER ITS FIRST PINBALL MACHINE, SEGA THREW IN THE HARDWARE TOWEL ALTOGETHER.

WHEN YOU LOOK AT THE COST OF CREATING A HARDWARE BRAND IN THE FACE OF OUR COMPETITORS, SEGA CAN'T COMPETE.

SEGA SPOKESMAN CHARLES BELLFIELD, 2000. THEREAFTER, THE COMPANY WOULD ONLY MAKE GAMES.

TELLINGLY, SOME OF THE LAST TRAFFIC ON SEGANET WAS GAMERS SET UP WITH *QUAKE III: ARENA* FROM PC STALWARTS ID SOFTWARE.

THIS UNDERSCORES THAT TO THOSE WHO DID THEIR GAMING ON PCS, THE ONLINE EXPERIENCE WAS HARDLY NEW.

FINALLY...A HIGH-PERFORMANCE 1200-BAUD MODEM FOR UNDER '400

THE "PERSISTENT UNIVERSES" OF MMORPGS--HUMBLY FOUNDED WITH MUD1 IN 1978--HAD BEEN GAINING GROUND EVER SINCE.

SONY'S OWN *EVERQUEST,* FIRST ONLINE IN 1999, WAS THE TOP-REIGNING MMORPG UNTIL *WORLD OF WARCRAFT* REACHED 4 MILLION SUBSCRIBERS IN ITS FIRST YEAR.

CHANGE WAS AFOOT. TRUTHS AND TRENDS WERE BEING REVEALED.

ON THE HOLY GRAIL QUEST TO MATCH THE ULTIMATE IN REALISM WITH THE ULTIMATE IN SWEEP-YOU-OFF-YOUR-FEET GAMEPLAY...

...CONSOLES WERE BECOMING A LOT MORE LIKE COMPUTERS-- *AND COMPUTERS LIKE CONSOLES.*

THE NEW BUZZWORD WAS "CONVERGENCE."

LIKE THE *BIBLICAL REVELATION* THAT TWO SEEMING INSEPERABLES-- *HEAVEN* AND *EARTH*--WERE TO BECOME ONE.

THE COMPANY WITH THE HIGHEST GRAVITATIONAL PULL IN THE WHOLE SOFTWARE FIRMAMENT TOOK NOTICE.

MICROSOFT, WHICH HAD THE BLOOD OF THE BUSINESS WORLD RUNNING THROUGH ITS VEINS, HAD OVER THE YEARS ERRATICALLY ATTRACTED AND REPULSED GAMERS.

BUT THIS SOFTWARE GIANT AMONG GIANTS HAD SEEN THE LIGHT. IT MADE PAINS TO ENSURE A HOME FOR VIDEO GAMES ON WINDOWS.

Microsoft
Microsoft
DIRECTX

BUT AS THE NEW MILLENNIUM DREW NEAR, THE THREAT OF PC GAME LOYALISTS MIGRATING TO PLAYSTATION WAS ALARMING.

JONATHAN "SEAMUS" BLACKLEY, A GAMER AND TRAINED PHYSICIST, WAS--AFTER A CHOPPY FIRST RUN AT GAME DESIGN--"HIDING OUT" WITH A MICROSOFT JOB.

WHILE RETURNING FROM A BUSINESS TRIP, HE REPORTED HAVING AN EPIPHANY AT 30,000 FEET.

ONCE ON THE GROUND AT 2 A.M., HE DIALED UP COLLEAGUE *KEVIN BACHUS.*

AND SO BEGAN A LONG AND ARDUOUS MARCH TOWARD A CONSOLE BUILT BY MICROSOFT.

XBOX

YEAR OF RELEASE (U.S.): 2001

COUNTRY OF ORIGIN: U.S.

CPU BITS: 32

RAM: 64 MB

CPU SPEED: 733 MHZ

MAX. DISPLAY RESOLUTION: SUPPORTS UP TO 1080I (1920X1080 PIXELS)

COLORS: 16.7 MILLION

MEDIA: CD, DVD, DIGITAL DISTRIBUTION

A SPLINTER CELL OF GAMERS WITHIN MICROSOFT BELIEVED THAT PC VIDEO GAME GRAPHICS WERE STILL TOP-FLIGHT--AND THAT A MICROSOFT-BUILT CONSOLE WOULD KEEP THEM THAT WAY.

THE XBOX STOOD AS A STIRRING SYMBOL OF PC/CONSOLE CONVERGENCE.

NO MERE MODEMS WITH THIS SIXTH-GENERATION CONSOLE. NOT ONLY DID THE XBOX HAVE A *BROADBAND* ETHERNET PORT FOR ONLINE GAMING, BUT IT ALSO WAS DESIGNED TO INTERFACE WITH *XBOX LIVE* FOR ONLINE PLAY, DOWNLOADABLE CONTENT, AND *VOIP* SUPPORT FOR CHATTING LIVE TO OTHER GAMERS.

THE XBOX WAS ALSO THE FIRST CONSOLE WITH A HARD DRIVE. 8GB ON BOARD? YES. NOW GAMERS NO LONGER HAD TO SHUFFLE WITH MEMORY CARDS IN ORDER TO SAVE GAMES AND THE LIKE.

EVEN GARGANTUAN MICROSOFT WOULDN'T ENTER THE HARDWARE FRAY WITHOUT LOOKING AT THE LESSONS OF HISTORY...

...AND LEARNING THAT, TO SELL CONSOLES, YOU HAVE TO HAVE GREAT GAMES.

5
Los Angeles

XBOX

SO MICROSOFT SNAPPED UP GAME DESIGNER *BUNGIE* WHICH HAD—AT THE 1999 MACWORLD CONVENTION— EXHIBITED A POTENTIALLY *TRANSFORMATIVE* PROJECT-IN-PROGRESS.

MICROSOFT HAD ACTED ON A QUITE FAVORABLE HUNCH.

BUNGIE
ACTION
SACK

XBOX   ONLY ON XBOX

HALO
COMBAT EVOLVED

MATURE
M
CONTENT RATED BY
ESRB

BUNGIE

HALO: COMBAT EVOLVED

GENRE: FPS

YEAR OF RELEASE: 2001

COUNTRY OF ORIGIN: U.S.

PLATFORMS: XBOX; OTHERWISE A WINDOWS EXCLUSIVE

DEVELOPER: BUNGIE

PUBLISHER: MICROSOFT GAME STUDIOS

THE SPRING-LOADED AND OFTEN OVERUSED PHRASE "KILLER APP" APPLIES UNRESERVEDLY TO THE HALO SERIES FOR XBOX.

IF IT TOOK *GOLDENEYE 007* TO HINT THAT A FIRST-PERSON SHOOTER COULD WORK ON A CONSOLE, HALO: COMBAT EVOLVED FIRED A PLASMA CANNON AT THE CONTROVERSY AND DISINTEGRATED ITS VERY MOLECULES.

THE GRAPHICS, ACTION, THE COMPETENCE OF ITS AI AND STORYTELLING—LINEAR BUT SOMEHOW STILL FEELING FLUSH WITH HIGH-STAKES POSSIBILITIES— RECEIVED AN UPROAR OF RAVES.

WE FINALLY HAVE A GAME THAT ENGAGES YOUR INTELLECT ON A WHOLE DIFFERENT LEVEL.

GAMES JOURNALIST *CHE CHOU*, 2002.

IF ANYONE INTIMATELY KNEW THE RELATIONSHIP BETWEEN MICROSOFT PRODUCTS AND GAMES, IT WAS GABE NEWELL.

AS A GAMES LOVER, HE HELPED PUT TOGETHER A PROJECT TO PORT *DOOM* TO WINDOWS 95.

BUT AS A BRILLIANT TECHNOLOGIST BEHIND DOZENS OF MICROSOFT PRODUCTS, NEWELL WAS SAID, BY THE MID-1990s, TO BE A BIT BURNED OUT.

IN 1996, NEWELL LEFT. HE HAD BEEN VALUED BY THE COMPANY--AND *MADE VALUABLE* BY COMPANY STOCK. BUT HE AND A COLLEAGUE FORSAKED SPENDING RETIREMENT IN KINGLY LUXURY.

MIKE HARRINGTON AND I BOTH HAD A LOVE OF GAMES, AND WERE ABLE TO *CON OURSELVES INTO BELIEVING* WE COULD MAKE A GO OF IT AS A GAME DEVELOPER.

EVEN THOUGH NEITHER ONE HAD EVER ACTUALLY WORKED ON A GAME BEFORE.

FOUNDED IN 1996, THEIR *VALVE CORPORATION* RECRUITED TALENT FROM THE PC GAMING "MOD" COMMUNITY.

WHIRR-R-R- CRUNK!

IN FACT, THE *COUNTER-STRIKE* (1999) SERIES STARTED AS A MOD OF VALVE'S BELOVED *HALF-LIFE* (1998).

BETWEEN 2001 AND 2002, THE UNITED STATES REACHED A TIPPING POINT: OVER 50 PERCENT OF INDIVIDUALS WERE USING THE INTERNET.

AI! NOT ANOTHER *AMERICA ONLINE* FREE TRIAL!

PCs HAD HARD DRIVES. SO DID THE XBOX...

(...AS WOULD ITS SUCCESSORS, THE XBOX 360 IN 2005 AND THE XBOX ONE IN 2013--TO SAY NOTHING OF THE PLAYSTATION 3 IN 2006 AND THE PLAYSTATION 4 IN 2013.)

VALVE HAD HAD TROUBLE COLLECTING ROYALTIES FROM ITS PUBLISHER. WITH THESE ADVANCES, THOUGH, VALVE SAW AN OPPORTUNITY TO *CUT OUT THE MIDDLEMAN* AND DISTRIBUTE GAMES DIGITALLY.

ITS STEAM PLATFORM WENT LIVE AND OPEN TO THE PUBLIC IN 2003.

IN 2006, SONY JOINED IN WITH PLAYSTATION NETWORK.

THE SIGHT AND SOUND QUALITY OF THE XBOX AND PLAYSTATION WERE SO HIGH, AND THE INTERNET WAS BECOMING SO FAST...

...THAT CONSOLIDATING *HOME ENTERTAINMENT*-- STREAMING MOVIES, MUSIC, TV, AND MORE-- INTO THE CONSOLES JUST MADE SENSE.

PLAYSTATION AND XBOX SOON WERE SPARRING NOT OVER DEDICATED GAMING SCREENS, BUT INSTEAD OVER THE *WHOLE LIVING ROOM*.

YET NINTENDO ZAGGED WHERE THE OTHERS HAD ZIGGED. IN 2006, IT INTRODUCED A CONSOLE THAT DIDN'T HAVE TO BE ALL THINGS TO ALL PEOPLE.

"WE" WOULD LIKE TO *PLAY*.

AND ITS REVOLUTIONARY INTERFACE HAD GAMERS DOING THINGS IN THOSE LIVING ROOMS THAT SONY AND MICROSOFT NEVER SAW COMING.

NINTENDO Wii

YEAR OF RELEASE (U.S.): 2006

COUNTRY OF ORIGIN: JAPAN

CPU BITS: 32

RAM: 88 MB

CPU SPEED: 729 MHZ

MAX. DISPLAY RESOLUTION: 480P (640X480 PIXELS)

COLORS: 16.7 MILLION

MEDIA: 512MB INTERNAL FLASH MEMORY; SD CARDS; PROPRIETARY

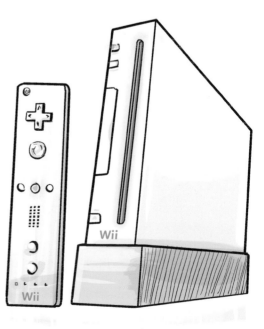

SHIGERU MIYAMOTO WAS, AGAIN, A LEADER OF THE DEVELOPMENT TEAM. HE WAS ORIGINALLY SHOOTING FOR A CONSOLE THAT WOULD BE ESPECIALLY ATTRACTIVE TO MOTHERS, AND COST ABOUT $100.

WHAT WAS SO ORIGINAL ABOUT THE WII WAS THE MOTION SENSORS AND INFRARED POINTER IN ITS WAND-LIKE CONTROLLERS. THESE ALLOWED PLAYERS TO USE THEIR BODIES TO CONTROL GAMEPLAY. THE PACK-IN GAME *WII SPORTS,* WAS THE PERFECT INTRODUCTION. THE INTERFACE, HOWEVER, WAS NOT QUITE PERFECTLY SEAMLESSLESS.

GAMERS WERE SO RECEPTIVE TO THE WII THAT OVER 100 MILLION UNITS HAVE BEEN SOLD TO DATE. THE WII BEAT ALL PREVIOUS NINTENDO CONSOLES, SAVE THE EVER POPULAR HANDHELD GAME BOY AND DS.

AS MOORE'S LAW PREDICTED, MICROPROCESSOR EVOLUTION KEPT PACKING POWER INTO EVEN POCKET-SIZED DEVICES...

...EXTENDING THE PHENOMENON OF CONVERGENCE INTO COMMUNICATION DEVICES AS WELL.

EARLY SMARTPHONE THE IBM SIMON PERSONAL COMMUNICATOR.

EARLY PDA (PERSONAL DIGITAL ASSISTANT) FROM *PSION*.

THESE WERE PERFECT CAPSULES FOR CASUAL GAMES--LIKE THOSE WINDOWS USERS HAD INDULGED IN FOR YEARS, LIKE *MINESWEEPER*.

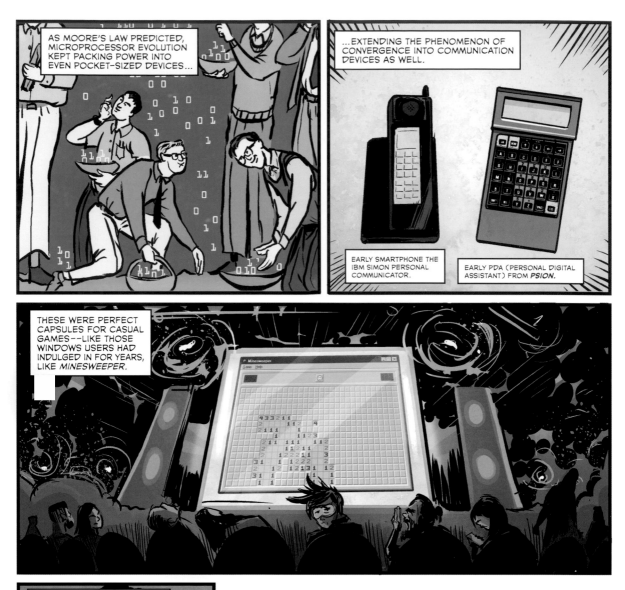

IN 1999, THE JAPANESE TELECOMMUNICATIONS FIRM *NTT DOCOMO* ROLLED OUT "I-MODE," THE FIRST FULL INTERNET SERVICE FOR WIRELESS PHONES.

USERS BEGAN DOWNLOADING AND PLAYING GAMES AT A RAPID CLIP.

THIS INCLUDED GAMES LIKE NEKOZONE'S *SHIT PANIC*, A VIRAL SENSATION INVOLVING CATCHING LUMPS OF EXCREMENT IN A MOVING TOILET.

SCORE: 30   00

THE TECHNOLOGY PUT COMPUTING-- *AND GAMING*--IN THE HANDS OF MOST EVERYONE ON THE PLANET, INCLUDING THOSE WHO HAD NEVER KNOWN *PAVED ROADS* OR *PLUMBING.*

POPULAR TITLES LIKE *SPACE INVADERS* AND *TETRIS* RAN CONVINCINGLY ALMOST FROM THE START.

BUT AS COLOR AND 3-D SUPPORT TRICKLED IN, MOBILE GAMES GREW WITH THE TECHNOLOGY.

AND *CLASSICS IN THEIR OWN RIGHT* EMERGED, NATIVE TO MOBILE PLATFORMS.

ANGRY BIRDS

GENRE: CASUAL

YEAR OF RELEASE: 2009

COUNTRY OF ORIGIN: FINLAND

PLATFORMS: IOS; PORTED TO ALMOST EVERY PLATFORM AVAILABLE

DEVELOPER: ROVIO

PUBLISHER: CHILINGO

JARNO VÄKEVÄINEN, KIM DIKERT, AND NIKLAS HED WERE STUDENTS AT HELSINKI, FINLAND'S UNIVERSITY OF TECHNOLOGY WHEN THEY ENTERED A MOBILE GAME CONTEST--AND WON.

THEY FORMED A COMPANY, LATER RENAMED *ROVIO.* BUT BY 2007, THEY WERE ON THE VERGE OF INSOLVENCY.

THE UNVEILING OF THE IPHONE GAVE THEM NEW HOPE. THE TEAM CONCENTRATED ON DEVELOPING A GAME FOR ITS MULTITOUCH SCREEN AND DAZZLING DISPLAY. *ANGRY BIRDS* WAS THE RESULT.

PHYSICS. PUZZLES. HUMOR. CUTENESS. THE WORLD OVER, MOBILE DEVICE USERS WERE TAKEN IN. ROVIO'S TWELVE EMPLOYEES HAD CREATED A HOUSEHOLD NAME.

THE LUDIC ELEGANCE OF *ANGRY BIRDS* ATTRACTED THOSE FOR WHOM THE MEGABUDGET, TRIPLE-A GAMES MADE BY HUNDREDS OF CODERS WERE UNAPPEALING OR OUT OF REACH.

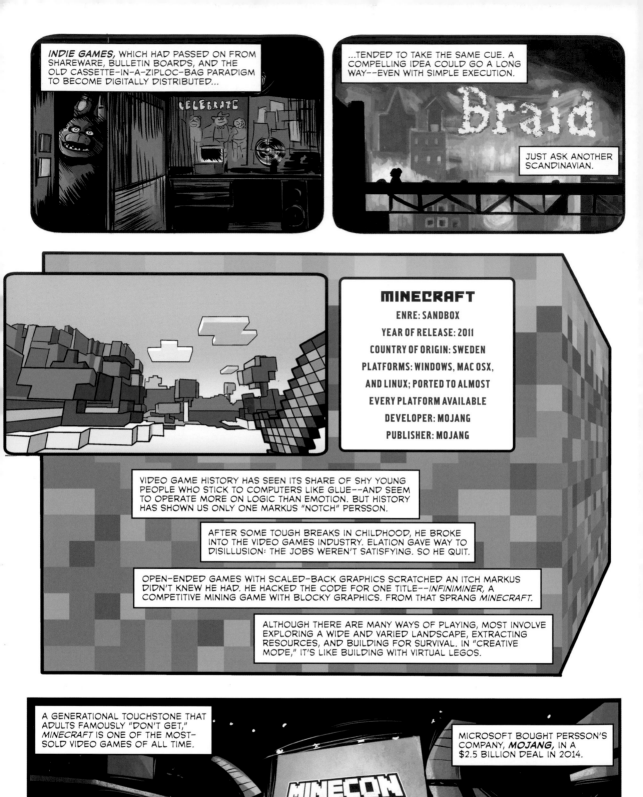

INDIE GAMES, WHICH HAD PASSED ON FROM SHAREWARE, BULLETIN BOARDS, AND THE OLD CASSETTE-IN-A-ZIPLOC-BAG PARADIGM TO BECOME DIGITALLY DISTRIBUTED...

...TENDED TO TAKE THE SAME CUE. A COMPELLING IDEA COULD GO A LONG WAY--EVEN WITH SIMPLE EXECUTION.

JUST ASK ANOTHER SCANDINAVIAN.

MINECRAFT

ENRE: SANDBOX

YEAR OF RELEASE: 2011

COUNTRY OF ORIGIN: SWEDEN

PLATFORMS: WINDOWS, MAC OSX,

AND LINUX; PORTED TO ALMOST

EVERY PLATFORM AVAILABLE

DEVELOPER: MOJANG

PUBLISHER: MOJANG

VIDEO GAME HISTORY HAS SEEN ITS SHARE OF SHY YOUNG PEOPLE WHO STICK TO COMPUTERS LIKE GLUE--AND SEEM TO OPERATE MORE ON LOGIC THAN EMOTION. BUT HISTORY HAS SHOWN US ONLY ONE MARKUS "NOTCH" PERSSON.

AFTER SOME TOUGH BREAKS IN CHILDHOOD, HE BROKE INTO THE VIDEO GAMES INDUSTRY. ELATION GAVE WAY TO DISILLUSION: THE JOBS WEREN'T SATISFYING. SO HE QUIT.

OPEN-ENDED GAMES WITH SCALED-BACK GRAPHICS SCRATCHED AN ITCH MARKUS DIDN'T KNEW HE HAD. HE HACKED THE CODE FOR ONE TITLE--INFINIMINER, A COMPETITIVE MINING GAME WITH BLOCKY GRAPHICS. FROM THAT SPRANG MINECRAFT.

ALTHOUGH THERE ARE MANY WAYS OF PLAYING, MOST INVOLVE EXPLORING A WIDE AND VARIED LANDSCAPE, EXTRACTING RESOURCES, AND BUILDING FOR SURVIVAL. IN "CREATIVE MODE," IT'S LIKE BUILDING WITH VIRTUAL LEGOS.

A GENERATIONAL TOUCHSTONE THAT ADULTS FAMOUSLY "DON'T GET," MINECRAFT IS ONE OF THE MOST-SOLD VIDEO GAMES OF ALL TIME.

MICROSOFT BOUGHT PERSSON'S COMPANY, MOJANG, IN A $2.5 BILLION DEAL IN 2014.

MINECON, 2015.

WITH ALL THE MASSIVE LEAPS VIDEO GAMES HAVE TAKEN, WHO CAN ANTICIPATE WHAT COMES NEXT?

WILL THE RUSH INTO VIRTUAL REALITY BE A GIMMICK, OR WILL IT REALIZE THE PERPETUAL FANTASY OF GAMES WHOSE VIVIDNESS WILL MATCH OUR FULL PERCEPTIONS OF THE REALITY?

WILL ALL OF A GAME'S COMPUTATION END UP IN "THE CLOUD"--WITH CONSOLES AND PC GAMING RIGS DISAPPEARING ENTIRELY--LEAVING GAMERS JUST A VARIETY OF DISPLAY DEVICES AND CONTROLLERS TO CHOOSE FROM?

WILL DATA COLLECTION BECOME SO HIGH-FUNCTIONING THAT GAMES WILL SELF-MODIFY IN REAL TIME--TO OPTIMIZE THEIR STRUCTURE AND CUSTOMIZE IT TO AN INDIVIDUAL'S TASTES? IF SO, WILL THIS LEAD GAMERS NOT TOWARD, BUT *AWAY* FROM EACH OTHER, INTO DEEP, PRIVATE RECESSES OF UNSHARED EXPERIENCE?

WILL AI IMPROVE TO THE POINT THAT GAME CHARACTERS WILL NO LONGER REQUIRE WRITERS TO PREPARE SCRIPTS FOR THEM?

WILL MOORE'S LAW COME UP AGAINST THE LIMITATIONS OF PHYSICS, CHILLING THE PACE OF INNOVATION GAMERS HAVE GROWN USED TO--AND PERHAPS EXPECT TO--CONTINUE FOREVER?

HUMANS HAVE FAR MORE OFTEN THAN NOT BEEN POOR PREDICTORS OF WHAT THE FUTURE WILL BE LIKE.

IF THE NEXT SEVENTY YEARS TAKES US THE SAME DISTANCE WE HAVE TRAVELED FROM THE CATHODE RAY AMUSEMENT DEVICE TO *CYBERPUNK 2077*, IS IT POSSIBLE TO EVEN *GLIMPSE* WHAT IT WOULD BE LIKE TO STAND UPON THAT HORIZON?

AS LONG AS WE REMAIN HUMAN, THAT ESSENTIAL URGE TO PLAY WILL NEVER DISAPPEAR.

IN ALL OUR THOUSANDS OF YEARS OF INVENTION, WE HAVE NEVER EVEN COME CLOSE TO THE SENSUAL AND EXPERIENTIAL TOOLBOX WE HAVE GIVEN OURSELVES WITH VIDEO GAMES.

WITH THAT ARTIST'S PALETTE, WE WILL UNDOUBTEDLY KEEP EXPLORING AND STIMULATING WHAT IS INSIDE US.

AND THROUGH VIDEO GAMES, WE WILL KEEP TRYING TO GRASP AT WHAT IS *OUTSIDE* US. TO PLAY WITH WHAT WE PERCEIVE AS REALITY IN OUR NEVER-ENDING EFFORTS TO MAKE THE WORLD FEEL THE WAY WE THINK IT'S SUPPOSED TO FEEL.

INDEX

Check out thecomicbookstoryofvideogames.com for detailed chapter notes, additional material, news, recommendations for further reading, and more.

Published in the United States by Ten Speed Press, an imprint of the
Crown Publishing Group, a division of Penguin Random House LLC, New York.
www.crownpublishing.com
www.tenspeed.com

Ten Speed Press and the Ten Speed Press colophon are registered trademarks
of Penguin Random House LLC.

Library of Congress Cataloging-in-Publication Data
Names: Hennessey, Jonathan, 1971- author. | McGowan, Jack
Title: The comic book story of video games : the incredible history of the electronic
    gaming revolution / Jonathan Hennessey ; artwork by Jack McGowan.
Description: First edition. | California : Watson-Guptill Publications, [2017] | Includes
    bibliographical references and index. |
Identifiers: LCCN 2016050499 (print) | LCCN 2017019087 (ebook) |
Subjects: LCSH: Video games—History—Comic books, strips, etc.
Classification: LCC GV1469.3 (ebook) | LCC GV1469.3 .H46 2017 (print) |
    DDC 794.8—dc23
LC record available at https://lccn.loc.gov/2016050499

Trade Paperback ISBN: 978-0-399-57890-8
eBook ISBN: 978-0-399-57891-5

Printed in China

Design by Chloe Rawlins

10 9 8 7 6 5 4 3 2 1

First Edition